RUNNING

SCARED

• • • • •

Masculinity

and the

Representation

of the

Male Body

In the series

CULTURE AND THE

MOVING IMAGE

edited by Robert Sklar

Temple University Press Philadelphia

• • • • • • • • • • • •

RUNNING

SCARED

Masculinity and the Representation of the Male Body

PETER LEHMAN

Temple University Press,
Philadelphia 19122
Copyright © 1993 by
Temple University.
All rights reserved
Published 1993
Printed in the United States
of America

Library of Congress
Cataloging-in-Publication Data
Lehman, Peter.
    Running scared : masculinity and the
representation of the male body / Peter
Lehman.
        p.   cm.—(Culture and the
moving image)
    Includes bibliographical references
and index.
    ISBN 1-56639-099-0 (alk. paper)
    1. Men in motion pictures.   2. Men in
popular culture.   3. Sex role in motion
pictures.   I. Title.   II. Series.
    PN1995.9.M46L45   1993
    791.43′652041—dc20   92-46733
                                CIP

FOR MELANIE

You turned around and walked away with me.

CONTENTS

PREFACE

Work on this book began long before I realized it. Its origins lie in many of my experiences growing up in the United States after World War II. Some of those experiences, such as having to swim naked in junior and senior high school gym classes at a time when adolescents are particularly self-conscious about their bodies, seemed somewhat bizarre to me then and still do. No doubt someone, or perhaps everyone, thought I and all the other boys would be better men for it. Those were also the years, however, when I took a special solace in listening to the music of Roy Orbison. That has not changed, and the title of this book is intended as a memorial tribute to a pop singer whose work has already lasted and grown in significance over a period of nearly forty years.

The direct origins of this book can be traced back to 1986 when I devoted a seminar at the University of Arizona to the male body in the cinema and when I was invited to organize and chair a special plenary session of the Florida State University Literature and Film Conference related to the conference theme of gender. Someone suggested a panel on *Victor/Victoria* and *Tootsie*, and while such a panel would no doubt have been productive, I wanted to do something different. I chose the topic of the representation of the male body in *American Gigolo*, and Patricia Mellencamp, Robert Eberwein, William Luhr, and Danae Clark all agreed to it. As far as I know, that was the first panel at any conference in the film field devoted exclusively to discussing the male body. There were two such panels at the 1990 Society for Cinema Studies Conference, and they have become a regular feature of conferences during the time I have been researching and writing this book. Some of the material in this book, in fact, grew out of other conference papers I presented. Although work on the sexual representation of the male body is now a fast-growing field, this book is for me a true beginning. Much work remains to be done before we can fully understand the rationale for and consequences of many of the ways in which we and other cultures have sexually represented the male body. And, for that matter, before we can understand why the Janesville, Wisconsin, public schools had the swimming rituals they once did.

ACKNOWLEDGMENTS

I feel that perhaps more than anything else I have written, this book owes so much to so many people. Among those who have alerted me to relevant material and pointed me in important new directions, I would like to thank Dennis Bingham, Jason Chen, Melody Davis, Robert Eberwein, Patricia Ehrens, Krin Gabbard, Jane Gaines, Mary Beth Haralovich, William Luhr, Edward O'Neil, Amy Rule, Rob Sabal, Robert Sklar, Mike Sottarelli, Diane Waldman, and Brian Watson. I particularly want to acknowledge the mature and candid responses that many students have offered over the years about the most taboo of topics in our culture. The way in which they have shared their perceptions and experiences has been invaluable in helping me think about a topic around which there has been too much silence for too long. The same is true for people in the profession. I am particularly indebted to several women who showed strong interest and patience in and support for what must at times have sounded like the unfathomable mysteries and obsessions of a man. Special thanks, therefore, go to Chris Holmlund, Chris Straayer, Laurie Schulz, and Susan Hunt. Susan Hunt and Chris Straayer supplied countless hours of conversation and criticism. Without them, writing this book would have been a lonely and scary project. As always, I am most indebted to Melanie Magisos, without whose editorial skill and valuable revision suggestions I would be lost. No book has ever benefited more from so much generosity from so many people. They, however, are in no way responsible for any of its limitations.

An earlier version of Chapter 6 appeared in *Cinema/Comedy/Theory*, edited by Andrew Horton (Berkeley: University of California Press, 1991), and I would like to thank Andy for his interest and support. Thanks also to the many conferences and journals that gave me an opportunity to present some of this material in an earlier and usually quite different form from what appears in this book. Those editors and conference organizers provided me with opportunities for valuable feedback, and this book is better for it.

Finally, I give special thanks to Janet Francendese at Temple University Press for her enthusiastic support and help. She and her colleagues stood strongly behind a manuscript that at times deals with controversial material. Their belief in this book has meant a great deal to me and I thank them for it.

RUNNING

SCARED

● ● ● ● ●

Masculinity

and the

Representation

of the

Male Body

1

INTRODUCTION

• • • • •

"WHAT HAVE WE DONE TO DESERVE THIS?"

Pedro Almodóvar's *What Have I Done to Deserve This* (1985) begins with a sequence in which a cleaning woman in a gym watches a group of men practicing the martial arts, including Kendo. As she looks at these men costumed in their athletic gear, wielding weapons, and boldly posturing in combat positions (1), desire arises out of her initial curiosity. Cut to the locker room where one of the men enters to take a shower after the workout. She and we see him from behind as he enters the shower (2). He becomes aware of her look, turns, and gestures for her to join him. She approaches, and in one shot we see her glance down directly at his genitals (3). He faces the camera as she walks up to him (4). They immediately begin to make love passionately. As he holds her and enters her standing up, she instructs, "Higher, higher." Seconds later, however, he is done (5), and in a long shot we see her walking away with a disappointed, dissatisfied expression. He walks toward the camera and stands naked, looking after her. Cut back to the empty gym, where she now wields the martial arts weapon.

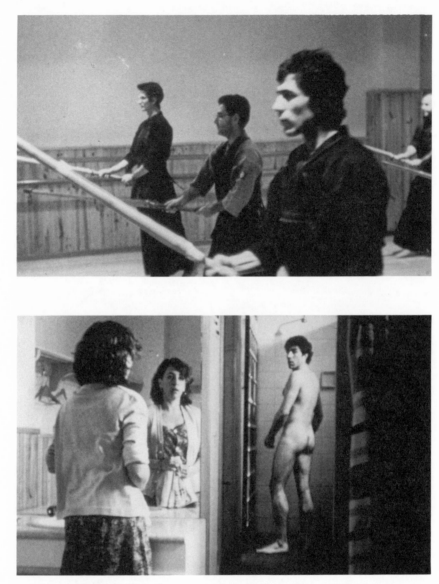

This brief sequence poses a number of crucial questions surrounding both the conventional sexual representation of the male body and the difficulty of creating significant alternatives. At the simplest level, the sequence reverses the usual structure of looks in the cinema that Laura Mulvey first described in gender terms, arguing in "Visual Pleasure and the Narrative Cinema" (1975) that within the classical structure men possess the gaze and women are its object. The male look is powerful, controlling, and desiring,

3

4

and within point-of-view editing patterns, it creates a circuit wherein the frequently fetishized image of the woman that follows is intensely eroticized.
A corollary of Mulvey's main hypothesis is that men cannot bear to gaze
on other men who are exhibiting themselves for that gaze and are thus not
similarly objectified.

Although I critique the limitations of this perspective, I want to emphasize that there are important contextual reasons for this near-total attention

5

to the woman's body, and as we may expect, this is not unique to film theory; it applies almost equally to literature, art, and photography. With important exceptions, such as Phylis Chesler's *About Men* (1978), feminism's initial agenda put primary emphasis on how patriarchy attempted to regulate women's bodies. Academic feminist film theory and criticism therefore prioritized understanding the alienating ways in which women's bodies were controlled in representation via such devices as fragmentation and fetishism. Politically it was much more important to understand and change the ways in which patriarchy, and primarily men within patriarchy, structured oppressive representations of women's bodies than it was to worry about how the same patriarchal ideology structured representations of men's bodies. Feminists were and still are very concerned that men not set the agenda for women. Issues around the male body may certainly be of more concern to men than women and thus not be a priority for feminists. This context is even more extreme when, as in this book, a man deals with the representation of the male body, appearing to privilege male concerns about the male body and thus raising the specter of the most traditional patriarchal discourse. I suggest, however, that the silence surrounding the sexual representation of the male body is itself totally in the service of traditional patriarchy and that critical work by men can complement, rather than displace or silence, feminist women's voices.

Indeed, we are faced with two highly paradoxical situations. From one perspective, film theory from the mid-1970s through most of the 1980s perpetuated the dominant cultural paradigm wherein women's bodies are displayed and men's bodies are hidden and protected. Countless pages have been devoted to analyzing how women's bodies are fetishized and controlled via the star system, fashion, lighting, camera position and cutting patterns, narrative structure, and so forth. Thus academics have replicated as well as deconstructed the very sexual ideology they are analyzing. Women's bodies have occupied the critical spotlight in a way analogous to which they have been center stage as a spectacle in the culture in which we live.

Patriarchy benefits from and may even be partly contingent on perpetuating the mystique of the penis–phallus. I employ both the word penis and phallus. The distinction is critical. The penis is the literal organ and the phallus a symbolic concept. As Barbara de Genevieve so succinctly notes while commenting on the double standard of nudity surrounding the male and female body, "To unveil the penis is to unveil the phallus is to unveil the social construction of masculinity. And *that* is a real taboo" (1991, 4). Since it is in the interest of patriarchy to ensure that men's bodies remain what Rosalind Coward has called the "dark continent," it is important to turn the light on those bodies. Only after thus centering the male body will it be possible truly to decenter it, for it is precisely when the penis–phallus is hidden from view in patriarchy that it is most centered. There is no way that we can move beyond the impasse surrounding the male body by simply ignoring it, since that is what patriarchy wants us to do and has, in fact, been quite successful in bringing about.

The following chapters show how both avoiding the sexual representation of the male body and carefully controlling its limited explicit representations work to support patriarchy. It is no coincidence that if scholars in gender studies continue to ignore the male body, arguing that we should neither look at it carefully nor analyze it, they will sound like the most traditional men. Like the congruent positions of antipornography feminists and the religious right, such congruent perspectives should give us pause. No doubt, paradoxes should also give us pause, but the paradoxes that, I argue, surrounded initial work on the female body and surround current work on the male body grow out of the fact that we cannot simply write from outside history and ideology; we must move through phases. The concluding chapters of this book point to some of the changes that may result from analyzing and challenging dominant discourses surrounding the male body. If this seems to place men and their bodies at the center and risks replicating patriarchal viewpoints, it is a risk I must take.

In the sequence in *What Have I Done to Deserve This?* described earlier, it is the woman who not only looks but desires the body on which she longingly gazes. Equally obviously, it is the man's body that is graphically displayed, first when he turns to beckon the woman into the shower and later when he stands looking after she has departed; she, in contrast, is fully clothed throughout the sequence. But the scene is not a simple reversal, such as male stripping and *Playgirl*. Simple reversals never address true power imbalances; while masquerading in society as liberating activities, they reinscribe the traditional ideological imbalance in ways that seek to contain any threat posed by the new activity. Almodóvar's scene is a complex reversal; nevertheless, it gets tangled in contradictory issues that it cannot satisfactorily resolve. Before carefully unpacking the sequence, however, I want to return to Mulvey's hypotheses and their impact.

Mulvey's article rightly became a watershed work in the history of film theory and criticism. It managed at one and the same time to be highly provocative and polemical, and its influence directly dominates a decade of work on gender and cinema. Mulvey's insights were astonishing, and like many other scholars, I am deeply indebted to her. Nevertheless, from the beginning I was disturbed by the implications that her argument had for issues surrounding the representation of the male body. It may be no coincidence that in an essay notable for its articulate, clear argumentation the sentences that most directly raise this issue have always struck me as awkwardly worded: "The male figure cannot bear the burden of sexual objectification. Man is reluctant to gaze at his exhibitionist like" (Mulvey 1975, 12). On the contrary, I argue in this book that man not only can but is driven to look at, and talk, and write, and joke about his "exhibitionist like." Similarly, he not only has carried the "burden of sexual objectification" but indeed wants to carry it. In short, Mulvey oversimplified both the history of the sexual representation of the male body and the nature of male subjectivity.

In 1985, Rosalind Coward remarked:

Under this sheer weight of attention to women's bodies we seem to have become blind to something. Nobody seems to have noticed that men's bodies have quietly absented themselves. Somewhere along the line men have managed to keep out of the glare, escaping from the relentless activity of sexual definitions. In spite of the ideology that would have us believe that women's sexuality is an enigma, it is in reality men's bodies, men's sexuality which is the true "dark continent" of this society. (1985, 227)

Since this observation was published in 1985, things have changed. Feminist scholars such as Miriam Hansen, Sandy Flitterman, and Chris Holmlund have analyzed the particular sex appeal for female spectators of such stars as Rudolph Valentino, Tom Selleck, Arnold Schwarzenegger, and Sylvester Stallone. Gaylyn Studlar has challenged Laura Mulvey's reading of the films of Josef von Sternberg by bringing to light the previously overlooked centrality of male masochism in those films. Linda Williams has analyzed hardcore pornography in relationship to the female spectator. In a manner symptomatic of these developments, Constance Penley and Sharon Willis have edited "Male Trouble," a special issue of *Camera Obscura* devoted to masculinity.

In addition to this feminist perspective, important work has been done from the gay male perspective. Richard Dyer's analysis of the male pin-up is a ground-breaking article. Tom Waugh is studying the history of gay male sexual representation and pornography. Steve Neale has analyzed the spectacle of masculinity and Paul Willemen the films of Anthony Mann. Dennis Bingham has analyzed the male spectator and such male stars as James Stewart, Clint Eastwood, and Jack Nicholson. There is also Paul Smith's work on Eastwood. Finally there is *Screening the Male*, edited by Steven Cohan and Ina Rae Hark, the first collection of essays on film devoted to masculinity and the male body.*

David Rodowick's *The Difficulty of Difference* supplies a brilliant re-reading of how film theory has misappropriated Sigmund Freud and Jacques Lacan and bears directly on the following chapters. Rodowick objects to the strong emphasis psychoanalytic film theorists have placed on binary oppositions such as male–female, active–passive, and sadistic–masochistic and attributes this to a misreading of Freud's work. Rodowick demonstrates that Freud saw these as fluid and necessarily related categories. They were not, as they have come to be in film theory, fixed categories associated with one

*As this brief survey indicates, during the 1980s a number of different strands of criticism surrounding the male body emerged, including a range of concerns from the perspectives of female, gay male, and heterosexual male spectators. Not surprisingly, this development has taken place in the other arts as well. Melody Davis has analyzed the male nude in photography. Finally, a whole new field sometimes called Men's Studies has emerged during the past decade, and such books as *The Sexuality of Men*, edited by Andy Metcalf and Martin Humphries, discuss masculinity and the male body in ways that relate to my concerns.

sex rather than the other. In film theory, for example, the psychoanalytic development of the fetishistic structure whereby one balances knowledge with belief is attributed solely to males as a result of dealing with castration anxiety. Relatedly, the ability to believe simultaneously in the reality of the image and distance oneself from it as only an image is attributed to males and a closeness to and overly emotional identification with the image to females. In short, film theory's notion of sadistic men who control a powerful gaze that retains visual distance and is built on a fetishistic regime of balancing knowledge of castration with a belief in the contradictory image of the woman as possessing a penis, as opposed to masochistic women who overly identify with the image and cannot maintain visual distance, is a simplistic, rigidified schematic account based on a misreading of Freud.

My response to the way in which film theory created the rigid male–female binary oppositions that Rodowick emphasizes was nearly the opposite of his. Rather than emphasize re-reading Freud and Lacan, I turned my attention to a detailed analysis of the sexual representation of the male body in a variety of texts; I closely read and re-read films, novels, paintings, photographs, popular music, and videos with the intention of exploring those texts in a manner that would maximize how they might shed light on the ideology of the representation of the male body. Although I employ Freudian thought and find it an invaluable critical tool, those close analyses, which constitute the following chapters, convince me that our rigid notions of male–female difference are oversimplified and that Rodowick is correct in conceiving of multiple, fluid, and contradictory positions. Men desire and fear, and sometimes desire what they most fear, in ways that confound any simple notions of male subjectivity. Before returning to these issues, however, I return to *What Have I Done to Deserve This?* a film that places the sexual representation of the male body in the foreground.

The film begins with the woman's desire being aroused by a clothed and very traditional image of men. Almodóvar further loads this image by making it athletic and thus competitive, combative and thus heroic—and one that involves wielding a big weapon and is thus overtly phallic. In her initial look, the woman does not see, let alone desire, a particular male body; she sees and is aroused by a highly phallic image of powerful, active masculinity. Part of what makes this sequence so interesting is that this symbolic spectacle and the desire it arouses carries over for the woman onto the literal male body, and here she is eventually disappointed. The way in which she returns to the gym and assumes the previous male position of wielding the weapon makes explicit the penis–phallus distinction.*

One of the main themes of this book is the way in which the phallus dominates, restricts, prohibits, and controls the representation of the male body, particularly its sexual representation. *What Have I Done to Deserve This?* makes clear that although the penis and phallus may be theoretically separable, they are linked in actuality, and linked in a way that has specific consequences for both the theoretical concept of the symbolic phallus and the literal male body and the penis. Most significantly, the woman can just as readily wield the phallus and its power as the man can. Neither men nor women, however, as Chris Holmlund reminds us, can possess the phallus, and in this sense masculinity is itself a masquerade. This is the importance of the scene in the gym immediately following the sexual encounter. The woman demonstrates that she can occupy what was previously the male position when she picks up the symbolic weapon and postures as the men have done. This in turn initiates a pattern in the film that culminates when she kills her oppressive husband by clubbing him over the head with a ham bone. At the end of the film, the detective assigned to solve the case is foiled by the woman in another scene in the gym where she stands wielding the phallus. Even her elderly mother collects sticks throughout the film, a mysterious act comically suggesting that women can and will occupy the presumed male role of wielding the phallus and its symbolic power.

But what of male nudity and the explicitness of the shower scene? On the one hand, it is a marked departure from the conventions of male nudity found in dominant cinema, photography, social pornography such as *Playgirl*, and hard-core pornography. In those forms, the explicit sexual representation of the male body involves a variety of structures that attempt to make it impressively dramatic. Foremost among these is an emphasis on large penises. Yet the actor in *What Have I Done to Deserve This?* is shown with a small,

*Lucy Fischer has brought to my attention some interesting resonances between the gym scene in *What Have I Done to Deserve This?* and a gym scene in *Gentlemen Prefer Blondes* (1953) in which Jane Russell admiringly looks at the bodies of Olympic athletes as they exercise. Her desires are unfulfilled, however, by the unresponsive athletes who are entirely self-absorbed in their exercise. In this context, a related gym scene occurs in Jean-Luc Godard's segment in *Aria* (1988) in which nude women dance around a weightlifter, who totally ignores them.

flaccid penis. This may at first appear to be a refreshing departure from the nearly compulsive need to make a powerful, phallic spectacle of the penis, but it works to reinforce that concept when we see that the man has failed to satisfy the woman. Thus his smallness marks his body with what we learn later in the film is his ongoing problem with impotence—the man turns out to be none other than the detective assigned to investigate the murder case involving the woman with whom he has attempted to have sex.

The fact that we later learn he is both a detective and impotent complicates the shower scene further. Originally perceived in a phallically powerful, athletic posture, he also represents the Law. It is precisely this patriarchal Law with which the woman will wreak havoc when she kills her husband and stymies the detective in his effort to arrest her. Thus, if the sight of the small, unerect penis signals the contrast between the penis and the phallus, it also implies that the small penis is somehow a sign of weakness and failure.

If the point of the scene is that the man cannot satisfy the woman because of premature ejaculation or, as we learn later, impotence, then penis size is irrelevant. Indeed, the important point is precisely that all penises are inadequate to the phallus, that none of them can measure up to it. Thus, Almodóvar at one and the same time makes fun of the inflated notion of the phallus and the Law and reinforces one of the most persistent notions about the male body that results from that cultural context. Indeed, Chris Straayer, who brought this film to my attention in relation to my 1991 essay on penis-size jokes in the cinema, noted that the predominantly gay male audience with whom she saw it erupted into laughter at the sight of the penis, which they interpreted as a visual rather than verbal joke. But there is, in her view, another layer of complexity here, since Almodóvar is a gay filmmaker addressing this joke to gay members of his audience. Thus it is not any man, but a man with a "hetero-egotistical" mentality that invests in and relies on a conflation of *macho* style, sexual prowess, and male sexuality who is the butt of the hostile joke. Whether one reads the scene as a joke or a noncomic moment, as I did, the fact remains that it is still caught in the contradiction of both challenging and reinforcing dominant sexual codes.

If the sexual representation of the male body in *What Have I Done to Deserve This?* at least departs from several norms and conventions of the classical cinema, how might we briefly analyze its antithesis? What then lies at the center of classical representations of the male body? The oft-filmed story of *Cyrano de Bergerac* supplies an intense distillation of crucial issues. Although the following analysis centers on the 1950 version directed by Michael Gordon, the number of versions of this film, the decades during which they were made, and the diversity of the countries in which they have been produced suggests that the story has deep resonance within twentieth-century Western culture. There are, to name just a few, a 1923 silent version made in France by Italian director Augusto Genina, an updated contemporary American version retitled *Roxanne* (1987), and a 1990 French version starring Gérard Depardieu, which shares a sexual ideology remarkably similar to that of the 1950 version. Steven H. Scheuer's capsule summary of the 1950 version calls it "the classic play" and describes José Ferrer's performance as "very moving and makes this perennial well worth seeing." The terms *classic* and *perennial*, along with the proclivity for remaking the film, raise the question of why this drama holds such fascination. Related to this is the question of the "moving" performance. Why does this particular character move audiences so deeply? The answer goes well beyond traditional aesthetics, taking us to the center of cultural assumptions about both the male body and the female gaze at it.

Cyrano de Bergerac tells the story of its title character (Ferrer), a military officer in seventeenth-century France who is equally renowned for his extraordinarily large nose and his prowess as a swordsman and a poet. Although Cyrano falls in love with his beautiful cousin Roxanne, it is William, a soldier assigned to Cyrano's regiment, who has caught her eye. Out of feelings for her, Cyrano determines to help the singularly inarticulate William woo Roxanne by supplying the words that make her fall in love with the handsome young soldier. They are married, but he dies in battle before they consummate their marriage, and she retires to a convent. Cyrano visits her weekly until his death, whereupon she learns the truth.

The opening scene in the film establishes a cluster of conventional associations around the male body. The large nose, predictably, has phallic associations. In a 1950s Hollywood version of the cultural myth that a man with a big nose has a big penis, Cyrano tells a man who stares at his nose that a great nose indicates a "virile" man. He establishes his skill as a swordsman in the same scene when he disrupts a play that the Count de Guiche wants to see and is warned that the count has "a long arm." "Mine is longer by three feet of steel," Cyrano replies. Cyrano may be ugly, but clearly he is to be feared and admired as a fighter whose body is appropriately marked as phallically powerful.

Cyrano's physical power is augmented by his remarkable verbal power. When another man criticizes his nose, he rebukes the man, not for the observation, but for the mundane wording of the insult. There are many clever uses of language to describe his nose with "wit," Cyrano tells the unfortunate offender before he engages the man in a duel, during which he shows equal skill at fighting and improvising a poem, killing the man as he finishes the poem. This brief dueling scene establishes Cyrano as totally in control of both action and language, the twin domains from which men assert power in a patriarchal culture. Thus the deficiency of his appearance (which, significantly, is marked by symbolic excess rather than literal deficiency) is overcompensated by his powerful actions and use of language. From the beginning, then, his looks seem a negligible component of his character, and in the metaphorical sense of sight in that common expression, he is an "attractive" character.

The remainder of the narrative works both to empower Cyrano further in the realms of action and language and to teach Roxanne that these things, rather than looks, are what really matter in a man. William supplies an extreme counterpoint to Cyrano, telling him, "I am never at a loss for words among men, but with any woman—paralyzed, speechless, dumb. I'm one of those stammering idiots who cannot court a woman." Cyrano not only empowers William with language but, in one exchange, links the images of battle with those of speech: "Those [words] are your weapon. How else do you conquer?" Elsewhere, musing on the desires of his life, Cyrano refers to "a voice that means manhood," while he ponders the dilemma "to fight or write."

How does the woman fit into all this? The first time William tries to woo Roxanne in person, he becomes tongue-tied and tells her that he grows "absurd." To which she tellingly replies, "And that distresses me as much as if you had grown ugly." At this point, Roxanne conceives of ugliness as a source of distress. She will soon learn better. Cyrano devises a way to prompt William as he woos Roxanne from under a balcony, but soon Cyrano, standing in the dark, speaks directly to her. "You need no eyes to hear my heart," he tells her, in what can be seen as a summary of the film's message to women about the role of their sight of and desire for the male body. The beautiful Roxanne learns that the appearance of a man's body means nothing; his power and skill with language and the sword mean everything. She learns her lesson well. "If you were less handsome, unattractive, ugly even, I should love you still," she tells William before he dies in battle.

Cyrano de Bergerac is a variant of "beauty and the beast" narratives, which always deal with an ugly or misshapen man and a beautiful woman. The television series aptly titled after the fairytale *Beauty and the Beast* perfectly fits this mold. A beautiful young woman falls in love with a creature who is literally part beast (his face appears catlike) and has special powers: He has both mental telepathy and unusual brute physical strength. In *Edward Scissorhands* (1990), the character played by Winona Ryder falls in love with the title character, a man-made, disfigured creature who has sharp mechanical hands that are powerful tools as well as an unusually adept and imaginative mind that informs his use of the hands.

While we are "moved" by the apparent humanistic message of these tales, it is a gendered message. Men, not people generally, should be valued and loved for attributes other than their bodies and appearances. Furthermore, the important character traits given to the misshapen man involve an intensification of traditional male patriarchal attributes, mental and physical powers, command of language, and so on. Thus, this supposedly universal tale cannot be reversed so that a handsome man learns to love a powerful, ugly, or misshapen woman. The ideology of these "beauty and the beast" narratives, moreover, sets up an extreme gender imbalance by making the woman particularly desirable for her beauty. This surfaces in a bizarre manner in *Edward Scissorhands*, which has a frame story in which the Ryder character is an old, shriveled woman who will not see Edward because she wants him to remember her as an attractive young woman. Similarly, in Jean Cocteau's *Beauty and the Beast* (1946), as a form of punishment, a young woman sees herself reflected in a mirror as an old woman who has lost her beauty. While the film audience desires the woman precisely because of what they see of her conventional beauty, she must learn quite literally not to see, or to see only with her heart. A man's appearance does not matter if he is overly endowed with substitute phallic powers. Indeed, *Cyrano de Bergerac* goes so far as to tell us that a woman must learn to stop looking at and seeing the male body while falling under the sway of powerful words and actions.

By way of contrast, it is instructive to shift attention away from the female gaze at the misshapen male body to the female gaze at the alluring male body. In *American Gigolo* (1980), a rather startling scene of a similar type to that in *What Have I Done to Deserve This?* occurred in the Hollywood cinema and shows just how contradictory and difficult such disruptions are.* *American*

American Gigolo received an R rating. Since frontal male nudity is rare in Hollywood films, many presume its absence is a simple ratings issue. Showing the male genitals does not mean an automatic X or NC-17 rating, and nearly all the Hollywood

Gigolo is one of the few Hollywood films that overtly disturbs central classical tenets about how the nude male body is shot, edited, and narrativized. Near the beginning, we see Richard Gere exercising in his apartment. There are three brief shots of views of the apartment, then a shot of two dumbbells lying on the floor. Gere walks into the frame, but we see only his legs from the knees down. He is wearing ankle grips, which he bends down and adjusts. Cut to a shot of a bar mounted on the ceiling as Gere's hands grab it, and we see him swing his ankles up and lock them onto the bar. Cut to a medium shot of Gere hanging upside down. He is wearing no shirt, and his upper body is visible. He engages in strenuous arm exercises with the dumbbells, and we hear his heavy breathing. Cut to a side-view mid-shot as we see his muscles straining from the exertion. He listens to a record designed to teach Americans to speak Swedish and repeats some of the phrases. Cut to an extreme long shot of his entire body. The camera slowly moves in as he continues exercising, breathing heavily, and repeating Swedish phrases. Cut back to the previous mid-view side shot. The phone rings. Cut to a shot of his forearms as he drops the dumbbells on the floor. Cut back to a full-body shot as he swings up to the bar, releases his ankles, and drops to the floor. The camera pans right as he answers the phone; he is still breathing heavily. He exercises and moves about as he talks on the phone. He walks away from the camera and looks at himself in a mirror as he continues exercising his upper torso and neck muscles. He walks toward the camera, then left, and the camera pans to follow him. He does two strong leg kicks. Only at the end of the shot does he very briefly stand still and then the camera frames him in a conventional head-and-shoulders close-up; none of his body is on display.

All the fragmented body shots emphasize the muscles either poised for action or in action. There is an emphasis on the athletic equipment characteristic of the props analyzed by Richard Dyer (1982) in photographs of male pin-ups. Even when he is talking on the phone, there is a need to show him

---

films that contain frontal male nudity are R-rated. Such noncontroversial films as *Drive, He Said* (1972) and *Buster and Billie* (1974) included full male nudity, as did such later mainstream films as *The Little Drummer Girl* (1984). Although Hollywood films include more frontal female nudity than male nudity, it is important to recognize that entirely different issues are at stake. In accordance with common patterns of male fetishism, Hollywood female nudity avoids the genitals and dwells on breasts and buttocks as a source of visual pleasure.

in constant action. The audible foregrounding of his breathing enlists the soundtrack in the service of stressing his exertion and activity. This scene can be read as a hysterical preparation and overcompensation for the static, passive display of Gere's body in a later lovemaking scene.

After Gere and Lauren Hutton make love, we have the seeming reversal of the classical Hollywood pattern. They are lying in bed talking when we see Gere in a medium shot. He is on his back looking up at the ceiling, then he sits up and gets out of bed. As he stands up, there is a cut to a previous extreme, high-angle, long-shot view of the room, which shows the entire bed toward the left of the frame and the wall and windows at the right. Naked, Gere walks across the room to the window, opens the venetian blinds, and looks out. Cut to a medium shot of him from a frontal angle as he continues talking (6). Except for briefly turning to look at Hutton, he looks out the window. The light from the window casts a strong bar pattern over his body. Cut to a medium shot from an angle behind Gere. We see the upper half of his body, and the camera is now positioned along an axis that approximates Hutton's view (7). The shot cannot be read as a point-of-view shot, however, since the camera is much closer to Gere than to Hutton. Cut back to the previous extreme long shot. As Gere talks, he turns toward his right, repositioning his body so that we now have an angled but full frontal view with his

7

8

penis visible (8). Hutton, who has been lying on her side while looking at him, now rolls over on her stomach. She continues to look directly at him as he finishes talking. The scene cuts abruptly to the next scene.

The apparent role reversal privileging the female gaze and objectifying the male body has to be qualified in several significant ways. In the full-body long shot, there is an unexpected cut back to an extreme distance from Gere. This obscures Gere's body at precisely the moment when it is most fully on display. This cutting pattern removes the view of Gere's body from being relayed through the woman's eyes, as the view of the woman's body is so frequently relayed through the male gaze. In fact, the camera has been placed so far back that Hutton's body is well within the shot near the left middle of the frame. In a traditional cutting pattern, her body would be absent or, at most, suggested by a neck-and-shoulders outline that would then mark the shot as a point of view. Furthermore, traditional spatial logic is broken in the extreme long shot, since earlier in the scene the cutting pattern has established an axis of cutting back and forth between the characters. Since neither character has moved, it is surprising to be pulled out of the established space. The added space is not necessary, in other words, to keep a character's actions in the composition. The cut back simultaneously denies the woman's point of view and deemphasizes the man's genitals.

What Gere is saying also deserves detailed analysis. After the lovemaking scene, Hutton initiates conversation with a reluctant Gere, who is looking out the window in a preoccupied manner that recalls another feature of male pin-ups analyzed by Dyer (1982). She asks him about himself; clearly uncomfortable with the subject, he is evasive. She then asks him, "Why do you sleep with older women?" "I prefer older women," he replies. "Why?" she persists. "What's the use of bringing some high-schooler to climax . . . some silly teenager that gets wet in the movies and goes home to masturbate? No challenge, no meaning." At the window, he recounts the following story:

> The other night, that night I met you at the hotel, I was with a woman, somebody's mother, her husband didn't care about her anymore. This woman hadn't had an orgasm in maybe ten years. Took me three hours to get her off. For a while there I didn't think I was going to be able to do it. When it was over, I felt like I'd done something, something worthwhile. Who else would've taken the time, enough to do it right?

Far from being reduced to an object here, Gere is in many ways the subject. The look of the woman, which the scene denies to the spectator, gets lost in admiration for male subjectivity. Gere delivers the lines, however, without a hint of braggadocio. Thus his sincerity can be read as articulating his true desire to bring sexual satisfaction to women. It can also be read as an affirmation of an extraordinary phallic male sexuality that is necessary for a woman's pleasure. Gere, then, is offered up and offers himself up as a gift to women. A mere man presumably could not have or would not have lasted the necessary three hours.

This structure, as we later see, may be extremely appealing for women. The man is offering up his body for the purpose of satisfying women, yet the film profoundly equivocates as it offers up Gere's body. It is no coincidence that Gere delivers this particular speech precisely at the moment in the film when the representation of his body momentarily and radically breaks with the usual codes of representing the male. Regardless whether one reads Gere as smugly offensive in his assertion of his sexual prowess or as attractive in his concern for women's pleasure, the fact remains that the speech foregrounds the male character's subjectivity even as the logic of the scene seems to objectify him and foreground the woman's subjectivity and her look.

Finally, the preceding lovemaking scene helps contextualize our response to the scene analyzed here. Gere actively makes love to Hutton. The scene is structured around very formally composed tight shots of the lovers' fragmented bodies. In nearly all the shots, Gere is actively moving over Hutton's body, kissing and stroking it. She is merely fetishized in the manner described earlier. Thus the reversal that takes place after they make love is extremely brief and atypical.

If the exercising scene can be read as a hysterical overcompensation and preparation for the later passive nude shot, the structure of the scene can be read as equally hysterical. This hysteria can be most simply seen in the cut back to the extreme long shot that follows no formal logic in this scene and that has no rhyme elsewhere in the film. It is a troubled moment resulting from the contradictory impulses of wanting simultaneously to show Gere's body and to cover it up.

Other signs of textual disturbance in the film result from the display of Gere's body. Julian, the character Gere plays, is identified with the traditional feminine position constructed by Hollywood and is frequently called "Julie." "Julie" is a prostitute, practicing a profession identified almost exclusively with women. He places an extraordinary emphasis on fashion; his closet is full of beautiful clothes. Perhaps most significantly, he is a victim who has to be saved at the end of the film—by a woman. A weak, out-of-control character for much of the film, he constantly asks women for help. He pleads with the older woman he was with at the time of a murder he is suspected of committing to be his alibi. He asks help of the woman who runs the prostitution service for which he works.

He begs Leon, a powerful black man who heads another prostitution service, to help him, and here the film reaches its logical extreme in Julian's character development. Leon, after refusing to help Julian, steps out on his high-rise balcony. Julian rushes him from behind and pushes him over the balcony, catching him by the legs as he is about to fall. Julian wants to scare Leon, but instead he panics about his inability to control the situation. Julian begs Leon not to fall, pleading that he needs him. Little by little we see Julian losing his grasp on Leon until the final horror—the sight of Julian clutching the empty boots as Leon falls to his death.

Here Julian fails at a moment of typical masculine action. Such a failure is unimaginable in a John Wayne or Clint Eastwood film. There are, of course, countless Hollywood films in which a male character risks the life of another character in order to get that character to do or say the desired thing, but I can think of no other such gruesome instance of a powerful male character failing so totally. The only other scene of typical masculine behavior by Julian occurs when he catches a senator's spy who is trailing him. He scares and humiliates the young man by violently writing a message on his forehead. The whole point of the scene, however, is that the senator has sent a comically inept kid who seems qualified to be a page but not a spy. But when faced with a real threat, Julian himself becomes almost comically inept. The image of him clutching the empty boots borders on grim comedy. Julian has been losing control throughout the movie, a loss that becomes explicit in this image. His powerlessness is the price he pays for standing nude while a woman and we, the spectators, look at him.

In the few instances when Hollywood shows the fully nude male, he is usually involved in action. In *The Deer Hunter* (1978), for example, Robert De Niro tears off his clothes and runs down the street. We see rear, frontal, and side shots of him; however, the camera distance and lighting in the frontal shot obscure his genitals. Just after he drops to the ground, a friend who has been following him catches up with him and throws a piece of clothing over his groin. Perhaps the most noted example of this pattern of male nudity occurs in the British film *Women in Love* (1969) when Alan Bates and Oliver Reed wrestle in the nude. Although their genitals can be seen, the male body is, using John Berger's distinction, naked rather than nude in both these films. In *American Gigolo*, Gere is nude rather than naked.

Referring to the male body in *American Gigolo*, Teresa de Lauretis has observed: "The body of John Travolta in *Moment by Moment* is not disturbing or exciting, but merely another pretty body on the Malibu scene; it even lacks the imaginary possibility, explicitly contained in the narrative of *American*

Gigolo, that the function of a man's body may be nothing more (and nothing less!) than to give pleasure to women" (1984, 83). Despite de Lauretis's enthusiasm, *American Gigolo* is intensely disturbed in its representation of Gere's character and body, perhaps precisely because of positing the function of the male body as being for the pleasure of a woman.

Until very recently, the notion that women should not look has been as entrenched at the level of critical intervention as it has been in artistic practice. This convention may seem somewhat surprising considering the importance of feminism in film theory during the past fifteen years, but feminist theory has been focused almost exclusively on the female body, leading Suzanne Moore to remark, "When I sought material on how women look at men, I discovered instead a strange absence" (1989, 45).

Laura Mulvey's work was primarily concerned with women and the representation of the female body, but it had strong implications for understanding the male body. For Mulvey, the male did not serve an erotic function but served as an active point of identification (the ideal ego, the more perfect body resulting from the misrecognition of the Lacanian mirror phase) for both male and female spectators; the male advanced the narrative, in the process demystifying, controlling, containing, and fetishizing females.* Even if true, the theory short-circuits questions about how powerful, active male characters are represented because Mulvey's explicit claim is that visual pleasure for both men and women spectators comes from the display of the female body; women are put in the position of adopting the male gaze. This argument, of course, relates to cultural arguments—put forward by John Berger (1972) and others at about the same time—that in our patriarchal culture women are brought up to survey their own bodies in comparison to the bodies

---

*Linda Williams's "When the Woman Looks" is an important exception, though in many ways it proves the rule (1984). Williams analyzes the look of the woman at the monster in a variety of horror films and concludes that the look creates a bond between the two; both the woman and the monster are the "other" of patriarchy, which uses the male body as the norm. Far from emphasizing a woman's desiring look at a beautiful body, the object of the look on which Williams focuses is deformed. Whereas in this genre, according to Williams, women see themselves mirrored in the monster, I argue elsewhere in this chapter that in various versions of *Cyrano de Bergerac* and *Beauty and the Beast* women must learn to ignore the outward appearance of the deformed male in order to love him for his inner qualities.

of other women and that this process is controlled by a male standard of desire. Thus, women derive pleasure from looking at other women's bodies, not from looking at men's bodies. Cultural evidence for this can be found in the fact that many women report pleasure in looking at *Playboy*. Once again, even if true, Berger's theory is inadequate to explain the complex issues of pleasure in cinema. Even if women are successfully enculturated to blind themselves to the male body—and I do not think they are—such cultural conventions cannot be applied to the cinema for the simple reason that all men and women are in some way objectified in the cinema. All of us, men and women, lesbians, gays, and heterosexuals, must look at the bodies of these represented men, even if only that we may identify with the male characters.

In other words, even if a case can be made culturally and psychoanalytically that women do not derive pleasure visually from objectifying male bodies in the way men do women's bodies, such a paradigm cannot be transferred to cinema because while watching a movie everyone is looking at representations of bodies in ways that include, but are not limited to, objectification. The cultural phenomenon surrounding the star system, for example, clearly indicates this. Even from the limited perspective of seeing the male protagonist as an active point of identification, features involving the objectification and eroticization of his body are not minimal. Marsha Kinder's personal response to Mulvey's argument makes this very clear:

> Despite the power of Mulvey's argument, I knew there were examples within Hollywood cinema of men functioning as the erotic object of the female gaze—not only Valentino in *The Shiek* or Gary Cooper in *Morocco*, but even John Wayne in *Stagecoach*. . . . I had experienced erotic pleasures at the cinema that were not explained by Mulvey's model and was unwilling to give them up. (1989, 201)

Mulvey makes an equally serious mistake in her theorization of the male spectator; she presumes that visual pleasure in the cinema for men lies exclusively in fetishizing the female form, in bringing the guilty woman under the control of the powerful male in the narrative, or both. But this is an error even from Mulvey's psychoanalytic perspective, since a male's development through the mirror stage establishes a powerful mechanism for pleasure in looking at the male body. I would argue that film theory has not only drastically underestimated the pleasure afforded women in looking at male bodies in the cinema but has also falsely presumed that, for the male spectator, issues of representation of the male body are the exclusive domain of gay theorists and critics. And while very important work has been done in that area by such critics as Richard Dyer and Robin Wood, this merely demonstrates an open acknowledgment on behalf of some gay men of their interest in representations of the male body. It tells us nothing about the viewing mechanisms of heterosexual men. As Scott MacDonald has admitted in his remarkably candid account of his experience with hard-core pornography as a heterosexual male, there is a "simple curiosity" for men in looking at erect penises: "In this particular context one of the primary functions of the female presence is to serve as a sign—to others and to oneself—that looking at erections, even finding them sexy, does not mean that the viewer defines himself as a homosexual" (1983, 14).

Left to their own devices, most heterosexual male theorists and critics may go merrily on their way forever minutely analyzing the representation of women's bodies. This may involve not only repression but also homophobia. Similarly, heterosexual men are not likely to acknowledge looking at other men in locker rooms. I am simply making the point that if we pay attention only to what most men say and write about these kinds of issues, we will be very much misled, since repression and homophobia play an important part in those articulations. A major premise of this book is that the sexual representation of the male body profoundly affects all men and women in our culture.

Indeed, Freud's work on paranoia and homosexuality implicates all heterosexual men in issues central to this study. Freud claimed that a man can transform the initial proposition "I love him" into four different variations: "I do not love him—I hate him"; "I don't love men—I love women"; "I don't love at all—I love only myself"; and "It is not I who love the man— she loves him." These variations deny and repress the original love for the man and ultimately replace it with hatred for the man, womanizing, self-love, or jealousy. All those forms of behavior repress homosexual love, and if Freud was right, all heterosexual men have repressed such love. This results from the passage through the stage of autoeroticism to object love, which includes a period of narcissism "which may be indispensable to the normal course of life" (Freud 1963, 163). This stage places particular emphasis on the penis: "The point of central interest in the self which is thus chosen as a love-object may already be the genitals. The line of development then leads on to the choice of an outer object with similar genitals—that is, to homosexual object choice—and thence to heterosexuality" (Freud 1963, 163).

Heterosexual men, therefore, do not simply bypass fascination with male genitals, although homophobia may make them characterize such interest as belonging exclusively to homosexuals.

Since this book is written from a heterosexual male perspective, it undoubtedly emphasizes some things that are totally alien to some heterosexual female perspectives, for example. Those concerns are not necessarily of interest only to heterosexual men, but some male concerns about the male body are exclusively the province of men. Tom Ryan, a practicing psychotherapist, notes that many men have concerns about their masculinity and that "one frequent manifestation of this is a preoccupation with the size of their penis" (1985, 16). Ryan argues that this is a symbolic as well as an anatomical concern and that many men exaggerate their smallness in accordance with their deflated masculine self-image. One of his patients "experiences his penis as small and shrivelled" (1985, 17). Clearly such perceptions of the penis are alien to women, who do not "experience" the penis in this way. Yet such male experiences seem to me not only to play a major role in the way in which men structure sexual representations of the male body but also, at times, to the way in which women respond to those representations or even create representations of their own.

The amount of fear and anxiety that I have found in a variety of forms among nearly all sexual representations of the male body might also be totally alien to women, but its pervasiveness certainly implies that all of us should attempt to understand it. As I argue in Chapter 8, however, there is a female flip side to the coin of these male preoccupations. Precisely because there is a symbolic dimension to the penis, as Ryan argues, the dominant patriarchal sexual ideology may have a pervasive impact on how some women respond to and create images of male sexuality. Although the experiences of the penis that Ryan describes are part of male subjectivity, they may very well be related, perhaps unconsciously, to female perception. Robert E. Becker, writing in *The Medical Aspects of Human Sexuality*, claims that "myths and misinformation" about penis size are shared by many females in our society, who "find a small penis to be less psychologically arousing" (1974, 170). Likewise, psychologists have claimed empirical evidence that both men and women respond to penis size similarly in ways that comply with cultural stereotypes (Verinis and Roll 1970). Although in the following chapters, I caution against the conclusions frequently drawn from this kind of medical discourse, it indicates how men and women may share the same ideological assumptions about sexuality and the male body. If this is true, we may expect that some women filmmakers, artists, and photographers, for example, may replicate many patriarchal assumptions about the male body, including those of power, size, and musculature.

But the arts and humanities are not the only areas in which new attention has been directed toward male sexuality, and it is instructive to turn to the sciences to elucidate an important parallel with the arts. In her paleoanthropological study *The Roots of Thinking* (1990), Maxine Sheets-Johnstone notes what she terms "a peculiar silence" (p. 174) with regard to the question of the evolution of the primate penis and that "the size of the human penis remains an unexplained mystery" (p. 174). She observes:

> If Martian scientists were attempting to understand male primate sexual behavior on the basis of the literature alone, not only would they not necessarily even conceive of a penis . . . but they would certainly not conceive of its spatio-kinetic transformational powers or its dynamic conformance to basic male sexual display behavior. Thus, to assume that the penis and penile erection can go without saying in accounts of primate sexual interactions on the grounds that explicit attention and description belabor the obvious skirts the point at issue. (p. 98)

Martian art, photography, and film critics are likely to be no more successful when dealing with the critical and theoretical literature on the nude male; logically, they should conclude that everything else in the image other than the genitals is important. In addition to presuming that we are dealing with the obvious, the arts have yet another way of skirting the issues of explicitness—good taste. It is impolite to notice such things or, more accurately, to talk about them. This climate of silence perpetuates, rather than challenges, patriarchal assumptions about the sexual representation of the male body.

Sheets-Johnstone argues that evolutionary scientists have not understood the crucial role of the penis in accounting for how hominids became bipedal. Her argument is that in a quadrupedal state neither the sight nor the size of the penis is of great importance; on the contrary, the female pudenda, not the penis, is the sight of significance. Nonhominid, quadrupedal sexual behavior revolves around posterior sexual presenting, and therefore changes in the size, shape, and color of the pudenda are important visual signals to males. The penis remains largely invisible. Only with the shift to upright posture does the display of the penis become important, and such display is constant with bipedality.

Paleoanthropologists and ethologists are reluctant, according to Sheets-

Johnstone, to "put the penis on the measuring line, not of reproductive competence, but of arousal, pleasure-giving competence" (1990, 175). Female pleasure resulting from tactile stimulation by the penis, she argues, played a major role in evolution. Males with larger penises "promised greater tactile-stimulatory competence" (p. 179). Females chose as their mates males with long penises and flexible hip joints, since these features gave them more pleasure through tactile stimulation resulting from thrusting during sex in ventro–ventral positions. Dorso–ventral positions, on the other hand, did not enhance the clitoral–labial–vaginal complex. Sheets-Johnstone argues that pleasure-giving competence, not competence in impregnating, explains the evolution of the male genitals.

A longer penis, then, served the dual purposes of being more visually prominent in bipedal males and facilitating the frontal coital positions that enabled stimulatory contact with the pleasure-giving zones of the female genital area. Females were no longer the static receivers of the male during characteristically brief sexual encounters (intercourse lasts between 8 and 12.2 seconds in chimpanzees); instead, ventro–ventral positions opened up immense areas of pleasure, including thrusting, embracing, touching, as well as tactile genital stimulation. Thus, Sheets-Johnstone concludes that "the evolution of human sexuality begins with an explanation of the move toward stark visibility of the primate penis, and the sizable increase in penile length and girth" (1990, 184). This emphasis on the visibility of the penis coincides with an inverse move toward greater invisibility of the female genitals, which culminates with the development of the labia majora covering the vaginal orifice.

Sheets-Johnstone also addresses the issue of circumference, noting that nonhuman primate penises differ in both length and girth from human penises. Chimpanzees, for example, have what she calls a pencil-thin penis and one that averages only 8 cm in length in comparison to 13 cm for the human penis. The evolution of the penis occurred in two rapid speciating events, the first involving increased length and the second increased girth. The importance of this argument for evolution cannot be overly exaggerated. Females whose genitals could accommodate the thicker penises had a reproductive advantage of a wider selection of mates and ultimately were able to accommodate infants with larger brains, from which speciation developed. The common assumption that the female body adapted to accommodate larger brains is mistaken. Similarly, Sheets-Johnstone argues that we have traditionally overvalued such traits as the ability to carry objects and expand visual range in explaining the move toward bipedality. Bipedality resulted from the increased pleasurability of ventro–ventral mating, and this move toward constant bipedality resulted from the continual display of the penis. The penis became an important visual signal, not just between males and females, but also among males. Indeed, Sheets-Johnstone draws the analogy with antlers, arguing that the male with the largest antlers emerges as the dominant one. Thus it is no exaggeration to say that in this argument, the evolution of humans as a bipedal, large-brained species depends on the centrality of the large penis for both its qualities as an impressive visual signal and its pleasure-giving competence for females.

I have discussed Sheets-Johnstone's argument in detail for a number of reasons. It certainly provides a striking example of the possible gains to be achieved by breaking the silence that protects the penis from any explicit attention. It also shows how unexamined assumptions can have far-reaching implications, in this case, skewing our entire account of evolution. The validity of Sheets-Johnstone's argument is not the issue here; that it was ever formulated and that it demonstrates the possible significance of explicitly analyzing the penis including its visual characteristics is, however, important. Sheets-Johnstone notes:

> While present-day humans might react quite differently to concealed genitalia of the opposite sex, it is reasonable to conclude that what is not tactilely or visually accessible in a nonhominid primate's corporeal world— what is not a readily available public sexual object so far as other animal bodies are concerned—is not a corporeal object commonly sought out for sexual touching. (1990, 173)

She has further stressed to me in personal correspondence that the conclusions she draws from her method of analyzing evolutionary developments of hominids millions of years ago bear no relationship to present-day females; that is, behavior today cannot provide explanations for evolutionary developments that originated long ago, nor can origins explain present practices or utility. Indeed, novelty plays a significant role in the origin and evolution of displays and bipedality created such sexual novelty. While she cautions against using her work to support the notion that present-day women respond significantly or even favorably to the visual or tactile stimulation of large penises, she does cite a 1979 study by Donald Symons that claims that women respond more erotically to photographs of men with erect penises than to those with flaccid penises because they suggest an actual sexual interaction rather than a possible one in the future. She also observes that the ethologist J. H. Crook, who itemized female contact signals arousing to men, includes genital sensation among them but does not itemize such contact signals arousing to women. She then notes:

> The same peculiar omission is found in the original Hite reports on female and male sexuality, with males being questioned explicitly about "the pleasure of the vagina on the penis," but females not being explicitly questioned equivalently about the pleasure of the penis in the vagina. While a reluctance to put the penis on the measuring line, not of reproductive competence but arousal, pleasure-giving competence, has, perhaps, been fed by the notion that "female animals are mere egg repositories waiting for something to happen," fixation on orgasm—on whether females have orgasms, and on where anatomically they come from—appears to blot out straightforward acknowledgement and investigation of the penis as a tactile stimulator. (Fixation on orgasm can also lead to preoccupations—and airy speculations—about the kind of mating system early hominids might or might not have enjoyed.) (Sheets-Johnstone 1990, 175)

This passage makes clear the reluctance to address publicly the possible pleasure-giving competence of the penis (although it certainly is a topic of private conversation), but it also reminds us of how, in our culture, we are prone to endless talk and speculation about such things as female orgasm. This preoccupation with the supposed mysteries of the female body has become so normative that we seldom give it a second thought, while avoidance of explicit analysis of the male genitals has become so deep rooted that merely to raise the issue makes it a preoccupation.

Sheets-Johnstone's claim that the response of ancient hominids is irrelevant to present-day human females slips when she leads up to her conclusion by citing the works of Symons, Crook, and Hite, three researchers who deal with the sexual response of modern women. Nevertheless, I think Sheets-Johnstone is absolutely right in pointing out how some contemporary sex research in anthropology, paleontology, ethology, and sociology manifests the same reluctance to address the penis that she has identified in paleoanthropology. But if there has been a peculiar silence about the penis in many areas, the one exception is, as we see in Chapter 7, sexology and the related sex manuals that have flourished in its wake. Here the situation is virtually reversed.

Sheets-Johnstone's work reveals both the possible gains to be made from and the dangers of directly confronting the taboo of the penis. Such work engages an extraordinary paradox: It challenges patriarchal prohibition, and at the same time, it risks reinscribing the penis at the center of things—precisely where patriarchy would want it. Indeed, in what appears to me an attempt to refrain from referencing feminism, Sheets-Johnstone is curiously silent herself on the subject of the cause of Darwin's silence (and the silence of all the evolutionary scientists who followed him) about the evolution of the human penis. Without exploring the underlying reasons, she simply points out that primate researchers have traditionally emphasized female genitalia and that the refusal to pay similar attention to penile erection may be linked to the fact that the display of the male erection in Western society is defined as a criminal perversion (1990, 93). Such a literal account is woefully inadequate. The medical profession in general and the sexology movement in particular showed no such aversion to studying penile erection. As we later see, the subject became a virtual obsession, and one that even permeated Western twentieth-century popular culture long before evolutionary scientists took up the issue. The history of science and medicine both involve frequent violations of the strongest cultural taboos and challenges to the deepest-held cultural beliefs. Indeed, Darwin is a perfect example. To argue that the taboo against representing the male erection would be respected because it is classified as a criminal perversion is to argue in a circular fashion, using as an answer something that itself needs to be explained. Certainly it takes more courage to challenge the biblical account of Creation than it does to study penile erection!

Throughout this book I confront the silence surrounding the male body, particularly the male genitals. Therefore I will repeatedly confront the following paradox: In a patriarchal culture, when the penis is hidden, it is centered. To show, write, or talk about the penis creates the potential to demystify it and thus decenter it. Indeed, the awe surrounding the penis in a patriarchal culture depends on either keeping it hidden from sight (as we see, for example, the classical cinema does) or carefully regulating its representation (as the pornographic film does). Since the penis bears a crucial, if frequently unacknowledged, relationship to the phallus, understanding this paradox is all the more critical. I would go so far as to suggest that the dominant representations of phallic masculinity in our culture depend on keeping the male body and the genitals out of the critical spotlight.

The films, videotapes, novels, photographs, artworks, and music I have chosen to explore in the following chapters reflect a variety of considerations.

In Chapter 2, I examine the repression of potentially disturbing sexual material in *The Wild Child*, *Kaspar Hauser*, and *Greystoke*, feral-child films that deal with the symbolic enculturation of males. Why was it so difficult for such diverse and highly praised filmmakers as François Truffaut, Werner Herzog, and Hugh Hudson to confront the sexual element inherent in their material? These films also bring into sharp focus the relationship between the literal and the symbolic, a distinction central to all the following chapters. If these films betray the difficult stakes involved in representing male sexuality and the male body during a transition into the realm of culture and the symbolic, the films of Howard Hawks supply an opportunity to survey what happens to that body once it is firmly within the symbolic. Chapter 3 focuses on *Rio Bravo* and *Rio Lobo*, two of Hawks's films that systematically explore the way in which assumptions about sexual difference structure the representation of men's and women's bodies with regard to such attributes as strength, beauty, power, and stature and how the loss of culturally sanctioned power for men and women is figured differently with regard to scarring, wounding, and aging of the body. Chapter 4 analyzes symbolic assumptions about power and the male body via an analysis of the casting of Edward G. Robinson in *Scarlet Street*. Robinson's short, rounded body signifies a failed masculinity that is ideologically related to Hawks's casting of him in *Tiger Shark* and to Fritz Lang's casting of Peter Lorre, an actor with a similar body type, in *M*.

Although film is the point of departure and focus of this book, many of the issues raised in the film analyses can be fully understood only in relationship to the other arts and media, and, ultimately, larger cultural discourses such as medicine. Chapter 5 analyzes Jim Thompson's *noir* novel *The Nothing Man*, which, like *Scarlet Street*, deals with a central character who lacks masculinity and like many Hawks characters has been wounded—the crucial difference being that his wound and his lack are both literally and symbolically linked to having lost his penis in combat.

The next four chapters deal with varying verbal and visual representations of the male genitals. Chapter 6 analyzes a widespread compulsion to joke and talk about the penis in Hollywood films of the 1970s and 1980s. These jokes point to the importance of humor as part of the sexual representation of the male body as well as the importance of considering what we hear in relationship to what we see or do not see in movies. Concurrent with the proliferation of penis-size jokes in U.S. films, there was a cycle of rape-revenge films in which beautiful, raped women extract graphic revenge on the guilty men's bodies. Both types of films were predominantly made by men and largely marketed for men. What pleasures accounted for the popularity of verbally and physically assaulting the male body and genitals?

If joking and banter seem like one of the few ways in which the penis is explicitly acknowledged in much of current culture including the media, the arts, and even scientific discourses, the exception lies in medical and sex-ology discourses and their popularized versions. The way in which the penis, and particularly its size, has become a focal point of twentieth-century sex manuals is a virtual return of the repressed. Chapter 7 traces this phenome-non, linking such disparate cultural products as the film *Porky's* and the popular best-seller *Everything You Always Wanted to Know about Sex—But Were Afraid to Ask*. My analysis of these jokes also relates to how heterosexual men may appropriate women characters to mask their homosexual preoccu-pations and how the work of such openly gay filmmakers as Almodóvar and Rainer Werner Fassbinder should not be marginalized as the sole province of gay theorists and spectators; such work is of central importance to under-standing crucial issues for both heterosexual male and female spectatorship.

In Chapter 8, I turn from film to video to analyze *Dick Talk*, an indepen-dent video production made by women and featuring women talking about the male body and sexuality. The tape introduces women's voices within the context of a serious discussion on a taboo subject that has traditionally been the province of male joking or male-dominated medical discourse. Once again, we listen rather than look, and while what we hear may seem quite unrelated to and at times, in fact, hostile to either male jokes or the medi-cal discourse on male sexuality, there are strong connections. The way in which the women speak raises the issue of what constitutes significant alter-natives to currently available erotic images of the male body in pornographic magazines and movies, something I then examine briefly in relationship to women's photographs of men.

Chapter 9 extends the investigation of several of these issues through an analysis of Nagisa Oshima's *In the Realm of the Senses*. Aside from pop medical discourse, hard-core pornography is the only place in contemporary media and popular culture where the penis is visually represented. Pornogra-phy thus supplies a vital area of investigation for the sexual representation of the male body. While *In the Realm of the Senses* includes explicit hard-core sex scenes, it differs significantly from both the Western hard-core feature as well as the Japanese erotic woodblock tradition of explicit sexual representa-tion of the male body. Referring to Japanese, Chinese, and Indian traditions, Chapter 9 examines Asian representations of the male body in comparison to

Western representations. Within this context, I also contrast ancient Greek representations of the male body with those of both Asia and the contemporary West. Oshima's unique film illustrates a true alternative to several cultural traditions, and I consider other such contemporary alternatives.

My concluding chapter begins with an analysis of Roy Orbison's music. Orbison's songs, singing style, image, and performing style all depart significantly from standard 1950s and 1960s norms of masculinity and the male body; open expression of intense male fear and anxiety lie at the center of his music and style. It is appropriate to conclude with his work for several reasons. Orbison reminds us that masculinity and representations of the male body are not as homogeneous as we might at first think, even in the world of Top-40 rock 'n' roll. Orbison's work points to the pervasiveness of male fear that underlies nearly all the discourses analyzed throughout this book: fear of measuring up either literally or metaphorically, castration anxiety, fear of women and homosexuals, or fear of loss of masculine power. Some of Orbison's music is startling for the way it revels in the masochistic pleasures of loss and loneliness and thus relates to the masochism that I find fundamental to many of the representations I have analyzed, including penis-size jokes, rape-revenge films, and *In the Realm of the Senses*. Orbison's music and persona also include rich images of the two poles that characterize so many representations of masculinity and the male body: the awesome phallic spectacle of power, and the vulnerable and frequently comic image of its failed opposite. The male body is trapped within the constraining confines of a polarity, which is something like the mother and the whore dichotomy that underlies so much of the sexual representation of women in our culture.

Studies of this kind can develop in different ways. One approach would be to hypothesize a single unifying theory and then apply it to various texts to prove its validity; this is the model Mulvey used in her influential essay on the representation of women in cinema. Among its strengths, the unifying theory approach provides a coherent and comprehensive account that both identifies previously ignored features of the works considered and explains their presence and significance. Before Mulvey, film scholars simply did not notice or comment on the prevalence of ways in which Hollywood cinema visually fetishizes women's bodies, narratively punishes and contains independent or threatening female characters, or both. Her Freudian–Lacanian theory offered an account of why men feared women and why their presence in the cinema posed problems that could be addressed through fetishism and narrative containment.

One of the model's great weaknesses, however, is that only those textual features supporting the theory will be noticed; thus, for instance, Mulvey and the many scholars who adopted her paradigms failed to notice how and how often men's bodies are eroticized in cinema and what kinds of looks characters possess. These oversights may be related, as we see in Steven Cohan's analysis of a scene in *Picnic* in which the relay of looks through the female gaze erotically objectifies William Holden's body as he showers. Once formulated, such theories are also frequently used in ways that distort textual features, making them appear to support the theory. Another drawback to posing a single theory with such vast explanatory force lies in its vulnerability. The model topples if its basic assumptions are proven wrong. If, for example, the Freudian–Lacanian account of psychoanalytic development or, more accurately, Mulvey's version of it is wrong, then its explanatory force disappears. If there is no such thing as castration anxiety, Mulvey's entire account of male spectatorship crumbles.

In practice, tests of theory rarely have such all-or-nothing results. If Mulvey were correct in identifying the pervasive patterns of women's representation in cinema but wrong in accounting for them, we would have to seek other explanations but retain the validity of the patterns. If she perceptively identified those patterns but disregarded other equally pervasive and important ones, we would need to identify additional patterns. Indeed, Steve Neale, in one of the first major essays to explore the representation of the male body in the cinema, proceeds, like Mulvey, to hypothesize and then apply a theory (1983). He argues that when the male body becomes an erotic spectacle, as in a film like *Spartacus*, it is brutally and sadistically punished. The sadism is a homophobic response to the erotic display of the male body, one that destroys its attractiveness. Although his account of looking and erotic objectification in the cinema is different from Mulvey's, Neale's argument is similarly structured and has similar explanatory strengths and weaknesses. Neale identifies a pervasive pattern, provides a psychoanalytic account (which is open to debate), and clearly overlooks important patterns of erotic display of the male body where no sadistic punishment occurs.

Neale also argues that when the male body is eroticized for the female gaze, it becomes feminized. Paul Smith's perceptive response to this claim shows the dangers inherent in such theorizing:

Neale's contention that in order for the male body to be thus objectified it has to be "feminized" is open to question, not least because it relies upon a sweeping generalization (increasingly doubted in film studies) about the conventions and apparatus of cinema—namely, upon the argument that they are oriented primarily and perhaps exclusively to the male spectator. Neale's argument is in a sense self-fulfilling, or at least circular. If it is assumed that the apparatus is male, geared to a male gaze, then any instance of objectification will have to involve the "feminization" of the object, so that the notion becomes so broad as to be useless. (1989, 93)

Indeed, all sweeping generalizations of the kind on which Mulvey and Neale base their theories have become increasingly suspect in film theory. Although I take a different approach in this study, I nevertheless feel there is a great value to their style of theorizing. It puts important issues on the agenda in a provocative manner and encourages their being tested, refined, and perhaps even rejected. As Smith's work on Clint Eastwood shows, such theorizing leads to more productive work, even from those who strongly disagree.

In writing this book, I have chosen not to hypothesize a single theory, psychological or otherwise, about the sexual representation of the male body. I do not, for example, propose that the pervasiveness of male fear in the texts I analyze can be explained by castration anxiety, though I employ that Freudian concept at times. Even when I address a more specific topic, such as masochism, I have resisted the kind of comprehensive account of it offered by recent theorists like Gaylyn Studlar and Kaja Silverman. Studlar's groundbreaking work on masochism led to a provocative refutation of Mulvey's reading of Josef von Sternberg's films starring Marlene Dietrich (1988). Studlar rejects the dominant Freudian–Lacanian model in film theory and argues for the importance of the powerful mother during the pre-Oedipal, oral phase of infant development. Silverman severely criticizes Studlar's psychoanalytic model as confused and inadequate, arguing instead for an understanding of masochism within an Oedipal framework. Silverman's emphasis at times falls on theoretically explaining male masochism, instead of merely analyzing and explaining its presence in artistic texts. I have chosen to bypass these debates for three reasons. First, I am a film and popular culture scholar, and my primary emphasis and expertise lie in explicating those texts and not in, for example, correcting Freud on his errors in accounting for masochism. If my textual analyses are perceptive, however, they should contribute to such highly theoretical projects. This leads me to my second reservation: If film theorists emphasize a particular psychoanalytic model in their work, the validity of their model, be it their reading of an extant one or their formulation of a new one, should be informed and evaluated not only by film theorists but also by medical professionals formally trained in those areas. The history of psychoanalytic film theory is as much, if not more, a history of misreading Freud and Lacan as it is of reading them. Furthermore, there is a vast psychoanalytic literature in addition to Freud and Lacan that, though seldom referred to by film theorists, relates to these issues. It is a dubious enterprise for Silverman to convince film theorists that her model of masochism is correct and Studlar's is wrong, since very few film theorists have read widely enough to evaluate these arguments. My point is not that psychoanalysts simply possess the "truth" nor that film scholars cannot contribute significantly to psychoanalytic literature but that, since both film studies and psychoanalysis are specialized disciplines, interaction between the two is essential to the success of such a project. Ironically, the entire masochism debate may be based on the questionable assumption, so dear to much film theory, that one of the positions is simply correct and has full explanatory force. Several psychoanalysts have indicated to me their belief that masochism is not an either–or proposition in relationship to the pre-Oedipal oral mother or the Oedipal father.* Masochism may have multiple and even contradictory origins. It seems to me premature at this point to accept Silverman's attempt to discredit Studlar's model; both have produced valuable insights. Thus, my third reason: A single account of the sexual representation of the male body is premature, as the subject has only recently received scholarly attention.

My approach gives primary emphasis to close textual analyses informed by a variety of critical methods, including formal analysis, feminism, psychoanalysis, auteurism, and cultural studies. I have used whatever method or combination of methods allowed the richest possible exploration of the texts and topics under consideration. The usefulness of this approach nearly reverses and, I hope, complements the usefulness of the approach employing a unified theoretical model. If my readings are insightful, they should encourage further exploration and theorization. It is my hope that such further work will be interdisciplinary and include professionals within the psychoanalytic community. Like Paul Smith, however, I would caution that "investigation of the representational strategies of film finally is capable of discovering more

*Members of the Film Studies Group of the New Orleans Psychoanalytic Institute expressed these views to me during a series of lectures I delivered in New Orleans sponsored by the Institute in February 1991.

about the availability of cultural ideologies than about forms of subjectivity" (1989, 101). We should not isolate elements of texts and simply presume that they demonstrate either male subjectivity or single, fixed spectatorial positions.

If I have used a plurality of methods without trying to prove a single theory, I have proceeded on a number of assumptions that explain the texts and topics I have chosen. Briefly, they are these: Even as work on masculinity and the male body has finally begun, there has been a virtual silence on the topic of sexual representation—how and when it is explicitly represented and, of equal importance, how and when it is avoided, covered up, displaced, and repressed. The cultural taboo concerning both the representation and discussion of the penis lies at the center of this topic. My primary assumption is that the representation of the penis and the taboo that usually suppresses its representation can be understood only by studying the relationship between the penis and the phallus. I am not talking here of any single notion of the phallus—Freudian, Lacanian, or any other—but about all these and more: the persistent and pervasive manner in which contemporary Western culture attributes profoundly important symbolic dimensions to the penis, at times even denying the connection between the penis and the phallus. Finally, I assume that in order to explore this topic it is necessary to abandon conventional distinctions between "high art" and popular culture (e.g., discussing Jim Thompson in the same breath as Ernest Hemingway and F. Scott Fitzgerald) and even between art and other forms of cultural discourse (e.g., the medical literature on and representation of the penis).

Most of this book, then, is composed of critical essays that explore a diverse but interrelated group of media and cultural texts, all of which touch on the sexual representation of the male body. My emphasis therefore is on male objectivity rather than subjectivity—the male body as object rather than the male as subject. Western twentieth-century film, media, and popular culture are my focus. Nevertheless, in order to understand those cultural products, I have found it necessary to contrast them with periods such as ancient Greece and the nineteenth-century West as well as with varying Asian cultures and time periods, just as I have had to contrast heterosexual male discourses with the discourses of heterosexual women, gays, and lesbians. I have explored the films and texts in a manner that I hope brings to light previously unexamined aspects of them. Although there is no single theoretical or historical argument underlying all these essays, they have been carefully chosen, arranged, and cross-referenced to encompass and develop many vital areas of exploration of the penis–phallus concept that so predominantly structures representations of the male body. Many theorists in the past have explored that relationship from the perspective of psychoanalytic theory, their goal frequently being either to affirm or to deny the psychoanalytic claim that there is no relationship between the literal possession of the organ and the symbolic concept on which so much in psychoanalysis depends. From this perspective, the purity of the concept of the phallus in psychoanalysis is at stake. My perspective reverses this emphasis. In this book, I am not concerned with psychoanalytic theory's relationship to the phallus but with the relationship of the symbolic phallus to the literal male body. For it is not just psychoanalysis, I would argue, that is tainted by the oft-denied connection between the penis and the phallus; it is also the male body and male sexuality. It is no exaggeration to say that men under patriarchy are not just empowered by their privileged position through the penis–phallus; they are also profoundly alienated from their own bodies, which are lost beneath its monstrosity. No wonder they are so often running scared.

"I WILL SUPPRESS NOTHING"

• • • • • •

SEXUALITY IN MALE FERAL-CHILD NARRATIVES

If being a "man" is part of a complex cultural process involving but also exceeding the body, feral-child narratives offer a particularly rich starting point for this study. By definition, such narratives are fascinating, with human–animal, culture–nature dichotomies and the process by which one moves from nature and the animal into culture and the human. Notions of sexuality, gender, and the body lie at the center of the human, as do matters of language. Since 1969, three major films about feral children have been made; from different countries, they reflect different cinematic traditions: François Truffaut's *The Wild Child* (1969), Werner Herzog's *Everyman for Himself and God against All* (1974, retitled *The Mystery of Kaspar Hauser* for its U.S. release and commonly referred to as *Kaspar Hauser*), and Hugh Hudson's *Greystoke: The Legend of Tarzan, Lord of the Apes* (1984). *The Wild Child*, usually classified as part of the French New Wave, and *Kaspar Hauser*, as part of the New German Cinema, both fall within the tradition of European Art Cinema, and *Greystoke* within the tradition of British Quality Cinema.

Feral-child narratives have been with us for a long time, yet their popularity tends to cluster at different historical moments. Although many supposed cases of feral children have been documented, few truly captured the popular imagination as did Victor of Aveyron, on whose life *The Wild Child* was based. Found wandering wild in the woods in France around 1800, Victor became a test case for then-current philosophical disputes centering on Jean-Jacques Rousseau's concept of the noble savage. Victor's medical treatment also revealed early nineteenth-century assumptions about the primacy of phonetic language and the inferiority, indeed the inadequacy, of signing as an alternative language system.

A clue as to why feral-child narratives have emerged so prominently at this point in the twentieth century can be found in Oliver Sacks's writings about events he witnessed at Gallaudet College in 1988, when students at the institution for the deaf successfully rebelled against the appointment of a non-hearing-impaired president: "Nor had I quite realized (even though I knew this theoretically) that sign language might indeed be a complete language. . . . I had to see all this, see it for myself, before I could be moved away from my previous 'medical' view of deafness (as a 'condition,' a deficit, which had to be treated) to a 'cultural' view of the deaf as forming a community with a complete language and culture of its own" (1988, 23).

We live at a time when social, intellectual, and scientific thought is preoccupied with the nature of language. Sacks, an eminent U.S. neurologist is, in this regard, like Claude Lévi-Strauss, Roland Barthes, and Jacques Lacan. Indeed, philosophical debates among French intellectuals formed an important part of the context in which *The Wild Child* was made.

Our culture is reconsidering the distinction between animals and humans. The cover of the May 23, 1988, issue of *Newsweek* featured a photograph of a dog with a cartoon balloon showing that the dog is thinking "$E = MC^2$." "How Smart Are Animals?" the headline asks. Answer, "They Know More Than You Think." Such a cover story is not surprising in a culture that became fascinated after Koko the gorilla reportedly went into mourning when All Ball, her cat friend, died. Many Americans believe that recent experiments prove that chimpanzees can use language. The previously cited French tradition of thought is strongly committed to a fundamental distinction between animals and humans and nature and culture based on the premise that only humans possess language. Animals communicate with each other by using signals, but only humans use symbolic language. Some consideration about the relationship between animals and humans is a constitutive feature of feral-child narratives. Frequently the child is literally raised by animals and is animal-like until integrated into a culture. Although he never had lived in the wild with animals, Kaspar in Herzog's film feels a closeness with animals; the first word he speaks is "horsey."

Most significant for my purposes, gender issues are an important part of the appeal of feral-child narratives for contemporary viewers and play an important structural role in them. For if such stories touch on what distinguishes humans from animals and the role language plays in that distinction, they implicitly (and sometimes explicitly) serve as a locus for examining sexual difference and the role that language plays in it. Feminist concerns with the positioning of women in relation to language are among the most important issues in current language debates. Is language within a patriarchal culture inherently masculine? Are linguistics and semiology male-ordered disciplines stuck within rigid patterns of oppositions that cannot analyze or understand the rhythmic complexities of feminine language that fall outside such categories? Some of these gender issues are addressed in the three films under consideration here. All three are about males, as are most feral-child narratives. This fact in itself reveals our culture's preoccupation with the male drama of the critical move from being outside culture with no language to being inside culture with language.*

François Truffaut's *The Wild Child* is based on Jean Itard's accounts of his work with Victor of Aveyron. Most of the film takes place in and around Itard's country home, where he takes Victor after encountering the boy in a Paris institution. Truffaut's recurring image shows Itard (played by Truffaut) observing Victor and then recording his observations in his journal. We hear his voice-over reading as he writes passages taken from the actual historical records. When *The Wild Child* was released, however, virtually no one knew that the film's narrative premise was entirely Truffaut's invention. Itard's own writings never mention that he brought Victor to his home, and Roger Shattuck, in *The Forbidden Experiment*, documents that it never happened.

*Such figures as Helen Keller and Fini Straubinger in Herzog's *Land of Silence and Darkness* are fundamentally different from those under consideration here. These women were either born blind and deaf or became so at an early age; they were always part of culture, and their stories are popularly seen as ones of heroically overcoming disabilities. Thus they are "remarkable" women, rather than near-animals dramatically entering culture and becoming human.

Truffaut had to have known this from Itard's reports, which present his contact with Victor fully within the conventions of a doctor–patient relationship, albeit an intense and long-lasting one. (Curiously, Harlan Lane made the same mistake as Truffaut in his study of the case a few years after *The Wild Child* was made.) Truffaut's departure from his source material is astounding because it is precisely his contextualization of Victor's treatment within the home and family (or lack thereof) that points to an ideological disturbance within this otherwise tightly controlled film.

By having Itard treat Victor at home, Truffaut poses a number of questions about Itard's motivations and his personal life. Perhaps most significantly, the film paradoxically raises the issue of sexuality through its very attempt to repress it. Itard is a bachelor who lives with Madame Guerin, his housekeeper. Truffaut cast Françoise Seigner as the housekeeper, an older woman who within the codes of the star system is strongly marked as holding no sexual interest for Itard or the audience. Her sole function is domestic: cooking, cleaning, and ultimately taking care of Victor within a traditional division of labor with her employer. All of Victor's emotional and physical needs are left to her; the doctor's total interaction with the boy is of a scientific and professional nature.

Madame Guerin is, in fact, based on Itard's accounts. According to Shattuck, "throughout his years of training, Victor lived in the Institute for Deaf-Mutes in a room above Mme. Guerin's. Itard had his own apartment in another wing" (1980, 211). She *and her husband* were Victor's guardians. Moreover, certain events arose that required Itard to make a crucial reference to the structure of Madame Guerin's domestic life:

> At about the same time, Madame Guerin's husband fell ill and was nursed away from the house without Victor being told of it. Having among his little domestic duties that of setting the table at dinner time, he continued to lay a place for Monsieur Guerin, and although he was made to remove it every day he never failed to set it again the next day. (Itard 1962, 90)

Itard goes on to describe Victor's response to his guardian after her husband died from the illness.

The point is not simply that Truffaut's strategy toward the adaptation blocks him from rendering this episode (which it does), but that he could not have been mistaken about the actual situation. Itard makes Victor's and Madame Guerin's domestic circumstances relatively clear in his 1806 report, which the film credits as its source, although there is only one reference in both the reports to the fact that the Guerins' apartment was in the institute. In making Madame Guerin Itard's housekeeper, Truffaut further decided to eliminate her husband, who is never mentioned in the film. She and the doctor are the only occupants of the home in which Victor is placed. Itard notes in his first report: "Several times during the course of the winter I have seen him crossing the garden of the Deaf and Dumb" (1962, 14). In his article "How I Made *The Wild Child*," Truffaut claims, however, that Itard "asked to take the boy home with him to his house near Paris and care for him" (1973, 12). At the same time he claims complete familiarity with both of Itard's reports and says that, although he created the adaptation strategy of Itard keeping a diary, throughout the making of the film he immersed himself in Itard's actual reports.

Truffaut's article thus complicates but does not fundamentally eradicate the question of why he changed the domestic situation; even if his essay had acknowledged that this did not happen, we would still be left with the film's assertion that it did. Another contradiction is raised when Shattuck relates Truffaut's explanation as to *why* he departed from the historical circumstances—overturning his own published statements that those events actually occurred. Shattuck simply reports Truffaut's explanation: "This departure from historical events was forced on Truffaut because he could set up his equipment in the institute only for a few days, and because he had to find a setting remote from Paris noise in order to use direct sound rather than post-synchronization" (1980, 211).

We must be cautious about accepting such a simple technological explanation. Why did Truffut not shoot exteriors and establishing shots at the institute and shoot interiors elsewhere? Why, in fact, does he privilege the "realism" of the actual institute over the narrative structure? Given a choice, nearly anyone approaching the subject from the perspective of faithfulness to the historical circumstances would decide that abandoning the actual setting was much less a violation of the true events than changing the fundamental relationships among the major characters! Indeed, we can even question Truffaut's need to privilege technology over narrative structure. Why should it be more important to shoot with direct sound away from Paris noise than to re-create Victor's actual circumstances? For that matter, why was Truffaut unable to find an institution in the country away from city noise? Certainly the decision to abandon Paris does not necessitate shooting the film in a country home.

Shattuck's acceptance of Truffaut's argument is naively inadequate, raising more questions than it answers and obscuring ideology in the process. Auteurist criticism maintains that Itard's relationship to Victor is analogous to André Bazin's relationship to Truffaut. As is well known, Bazin "adopted" Truffaut when he was a troubled teenager. In this film, Itard similarly "adopts" Victor. Victor thus becomes another troubled, homeless child in Truffaut's work, like the main character in Truffaut's first feature film, *The 400 Blows*. This account does not address ideological issues any more than Shattuck's does, but it may help explain why Truffaut took the approach to adaptation he did.

The lack of traditional family structure in Itard's home is highlighted by a scene in which Itard takes Victor to visit friends, a husband and wife with children. Here Truffaut supplies an image of traditional family life that contrasts sharply with Itard's. He seems to share none of the culturally normative basic rewards of wife and family. All Itard cares about in this film is Victor. Victor becomes a virtual obsession defining Itard's existence. Why?

Had Truffaut followed his source, none of these questions would have arisen. We would have seen Itard working with Victor in an institution and would not have wondered about his home life because we would have simply presumed it to be irrelevant to this case, which would have been one among many. Instead, we are faced with the image of a sexually repressed man who, under the guise of detached scientific inquiry, invests too much in a boy's treatment. And here we encounter Truffaut's other significant departure from his source—the child in the film appears to be prepubertal, although the real Victor was at the age of puberty. The historical documents include information on Victor's body and speculation on whether his feral state retarded his genital development: "His sexual organs are moderately developed, a little less than those of children of the same age living in the city, for social development hastens their growth" (Lane 1976, 37). Truffaut includes scenes based on those medical examinations but omits any references to Victor's genital development or his approaching puberty. Thus the child, like the doctor, seems entirely nonsexual. He is, as it were, the perfect object of pure scientific scrutiny. But Itard's reports make clear that this was not the case. In a remarkable passage at the end of his first report, Itard writes:

A very similar reason has prevented me, when speaking of young Victor's varied development, from dwelling on the time of his puberty, which has shown itself almost explosively for some weeks, and the first phenomena of which cast much doubt upon the origin of certain tender emotions which we now regard as very "natural." (1962, 51)

Indeed, Itard feared drawing conclusions that "tend to destroy those prejudices which are possibly venerable and those illusions of social life which are the sweeter because they are the most consoling" (1962, 51). Although he does not expand on it here, Itard seems to suggest that the belief in the naturalness of heterosexuality is one such consoling, sweet illusion.

Earlier in the same report, Itard had written much more directly about Victor's sexuality. As part of an exercise to make Victor more sensitive to temperatures, Itard gave the boy baths:

To the administration of the baths I added the use of dry frictions along the spine and even ticklings of the lumbar region. This last means was more exciting than most. I even found myself obliged to reject it, when its effects were no longer limited to producing movements of pleasure but appeared to extend further to the generative organs and to add the threat of perversion to the first stirrings of an already precocious puberty. (1962, 17)

This passage may be the only way to make sense of Itard's later reference in the same report to his fears of alarming people by undermining their confidence in the natural.

In the 1806 report Itard wrote more directly about Victor's sexuality and left no doubt as to his speculations: "But what appears still more astonishing in the emotional system of this young man, and beyond all explanation, is his indifference to women in the midst of the violent physical changes attendant upon a very pronounced puberty" (1962, 96). Moreover, Truffaut could hardly misread the following passage from the same report because Itard's precise language is so revealing: "I waited each day until some breath of that universal sentiment which moves all creatures and causes them to multiply should come and animate Victor and enlarge his mental life" (1962, 97). Itard's use of the word "universal" here suggests that he requires the consolation of believing, in the face of evidence to the contrary, that heterosexual monogamy is "natural." Itard notes that Victor does "prefer the society of women to that of men," although the boy seems to get more agitated in the process, finally pushing the woman he has been with away from him (1962, 97). The passage is itself somewhat contradictory, decrying Victor's "indifference to women" and at the same time deploring his lack of involvement of the "heart" and his failure to show a "preference for any woman" (1962, 97). Itard seems to interpret Victor's sexuality as vaguely heterosexual. Itard goes so far as give up Victor's sexual training for fear that the "savage" might attempt to satisfy his sexual desires "as publicly as his other wants and which would have led him to acts of revolting indecency" (1962, 99).

In his second report, then, Itard seems to assert out of fear the very thing he attributes to others in his first report, namely, accepting the universality of heterosexuality. Yet, writing on the subject of Victor's sexuality, Itard boldly declared, "I will suppress nothing" (1962, 96). However we respond to Itard's somewhat contradictory and seemingly fearful interpretation of Victor's sexuality, it is immediately clear that Truffaut suppressed everything, as it were, and the consequences of this are even stronger than his decision to rearrange Itard's circumstances. Shattuck concludes:

> Itard leaves no doubt that one of the principal reasons why Victor's training could not go on was that the boy did not know how to direct his developing sexual responses toward any particular object. He had no idea of "the other sex," and Itard did not find a way to instruct him. Itard discreetly yet emphatically tells us that the boy's immodesty and the onset of puberty posed insuperable problems that no one had adequately foreseen. Truffaut passes over the whole question. Sex does not exist in the film. (1980, 212)

Although Shattuck's interpretation of Itard's reports is very precise, he offers no explanation for Truffaut's decision. Whereas he attributes the film's first major departure from its source to technological imperatives, he simply notes and dismisses this one. We can, however, make several observations and offer some possible explanations.

At the simplest level, the first strategy of adaptation affects the second. Raising the specter of "perverse" and "unnatural" sexuality in Itard's home is connotatively different from doing so in an institution. This is in turn complicated by the way in which Truffaut represents Itard as a bachelor with no interest in women or sex. And as if more complications are needed, they are supplied by Truffaut's decision to cast himself in the part of Itard. Were he to include, for example, the bath episode, we would see the bachelor Itard/Truffaut sexually arouse the pubescent boy in his own home.

This predicament leads to the second explanation for Truffaut's decision. The sexually explicit male body has always posed a problem for the cinema, including the European Art Cinema. In the opening shots of *The Wild Child*, for example, we have a traditional solution to representing the nude male; he is in constant action. Furthermore, the actor is prepubic, and the genitals are barely glimpsed. The bath episode would have focused attention on the genitals. Truffaut could easily have solved this problem in yet another conventional manner. We could have seen the doctor bathing the boy with the tub blocking the view of the genitals, or we could have had reverse-angle shots of Itard. In either event, we could have heard of the procedure during the voice-over journal entry. This would have bypassed the problem of visually representing the male body while still including the episode.

The third explanation involves the relationship between sexuality and language and is, I think, the most profound of the three. Remember that Truffaut acknowledged the decision to convert the two separate scientific reports into a journal-writing process because he felt it would facilitate narration. But most narrative filmmakers would dismiss repeated images of a man writing as obstacles to narration, since neither they nor their audience are likely to think of such images as "cinematic." Indeed, such images seem closer to stopping the narrative action than easing it along. But it is precisely the image of Itard writing that lies at the center of the film. We repeatedly see him standing by his writing table as he records the results of a just-completed experiment. *The Wild Child* represents the doctor as a powerful man of science, one who observes, knows, and writes. For him, language is in the service not only of "knowledge" but also of politics; his writings are intended to convince his superiors that he should be allowed to continue working with Victor. Shattuck observes of Itard:

> He never shows distress or passion, and keeps writing soberly his daily account of the training program. . . . Truffaut keeps the scientific, case-history tone even where Itard's prose becomes personal or sentimental. Madame Guerin has the most human part, a simple understanding woman willing to dedicate herself to an almost inhuman boy. The film restores her to a central role sometimes passed over or taken for granted in the reports. Without her warm heart, the film would not be believable. (1980, 211)

Whereas earlier he revealed a naive technological determinism, Shattuck's analysis here betrays a naive realism: Madame Guerin makes the film "believable." Even more surprising, Shattuck claims that the representation of the housekeeper–governess gives her a centrality that Itard denied her.

Shattuck is correct in contrasting the image of the passionless, diary-writing scientist with the woman who cares for the boy's emotional needs, but we cannot accept the relationship on the grounds that it makes the film "believable" (which it may do) or that it restores the woman to her rightful place in the narrative (which it does not do). Instead, it functions as part of a representation of language that places the woman outside language.

Itard's reports do not, of course, contain descriptions of himself writing reports. Truffaut's approach to adaptation makes central the representation of the act of writing. A more conventional approach would have simply shown or alluded once to the fact that Itard wrote reports of his work with Victor. For Truffaut, the focus of the drama is the man of science wielding language in a purposeful way. Madame Guerin, in contrast, is positioned outside language, and this contrast is central to the film. Rather than restore her to her "rightful place," Truffaut delineates what that place is, thus opening up the possibility of both questioning it and its relationship to the place of the powerful man.

Had the film been set in the institute and had Madame Guerin been married, this would have been difficult. In *The Wild Child*, Truffaut needs to situate language and sexuality within his central character's life because he wants us simultaneously to marvel at the doctor's noble work and, perhaps unconsciously, observe the cost of that male language and power. Itard's mastery of scientific language is based on total sexual repression and marked sexual difference. Madame Guerin is a silent reminder of what Itard's view of language has nothing to say about and what Truffaut's view of language can acknowledge but about which it can do nothing.

Werner Herzog's approach to Kaspar Hauser is similar to Truffaut's treatment of Victor. Once again, the film relates to a famous historical case (feral-child narratives in general seem to require this documentation to lend credibility, with films in particular turning on documentation–adaptation) where the original report included attention to the feral-child's sexual development. The film is based on Anselm von Feuerbach's 1832 publication, *Caspar Hauser: An Account of an Individual Kept in a Dungeon, Separated from All Communication with the World, from Early Childhood to about the Age of Seventeen*. Issues of sexuality enter Feuerbach's account several times: "He distinguished animals from men only by their form, as men from women only by their dress; and the clothing of the female sex was, on account of its varied and striking colors, far more pleasing to him than that of males; on which account he afterwards frequently expressed his desire to become a girl; that is, to wear female apparel" (1942, 298). From the contemporary perspective, of course, we should not be too quick to accept Feuerbach's simple explanation of Kaspar's behavior, though the important point is that

Herzog omits any reference to Kaspar's refusal to accept his culture's gender definitions; never in the film does he dress like a girl or express a desire to be one.

Feuerbach also observes of Kaspar:

It is particularly farcical to hear him speak of the future plans of his life; of the manner in which, after having learned a great deal and earned money, he intends to settle himself with his wife, whom he considers as an indispensable part of domestic furniture. He never thinks of a wife in any other manner than as a housekeeper, or as an upper servant, whom a man may keep as long as it suits him, and may turn away again, if she frequently spoils his soup, and does not properly mend his shirts or brush his coats, &c. (1942, 352)

Once again, from the contemporary perspective the passage is interesting because it implies that Kaspar lacks sexual desire, never having developed heterosexual, genital sexuality. And once again, Herzog omits any reference to Feuerbach's observation.

Paradoxically, he includes a scene in which Kaspar asks a housekeeper, "What are women good for? Can you tell me that, Katy? Women are not good for anything but sitting still! Why are women allowed to only knit and cook?" Katy merely smiles and says kindly, "You'll have to ask Mr. Daumer [Kaspar's benefactor and her employer] that. He'll know a decent answer for you." She is so removed from power and language that Kaspar's question does not even strike a responsive chord in her. In the scene, Herzog shifts the emphasis away from Kaspar's personal sexual development (the film never hints that he thinks of getting married) and makes a critique of the place of women in nineteenth-century German society.

As with *The Wild Child*, *Kaspar Hauser* carefully situates women outside language, which is the province of the symbolic Father and the Law. Early in the film, when Kaspar is found in Nuremberg, he is taken to a stable where he is interrogated by a military officer in charge of the town's affairs. The entire interrogation is recorded by the town scribe. During the proceedings, Herzog cuts to a shot of an unidentified woman who silently looks on as the powerful men who control language seek the truth and make decisions. The shot comes as something of a surprise because we do not even know that she is present; she never speaks or moves and serves no additional narrative function.

Another scene involving the housekeeper crystallizes this positioning of women. A professor of logic comes to test Kaspar's powers of understanding. Katy sits between Kaspar and the professor. As the professor tells a complicated riddle, she first objects that it is much too difficult. Then, while he awaits Kaspar's answer, she remarks that even she could not resolve the riddle. Finally, when Kaspar gives a solution that defies the rules of logic the professor will accept (the professor's solution depends on tricking a speaker into using a double negative, a sophisticated language skill), Katy smiles in sympathy with Kaspar as the outraged professor vehemently rejects Kaspar's solution. She even defends Kaspar's reasoning, saying that it makes sense to her. Katy thus aligns herself with the feral child who is outside language. Although Herzog carefully develops this theme of gender in relation to language and power, he never for a moment presents Kaspar as grappling with any personal sexual desires, urges, or confusions; he is entirely a nonsexual being.

If the cinematic Victor and Kaspar are nonsexual characters, Hugh Hudson's Tarzan in *Greystoke* is the normative heterosexual par excellence. The two elements most associated in the American imagination with the figure of the B-movie Tarzan are his signature cry and the phrase "Me Tarzan, you Jane." Indeed, the copy on the video box for the release of the 1932 film, *Tarzan, the Ape Man*, begins: " 'Me Tarzan, you Jane'—the immortal words spoken by *Tarzan, the Ape Man* as he wins his lady Jane," though, in fact, Tarzan does not speak those words in the film. These two elements, so strongly fixed in the popular imagination, represent antithetical poles of language; the inarticulate cry that precedes Tarzan's interaction with civilization and the first words he speaks as he clumsily tries to master language. And those words, of course, are bound to the other central image of the series: the character of Jane. We can hardly think about Tarzan without Jane, so central is their relationship to the B-film tradition in which normative heterosexual romance goes hand in hand with language and civilization.*

From its inception, however, the Tarzan series never took issues of language and culture seriously. *Tarzan, the Ape Man* assumes the form of an adventure and romance, and nearly all the narrative is devoted to one or the other. Jane visits her father in Africa and discovers that he and his young

---

*From one perspective, Tarzan is an opposite rendition of the beauty and the beast narratives discussed in Chapter 1. Although in both cases the man–animal is active and powerful, Tarzan is sexually attractive and, in opposition to deformed characters like Cyrano, entirely lacks the power of language.

associate are about to embark on a quest to find valuable elephant burial grounds. Jane accompanies them, much to the delight of the young partner. Before they meet Tarzan, their journey is fraught with the dangers of climbing mountains with treacherous trails overlooking seemingly bottomless abysses (into which, predictably, a number of natives fall), crossing rivers infested with crocodiles, and interacting with exotic savages who materialize at night out of the jungle. Nor do things change much once Tarzan appears. The adventures continue, compounded now by Tarzan's battles with wild animals. Jane quickly falls under Tarzan's spell. The film climaxes when the expedition is captured by "pygmies" who are about to drop their captives into a pit with a man-eating gorilla (who has, of course, already consumed a number of natives) when Tarzan appears and saves the day. As they flee, a dying elephant leads them to the burial grounds. The father and his partner decide to return to civilization to set up a business to exploit the rich ivory source. Jane stays behind with Tarzan, the last image of the film showing them and Cheetah bound together in the perfect image of a nuclear family.

Against this tradition, Hudson made *Greystoke*. As the title indicates, Hudson turned to Edgar Rice Burroughs's 1912 novel, *Tarzan of the Apes*, which is formally acknowledged in the opening credit sequence. In accordance with the British Quality Cinema tradition, *Greystoke* promises an artistic seriousness entirely absent from the American Tarzan series, something strongly marked by casting Sir Ralph Richardson as the Sixth Earl of Greystoke and giving him the first acting credit. Similarly, the music is recorded by the Royal Philharmonic Orchestra.

The U.S. reception of the film included an interview on PBS's "All Things Considered" with experts who described the accuracy of the research that went into the film's re-creation of ape language. Several critics, in fact, saw the film as remaking Tarzan in the tradition of *The Wild Child*; this, they argued, was a more serious Tarzan and dealt intelligently with themes of language and culture. Hudson draws on the widely publicized films of the European Art Cinema as additional sources for his remake of the lowly Hollywood B film. Several major ideological consequences emerge from this attempt to bring the Tarzan legend into the serious European feral-child-narrative tradition by remaking the series and, in the process, readapting Burroughs's original text.

Burroughs's novel is part of another feral-child narrative tradition that has its main antecedent in Rudyard Kipling's *The Jungle Books* (1894 and 1895) and its central character of Mowgli, a child literally raised by wolves. In these stories, animals have their own languages, and they speak like humans. In this highly anthropomorphic characterization, animals also live in social structures similar to those of humans. Indeed, Kipling's emphasis on the Law of the Jungle (with a capital "L") seems today like a virtual parody of the Lacanian concept of the symbolic. The animals in Burroughs's *Tarzan of the Apes* also have names and language. Tarzan is raised by apes but, as with Mowgli, he finds himself within a form of cultural organization that resembles that of humans. And, like Mowgli, his life in the jungle is characterized as totally nonsexual.

Greystoke occupies a curious position in relation to these conceptions of language and culture. The seriousness with which the film develops a language theme seeks to distinguish it from both the B-movie tradition in which adventure and romance overwhelmed any pretense of interest in such themes and from Burroughs's novel in which apes possess an anthropomorphic language. Yet *Greystoke* participates in an equally crude ideology of language and culture that is so successfully masked that it raised no comment at the film's release. Hudson offers his film as a more sophisticated account of Burroughs's conception of language: We all "know" that animals do not possess a crude form of our language. This added "realism" is what seemingly aligns the film with *The Wild Child*.

Hudson establishes what appears to be a well-informed critical perspective through the use of a narrator, Phillippe D'Arnot (Ian Holm). In the scene that introduces the expedition of whites who will discover Tarzan, D'Arnot, a Belgian and the only non-British member of the party, remarks, "My companions consider themselves to be the foremost among God's creatures and treat Africa and all things African with an unwavering contempt. If I was not under orders, I would have abandoned them in the first week and gone home to Brussels." The scenes that follow support D'Arnot's critique of the arrogant smugness of British imperialism and further mark this film's difference from the Hollywood serial, where racism is never questioned; the whites in Hudson's *Greystoke* are indeed presented as God's superior creatures. Astonishingly, Hudson recapitulates one of the central racist elements of the Tarzan legend: Only when Tarzan encounters a white woman does he become a sexual being—and a highly normative one at that.

Tarzan, the Ape Man brings Jane into the jungle, where she and Tarzan instantly fall in love. Hudson, following Burroughs's novel, has Tarzan brought to England. Once again, Hudson's strategy seems to be entirely on the side of seriousness. Instead of the silly spectacle of Tarzan and Jane taking up living together in a tree house surrounded by Tarzan's animal friends, we have Tarzan faced with the task of integrating himself into British society.

Tarzan (Christopher Lambert) is a fully grown man by the time D'Arnot meets him. In the first part of the film, Hudson uses an extended montage sequence to show the child growing up in the jungle. Predictably, the sequence presents the male body in a variety of traditional ways. As the boy reaches puberty, he is shown only in action, such as swinging on vines, or, if he is at rest, the genitals are carefully covered or obscured by camera distance and lighting. This is the traditional phallic male body, powerful and "impressive." Tarzan, growing up in the jungle, outside language and culture, magically transforms in front of our eyes into a "man." Presumably this "man" has encountered the natives with whom he shares the jungle. Thus he would have seen women, and nearly naked ones at that. But they have not aroused any desire within him or even had any apparent impact on him. He is totally nonsexual, awaiting the white woman.

As if by a great racist universal law, it is only when Tarzan (now called "Johnny") meets Jane (Andie McDowell), a conventionally beautiful woman by contemporary standards, that he becomes a sexual man. Jane, an American living in Greystoke's mansion, undertakes Johnny's education immediately on his arrival. In one scene, she stands in front of a blackboard teaching Johnny how to conjugate a phrase about love. As these scenes progress, Johnny and Jane obviously fall in love with each other. But Jane has a suitor, Charles, who proposes marriage to her. She declines, leading him to remark, "Three months ago before Clayton [Johnny] returned, I doubt you would have hesitated." Charles's place in the narrative is structurally very similar to that of the young business associate in *Tarzan, the Ape Man*. In both films, Jane is not responsive to the romantic intentions of the suitor; she falls under Tarzan's romantic spell almost immediately; and the rival suitor becomes jealous. Thus the feral apeman instantly has or quickly develops our culture's ideal characteristics of masculinity, so much so that he displaces Jane's previous suitors. These traits of manhood appear natural; they are not contingent on processes of language acquisition and symbolic cultural interaction such as Oedipal family structures.

Ironically, this strand of the film culminates in a lovemaking scene between Johnny and Jane, ironic because the second half of the film is dominated by a maudlin Oedipal narrative. Greystoke, now an old man, is obsessed with Johnny's presence; on several occasions he even confuses his grandson with his son, who he thinks has returned home. Clearly we are supposed to be moved by the development of this father–son bonding, which ends with Johnny's anguished response to Greystoke's death. On the night of the funeral, he seeks comfort from Jane.

The sequence begins with Jane dressed and groomed for bed. We see highly fetishized shots of her as a servant brushes her hair. Johnny enters the room, apelike, on all fours, and Jane dismisses her servant. Johnny hops on the bed and undresses her. She succumbs immediately to his apelike behavior as he jumps around on the bed making animal noises. Several shots show Jane in a romantic passion with her eyes closed. These shots, not unrelated to the way in which women's pleasure is represented in hard-core pornography, use the pretense of her pleasure as a way to intensify her fetishistic representation; her pleasure is both narratively a sign of the power of the man on whom it is contingent and representationally a device for intensifying her desirability for those who look at her. In this film, the fetishism is also implicitly racist because Hudson never questions why a white woman who personifies our current image of Western desirability should so quickly and naturally arouse heterosexual desire in Johnny in a way that no black woman has. In this sense, *Greystoke* has not transcended the simplistic and racist assumptions about sexual difference operative in *Tarzan, the Ape Man*, when Tarzan carries Jane to his home, then puts his hand to hers and notices the difference in size. She remarks, "Yes, there's quite a difference. You like that difference? You've never seen a woman like me before, have you?"

The lovemaking scene in *Greystoke* ends with a shot of Jane falling back in the bed with Tarzan on top of her. In accordance with the conventions and requirements of a PG-rated film, the scene ends with a fade-out. Although we do not see what follows, clearly we are left with the impression that Johnny skillfully makes love to Jane. Not only has his desire been awakened, but her closed eyes combined with the way in which she falls back in the bed imply that he can satisfy her desires: Johnny is a good lover. The fact that all this occurs on the night that Johnny has buried his "father" needs no further comment; Johnny is now a complete "man."

In the Lacanian view, it is precisely the absence of language and its attendant symbolic cultural organization that distinguishes animals from humans. From this perspective, the acquisition of language and sexual identity are so strongly intertwined that becoming a speaking subject is inseparable from castration, the phallus, and the Law of the Father. This is obviously a different framework from that in which Kipling and Burroughs approached their feral-child narratives and one in which a figure like Tarzan, found in the jungle in his mid-twenties possessing no language and without having had any human contact, would be almost unrecognizable to us as a "man." Learning language, the symbolic place of the Father, desire, and normative heterosexual genital sexuality would be a long and arduous struggle. Nor would the image such a figure cut be one that would inspire romantic and sexual desire within a young woman such as Jane.

My point is not to criticize *Greystoke* for being unrealistic but to show that the film's treatment of language and culture is simplistic. Hudson replaces apes that talk with actual apes or apes that gesture and make noises like actual apes, but rather than come up with a more complex or sophisticated view of language and culture than Burroughs had in 1912, Hudson merely relocates crude, unexamined cultural assumptions about language and sexuality elsewhere in the narrative. Thus the apparent sophistication of the way in which the jungle is represented in the first part of the film and culture in the second part lends credence to the film's overall thematic development. Both *The Wild Child* and *Kaspar Hauser* offer much more complex (though widely differing) accounts of language acquisition and the enculturation process than does *Greystoke*. All three films, however, contain an extreme degree of sexual repression.

In half a year, Hudson's Tarzan goes from not believing his mother was anything other than an ape to making love to a beautiful white woman on the night of his grandfather's funeral. Clearly Hudson does not repress sexuality in the way Truffaut and Herzog do, but his representation of Tarzan's sexuality is merely the other side of the coin: He represses all indication that there would be any departure from our culture's normative notions of heterosexuality in a feral-child's development. Tarzan of the jungle in the first part of the film is totally nonsexual; Johnny, heir to Lord Greystoke, in the second part of the film, is a "normal" heterosexual who never shows any signs of difficulty in controlling unacceptable sexual urges or in developing heterosexual desire and focusing it on one woman. In this account, although Tarzan seems to be a fully sexed character, his portrayal is achieved by repressing everything that would be the least bit disturbing or call into question any of our currently cherished notions of normative heterosexuality.

If this were in reality the kind of sexual development a feral child would undergo, one might wonder why Truffaut and Herzog are so rigorous in their repression of all things sexual in their films. Since their sources, however, are accounts of actual cases that contain disturbing elements, they must either repress those elements or confront them. Hudson's sources are a novel and a B movie that do not contain equivalently disturbing elements so that there is nothing for him to repress; he simply creates a totally comforting, fictional account of Tarzan's sexuality. Nevertheless, in all three films we are left with the disturbing realization that in an era when filmmakers are incessantly drawn to male feral-child narratives, none of them can maturely acknowledge and confront the component of their material that centers on the male body and its sexuality. Truffaut and Herzog present intelligent investigations of the process of language acquisition and enculturation, but they totally ignore the integrally related area of sexual development. Hudson emphasizes the sexual component of the story (advertised recently on television as a great "romance"), but does so by affirming and universalizing a white racist, patriarchal account of normative heterosexuality, and he accomplishes this under the guise of the Quality Cinema's triumphant remake of the lowly B film. As such, all three films dealing with the pivotal transition from animal to human and from nature to culture point to a repression about the sexual representation of the male body that is deeply embedded in twentieth-century Western culture.

"I LIKE SCARS, REALLY"

• • • • • •

MEN CALLED SCARFACE, SCAR, AND STUMPY

We saw in the last chapter that for the male feral child the movement from nature to culture is marked by sexual repression and disturbance. In psychoanalytic terms, the fully enculturated male has to pass through and resolve what Freud termed the Oedipal complex and enter what Lacan termed the Symbolic. In preparing the ground for later chapters that deal with overt aspects of male sexuality, this chapter deals with symbolic issues. Not surprisingly, critics have dealt much more extensively with symbolic issues than with the openly sexual representation of the male body; since it is my premise that the two are intimately linked, I want to lay out some crucial features of how our culture represents masculinity and the male body in ways that are not overtly sexual. In this chapter I concentrate on three films by Howard Hawks, *Rio Bravo* (1959), *Scarface* (1932), and his last film, *Rio Lobo* (1970), which together schematize central issues about masculinity and its relationship to the male body in an extremely condensed form. My main interest is not to add to the already rich body of work that exists on Hawks's films, but to show how his oft-noted concerns with issues of masculinity can help us better understand cultural assumptions about not only the male body but also its relationship to the female body.

Robin Wood's justly celebrated work (1981) initially articulated Hawks's central concern with a particular concept of masculinity and showed the complex relationship between the director's comedies and male action films. Wood's premise is that social responsibility is maintained in the adventure films and abandoned in the comedies, in which male mastery is lost. The comedies are thus the inverse of the adventure films. Building on Wood's division of Hawks's films, Peter Wollen later emphasized the distinction as one between dramas that uphold and celebrate male virtues and the world of masculine endeavor and comedies in which the feminine overruns and ridicules those male values. In comedies, men are frequently placed in the position of women and children; in the dramas, the threat posed by women is controlled and contained. In a remarkably perceptive way, Wood argued that *Scarface*, a gangster film, is in reality a comedy and not a male action film, an observation that, as we later see, is related to understanding the scarred face of the title character in that film. But first, *Rio Bravo*.

Rio Bravo tells the story of a town under seige by outlaws. Sheriff John T. Chance (John Wayne) arrests Joe Burdette (Claude Aikens), who has killed a man in cold blood. Joe's brother Nathan plots to free him. Chance deputizes Dude (Dean Martin), a former deputy who has become the town drunk. Along with Stumpy (Walter Brennan), Chance's old sidekick, and Colorado (Ricky Nelson), a young cowboy, they plan to hold their prisoner for trial. A subplot develops when Chance, mistakenly thinking he has caught Feathers (Angie Dickinson) cheating in a card game, orders her out of town. She does not leave, however, and Chance falls in love with her. Much of the action takes place in the town hotel, which is run by Carlos (Pedro Gonzales) and his wife Consuela (Estelita Rodriguez), who are constantly engaged in a marital contest of wills. Eventually Chance, Stumpy, and Colorado seek refuge in the jail with their prisoner, but when Nathan Burdette succeeds in taking Dude hostage, Chance agrees to trade Joe Burdette for him. A shoot-out ensues, and Chance's men are victorious. The film concludes with Chance and Feathers locked in a romantic embrace.

Rio Bravo can be seen as a drama about masculinity with its four major male characters representing different levels of masculinity. John T. Chance is the ideal figure of strength and power, which is further underscored by casting John Wayne in the part. In the 1950s Wayne was at the height of his career, his name and image virtually synonymous with the quintessential Western hero. In contrast, Dude was once a figure of ideal masculinity, but drinking has destroyed this. At the beginning of the film, he is groveling, ill shaven, poorly dressed, and overly nervous. His drive to regain his masculinity is treated very seriously in the film; indeed, it becomes a minidrama of masculinity lost and regained. As he progresses toward overcoming his drunkenness and making himself a useful member of the group defending the town, he first regains his guns (obvious phallic images) and later his clothes, which Chance has been holding until they "fit him" again (i.e., until he is man enough to fill them). Similarly, he earns the right to go in the front door of the saloon, something he lost in his state of pathetic drunkenness. After the transformation, he is a good-looking man, calm in the face of danger.

Stumpy's age has eroded his masculinity. In many ways, he fulfills the traditionally feminine function within the group; he cleans, cooks, and keeps house. His limp is a physical sign of his loss of masculine power, and his constant chatter about unimportant things further associates him, through convention, with women. Colorado is the opposite of Stumpy; he is the youth with the potential to become, like his father and Chance, the ideal figure of masculinity—a promise he fulfills during the course of the film.

The women characters are a threat to these men. Significantly, we learn that it was a woman who was responsible for Dude's drinking. Feathers poses a similar threat to Chance. She mocks his masculinity when she unexpectedly walks in on Carlos holding a pair of red women's underwear up to Chance and imagining what they will look like on his wife. Her open use of sexuality embarrasses Chance and puts him on the defensive. After he accuses her of cheating in a card game, she says, indicating her bosom and undergarments, that he will have to search her. Indeed, he suspects her, in part, because she fits the description of a criminal on a handbill. She is, in other words, marked as a "guilty" woman, which seemingly motivates Chance's desire to have her put on the stage and run out of town. Within a comic subplot, Consuela, Carlos's wife, poses both verbal and physical threats to her husband.

As Wood and others have noted, the proof of masculinity in Hawks's films is based on how "good" a man is at what he does, and the characters in *Rio Bravo* talk a great deal about how "good" someone is. Masculinity becomes a virtual division between professionals and amateurs. Indeed, when Pat Wheeler (Ward Bond) offers Chance the help of his men, Chance calls them "well-meaning amateurs," whereas he calls Burdette's men "professionals."

The concept of "good" masculinity is not merely physical; it also involves the careful control of language. At one extreme, powerful men do not need language. The entire opening barroom sequence is shot without dialogue. Dude begs for money and is about to pick a coin out of a spittoon where Joe Burdette has tossed it. Chance kicks the spittoon away, but Dude, from behind, knocks him unconscious. In the ensuing confusion, Burdette shoots an innocent bystander who tries to stop him from further violence, then leaves the saloon and walks down the street into another bar. No one says a word. They do not have to because this is a world of male interaction structured solely on physical power. Language has no place in it.

The entire sequence lays out shifting power relations in a bizarrely condensed form. Every moment shows an unexpected shift. Chance, for example, appears to be a powerfully dominating figure as he kicks away the spittoon to prevent Dude from reaching for the money Burdette has sadistically thrown into it. A moment later, however, Chance lies unconscious on the floor after Dude hits him over the head from behind. The shifting fortunes of the cowboy who intervenes is just as quick; one moment he lays his hand on Burdette and turns him around—a moment later a look of disbelief crosses his face as he slumps to the floor where he dies after being shot by Burdette. Walking along the street to the other bar, Burdette passes a woman; without saying a word, he grabs her, turns her around to inspect her. Finding her unattractive, he releases her and continues on his way. Burdette inhabits a world where everything from male interaction to sexual interaction with women proceeds without language; it is all brute power and action.

At one point, Pat Wheeler, referring to how Nathan Burdette is responding to his brother's being jailed, asks Chance, "What does Nathan say about this?" "Nothing. Not talking, just doing," comes the terse reply. Powerful men hold language in reserve, and when they use it, it has impact. The strong, silent type in the male action cinema thus bears a relationship to language that is nearly the opposite of the oft-noted positioning of women "outside" language, which is operative in *The Wild Child* and *Kaspar Hauser*. In these films, the women's silence marks their position on the periphery of power; they do not speak because they are excluded from decision making. The men's silence stems from their excess of power; they do not talk much because their actions speak louder than words.

Indeed, within such a world, men who talk too much are marked as weak. When the friendly rancher Pat (Ward Bond) talks too much about Dude's drinking in front of Dude, upsetting him, Chance remarks, "Wasn't good." Pat even gets killed because he talks too much. Not surprisingly, male comic characters are marked by excessive talking. Stumpy runs on and on, and at several points others beg him to shut up. Chance links Stumpy's constant babbling to fear; he tells Dude that Stumpy talks too much because he is afraid. Carlos also talks a great deal and is comically associated with a failed masculinity. That he is extremely short and slight of build is emphasized in a number of two-shots with Chance and Carlos where Chance looms over Carlos; when Carlos shoots a shotgun, the kick from the blast nearly knocks him over. He gets a black eye from his wife when he fails to put Feathers on the stagecoach, a double marking of masculine failure because the black eye not only shows that his wife hits him but also that he failed to get rid of the threatening, "guilty" woman.

At several points in the film, the use and control of language arises directly in terms of masculine–feminine relationships. Carlos pleads to his wife, "Please, Consuela, do not say more. You already say too much." "I guess I talk too much," Feathers says after an interaction with Chance. Their entire relationship plays with language and misunderstandings. At times she cannot get Chance to say what she wants and is frustrated and angered by his silence, as in the famous last scene where Chance threatens to arrest her if she performs in public in a skimpy outfit. When she joyously blurts out that she thought he would never say it, he asks, "Say what?" "That you love me," she replies. "I said I'd arrest you," he responds, and she, in an oft-quoted line, says, "It means the same thing." At other times, such as when Feathers walks in on Chance as Carlos holds up the underpants, and when Chance angrily discovers that Feathers has stayed up all night guarding his room, Chance cannot get a word in to explain or correct a false impression. At these moments, the comedy works against Chance's power by indicating a temporary loss of it; his inability to speak here is far removed from the powerful male reserve of language evident in the opening scene.

Rio Bravo, then, articulates a number of central cultural assumptions about power, masculinity, and the male body. Powerful men frequently hold language in reserve, not because they are excluded from it, but because they do not need it. Moreover, they literally embody their power as reflected by stature and muscularity; to be powerful is to be able to exert yourself physically over others. Aside from the symbolic associations of castration, to which I return, Stumpy's bad leg is also a sign of his weakness; he cannot run as fast or move as nimbly as other men. Similarly, Carlos's diminutive stature, within cultural codes, marks him as someone who can be physically dominated by an angry wife or the kick of a shotgun blast.

Women, of course, have traditionally been told that their power comes from their beauty and their appearance, not their physical strength, just as they have been told that they, like children, should be seen and not heard (i.e., be at the periphery of language). Casting Angie Dickinson as Feathers conforms as fully to cultural notions about gender and the body as does casting John Wayne as Chance. Feathers uses her beauty and her sexuality as the source of her power. We see this literally when she dissuades Chance from searching her by provocatively displaying her body, and in the final scene where she forces him to declare his love for her by preparing to perform in an erotic costume.

Rio Lobo makes graphically clear in an astonishingly condensed manner the major consequences for both men and women who live within this sexually imbalanced framework of power and the body. *Rio Lobo* has received little critical attention because auteurists consider it by far the weakest of the Hawks trilogy of which *Rio Bravo* and *El Dorado* (1966) form the first and second parts. From the perspective of issues about the representation of power and its loss in relationship to sexuality and the body, *Rio Lobo* not only expands on the previous two films but also crystallizes those issues in a manner unique within the male action cinema.

Rio Lobo tells the story of a group of men and women who, for entirely different reasons, join forces against Ketchum (Victor French), a crooked landowner, and Sheriff Hendricks (Mike Henry), who works for him. The group is led by Cord McNally (John Wayne) and includes Shasta (Jennifer O'Neil) and Amelita (Sherry Lansing). A complicated plot is resolved when, after each side has taken hostages, they meet to exchange them. In the ensuing fight, McNally's group succeeds in defeating Ketchum's men, and both Ketchum and Hendricks are killed in the process.

Rio Lobo bears similarities to *Rio Bravo*, especially in the heroes' seeking refuge in a jail and in the exchange of hostages at the end. On issues of masculinity, once again we have an all-male group that wants to be free of women, but cannot be. Shasta is the "guilty" woman, the "come-on" for a medicine show that is the equivalent of the card-cheating, saloon woman in *Rio Bravo*. Like Feathers, Shasta owes her position to a bad husband, one whose masculine failure is marked in terms of how he fails to be good. Shasta says of him, "I was married and it wasn't a good marriage. He couldn't drink but he did and when he did, he wasn't good." Much like the attempt in *Rio Bravo* to get rid of Feathers by putting her on the stagecoach, the male group in *Rio Lobo* fails repeatedly to go on without Shasta. Similarly, much to the surprise of the men, Amelita, who has been sadistically scarred by Hendricks, is present at the shoot-out at the end and is the one who kills Hendricks, something that McNally has specifically told her he intends to do.

Shasta and Amelita, like Feathers, derive their power from their beauty. But Amelita is brutally scarred when Hendricks cuts her right cheek from her ear to her jaw. This sudden alteration in her body is compared with the wounding of Hendricks and McNally in the final sequence. The hostage exchange begins with McNally sending Ketchum over to Hendricks, the corrupt sheriff. When the trouble starts, Ketchum is killed in the ludicrous and humiliating position of trying to hold up his beltless pants. As he tries to cover his body, he pathetically pleads with Hendricks for his life. As soon as the shooting starts, Hendricks and McNally both suffer a leg wound, which is emphasized by a shot of one grabbing his leg followed by the other doing the same thing. Throughout the ensuing battle, they limp. Indeed, in a remarkable image, Hendricks uses his rifle for a crutch, in the process packing the end of the barrel with dirt. When he next takes aim and shoots, the rifle backfires, and we see his bloodied face as he screams in terror after blinding himself. When Amelita shoots him, we are faced with the spectacle of a once-beautiful woman killing a once-powerful man now reduced to a limping, blinded, bloody mess. Moments later, the film ends with one of the most unusual images of coupling in all of Hollywood cinema, as McNally limps down the street with his arm around the scarred woman.

The final moments of the film summarize the entire ideology of power, gender, and the body that underlies the classical cinema. To disfigure the woman, whose power comes from beauty, is to mark her loss of power. Critics have noted that when women's faces are damaged in films, the mark is frequently confined to one side only. This is true, for example, in *The Big Heat* (1953), when Lee Marvin throws scalding hot coffee in Gloria Grahame's face. There is a remarkable moment in *Peeping Tom* (1960) when what appears to be a beautiful porn actress, introduced in profile, turns her head and reveals that the other side of her face is horribly disfigured. The moment makes clear the structure that underlies this scarring of the woman's face; the shocking contrast between beauty and its loss is heightened. We are reminded of the beauty she once had and, in films like *The Big Heat* and *Rio Lobo*, how she is ruined for life by its loss. In contrast, the male's loss of power is marked not by a disfigurement but by a crippling, that is, a limitation of the power to act. For this reason, leg injuries are probably the most common male equivalent of the female scarred face. In the action cinema, men rely on their legs for their agility and strength in life-threatening situations; a leg wound literally disempowers them. But it does something more; it also symbolically robs them of phallic power.

The symbolic weight of leg wounds is emphasized when McNally and Phillips, trying to scare Ketchum into giving them the deeds, set his legs on fire. Through the metonymic process in which legs become associated with the penis–phallus and the loss or wounding of a leg symbolically castrates a man, the way in which Hendricks and McNally suffer leg wounds clearly marks both as unexpectedly weak. But with Hendricks, the symbolic wound is doubled. First, he uses his rifle as a crutch. Guns normally are the most common phallic image in Westerns, as Hawks makes clear earlier in the film when Shasta shoots one of the villains with a tiny derringer. The small gun is associated with the woman and contrasted with the pistols and rifles the men carry, a point to which I return in discussing *Scarface* and in Chapter 6 in relation to *McCabe and Mrs. Miller*. As if the image of Hendricks trying to support his crippled body with his phallic rifle were not enough, Hawks carries it to its logical conclusion by having the man blind himself with his own rifle; next to or perhaps equivalent with leg wounds, blinding is the most common symbolic mark of male castration. As Stephen Heath has pointed out, such a use of blindness informs everything from the Lady Godiva myth, wherein any man who looks at the naked woman will be blinded, to hysterical blindness, where a character loses sight for no physiological reason. Within such a logic, Hendricks looks like a man who is ready to be killed by a woman: He limps, he incompetently uses his rifle as a crutch, and he blinds himself. The shot of his bloody face after his gun has backfired even includes a view of the bent, ripped barrel. Everything marks this man as castrated and powerless, the equivalent of the once-beautiful woman who kills him.

But what of McNally? Throughout the film, McNally is a man who is losing his physical agility and his sexual potency due to age. In some ways he is a less exaggerated version of Stumpy in *Rio Bravo*; but we can still see that he was once the embodiment of the ideal male figure. Again, the star system works interestingly here. Wayne had aged beyond the point where he could plausibly play the same physically powerful characters he had in such films as *The Searchers* (1956) and *Rio Bravo*. In this film, McNally is excluded from both the main action sequences (such as the opening train robbery) and the romantic subplot, which turns on the developing relationship between Pierre Cordona (Jorge Rivero) and Shasta. At one point, Shasta seeks refuge from Pierre by sleeping with McNally because his body is "comfortable."

In a word, age has made him safe from the active threat posed by younger members of the male group. There is, then, a logic of once-powerful bodies marked by loss, which links McNally and Amelita and forms them into the unusual couple in the film's final shot. In fact, there has been no prior development of any love interest between them, but in the final shot they look like the typical couple that ends so many Hollywood films, including *Rio Bravo*. McNally and Amelita, however, are united not by romantic love but by the ways in which their bodies bear the marks of loss of power: McNally's limp and Amelita's facial scar. He is no longer simply strong, and she is no longer simply beautiful. What the final shot of *Rio Lobo* makes clearer than any equivalent image I can think of in the cinema is the different and unequal ways that power and its loss are marked on male and female bodies in a patriarchal culture.

Nothing illustrates this better than comparing Amelita's scarred face with the scarred face of men in other action films. If, in fact, beauty is not the source of male power in patriarchal culture, then an acquired physical mark such as a scar that mars the aesthetic surface of the body should signify much differently on the male body from the female body. In the cinema, a scar on a man's face frequently enhances rather than detracts from his power, providing a sign that he has been tested in the violent and dangerous world of male action and has survived. He is not easily defeated or killed. He may not be perfect, but he perseveres. If he has done so in the past, he can do so again. Instead of (or, in the case of villains and enemies, in addition to) being ugly, he is more powerful for having been scarred.

John Ford's *The Searchers* illustrates this kind of male scarring clearly. At the beginning of the film, a white family homestead is attacked by Indians, who rape the mother and then kill the entire family with the exception of a teenage girl and her younger sister, who are kidnapped. The teenager is soon raped and killed, and her sister raised as an Indian. These raping, murdering, scalping Indians are, in short, the epitome of a common racial villainy depicted in Westerns.* The white men who search for the kidnapped girl learn that the name of the chief who leads these Indians is Scar. At various points in the film, the name is pronounced with ominous emphasis. At one point, the chief is called Cicatrice, and one of the searchers misses the significance until the other translates Cicatrice as Scar, again emphasizing the name. When the searchers finally find Scar, and he is reintroduced after only

*For a discussion of racism in the film, see Lehman (1990).

a brief glimpse of him at the beginning of the film, one of the searchers re-marks, "Easy to see how you got your name." Scar turns out to be not a weak man but a formidable opponent. And when he talks with the searchers, his status as a survivor emerges; he attacks the whites not out of some intrinsic evil but because of what the whites have done to him and his family. He fights back, in other words, and is not easily defeated. Indeed, his strength is em-phasized in many ways including physically when his powerful body seems the mirror image of John Wayne's, who plays one of the searchers. Everything about his name, about how he got it, and about his appearance combine not to emasculate him but to empower him as a particularly terrifying presence.

The same cannot be said for the white male gangster after whom the film *Scarface* is named. Instead of a large, disfiguring scar, Tony Camonte (Paul Muni) derives his nickname from a small **X**-shaped scar on his left cheek; since it is barely noticeable, it does not contribute to making the character more ominous or threatening. The origin of the scar is even more interest-ing than its visibility. When asked by a woman where he got the scar, Tony maintains that he received it during the war. Another gangster intervenes: "Yeah, some war with a blonde in a Brooklyn speakeasy." Tony's answer con-forms to the notion of the scar as evidence that the marked man has tested himself in the realm of male combat and survived. The truth is that Camonte was marked by a woman. Rather than make him appear stronger, this scar fulfills the unusual function of making him appear weaker; he cannot control the threat posed by women. Tony's scar, which Wood does not mention, is further evidence for the validity of his claim that the film is a comedy due to the loss of male mastery.

The men in *Scarface* are frequently marked as feminine. The most direct instance of this occurs when Poppy (Karen Morely) tells Tony that his style of dressing is "effeminate." Not knowing what the word means, he proudly responds, "Yeah, ain't it." His failure of language is another sign of his direct association with the feminine. Male mastery of language, as we have seen, may involve reticence, but such powerful reserve is a far cry from its in-competent use, which we see in *Scarface*. This is most evident with Tony's secretary. The fact that the character is even called a secretary is interesting, since the term has cultural connotations of being a woman's job. But it is also a job associated with the use and control of language, something that Tony's secretary cannot do. The man cannot write or even speak on the phone. Both he and his boss are comically inept in the realm of language in a way that contrasts sharply with the dramatic silence in which men like Chance and Burdette act. Remarkably, Hawks directs this early sound film so that at times the actors' speech connotes femininity. The scene in which Guino Rinaldo (George Raft) is killed begins, as Wood notes, with Cesca singing a childish song to her new husband. Wood does not, however, mention the strikingly "effeminate" way in which Rinaldo talks to Cesca; his voice is soft and passive—the sound equivalent of the passivity he showed at the beginning of his relationship with Cesca, when it was she and not he who was the instigator. The scene also emphasizes the small, ornate pistol he carries, contrasting sharply with the phallic machine guns used throughout the film.

Hawks's Westerns are marked by an unusual emphasis on phallic rifles, as opposed to pistols, though guns in general are clearly phallic. In a remarkable scene in *Red River* (1947) two young men show each other their pistols, talk about them, exchange them, and impress each other with demonstrations of their use. Within a world of phallic mastery of weapons, Rinaldo's small, ornate pistol seems closer to Shasta's derringer than McNally's rifle. And within a world of such limited and failed masculinity, Tony's scar links him more to Stumpy than to Chief Scar.

Like the war he lost with the blonde in the Brooklyn speakeasy, Tony will lose the war with his sister over keeping her in the home and out of the world of male violence. Neither Wood nor Gerald Mast, who has written a detailed analysis of *Scarface*, mentions one of the most extraordinary appearances of the **X** motif when it migrates onto Cesca's body. Tony is furious to find her at a club that is a hangout for gangsters. When he angrily confronts her, she turns around to reveal a large **X** boldly formed on her back by the black straps of her gown. After Tony forces her to return home, the **X** is emphasized as she stands gazing out her bedroom window. This sequence does more than foretell her death; it crystallizes Tony's failure to keep his sister separate from his world of male camaraderie and violence—that is, the distinction between the masculine and the feminine realms breaks down completely, as we see when Cesca dies in Tony's fortress. As Wood rightly points out, the **X** motif is present in the balcony railing that frames the first meeting between Cesca and Rinaldo and is present when she dies. If the feminine world cannot be controlled in comedies, then most assuredly *Scarface* is a comedy, though one in which Tony, physically marked by one woman and unable to control another, will lose his life.

Whether or not we classify *Scarface* as a comedy, it is worth briefly calling attention to how much it has in common with adventure dramas, for in those the world of the feminine threatens and intrudes more upon the masculine than either Wood or Wollen acknowledges. In much the same way as Tony cannot keep Cesca at home, Chance cannot send Feathers out of town and McNally can neither lose Shasta nor prevent Amelita from coming to the final shoot-out and killing Hendricks. In fact, Amelita's totally unexpected presence in the scene parallels Cesca's presence at Tony's shoot-out with the police, and the distinction between the uncontrolled activity of the two women is perilously slim, as are other distinctions between the comedies and dramas. In *Rio Bravo*, Chance loses his power in one scene by tripping over a rope and in another by being fooled by a ruse, and he even requires help from a woman and a youngster in another scene. The powerful men in Hawks's action films are never quite so powerful and secure as they may seem; Chance and McNally are not that far away from Tony Camonte.

The unusual handling of the scar in *Scarface* bears comparison with that in *The Enchanted Cottage* (John Cromwell, 1945). Indeed, that love story supplies within its genre a uniquely condensed treatment of exactly the issues condensed in *Rio Lobo*, but the differences between the male action film and the female love story are revealing. *The Enchanted Cottage* tells the story of Oliver (Robert Young), who rents an isolated seaside cottage in anticipation of his honeymoon. On the day of his planned marriage, he is called away to fight in the war. Returning scarred and wounded, he seeks refuge in the cottage where he falls in love with Laura (Dorothy McGuire), an unattractive maid. After they marry, a magical transformation occurs: Oliver's body is restored, and Laura becomes beautiful. Later we learn that the transformation occurred only in their own eyes.

Oliver's war wounds take two forms; one side of his face is horribly scarred from the ear to the mouth, and the disfigurement is heightened by the way in which his mouth and lips are drooped and twisted. One arm is also crippled, useless, and motionless at his side. The facial scars work in direct contradiction to those described earlier, wherein the man appears as a strong survivor of a test of his power. Oliver is ugly, not menacing. Like Amelita's in *Rio Lobo*, his looks are marred. Indeed, the form of his wounds creates a contrast between the two sides of his face; as we look at the ugliness, we are reminded of the former beauty. The crippled arm is the typical male wound that indicates loss of both literal and sexual power. The reference to a loss of sexual power is implied, within the censorship codes of the time, when Oliver rages against his condition by pointing to his ugliness and indicates something additional that he is about to say when he is interrupted. How can we account for this odd combination of wounds and scars?

In her discussion of 1940s love stories, Mary Ann Doane observes, "The male stars who tend to play the romantic leads in these films—Charles Boyer, John Boles, Louis Jourdan, Paul Henreid, Leslie Howard—were clearly not chosen for their 'masculine' qualities" (1987, 116). Whereas Tania Modleski attributes this feminization of the male to his characterization as an alternative to patriarchal authority, Doane attributes it to narcissism. The women in these films, in other words, love men who mirror themselves. In either case, it is precisely the feminization of the man in this genre, I would argue, that accounts for the patterns of scarring and wounding on Oliver's body. Robert Young is like those actors cited by Doane and not at all like Chief Scar or Scarface; his facial scars primarily mar his beauty. Indeed, the unusual nature of this aspect of the 1940s love story emerges in an odd bit of dialogue after the "transformation" has taken place. Laura tells Oliver how "beautiful" he is, and Oliver responds by telling her that men are not beautiful, they are "handsome." Yet Laura's word usage makes clear how, in this genre, the feminized male departs from the usual hero.

Doane's passing reference to *The Enchanted Cottage* takes place within a discussion of the way in which the love story represents the dangers of unbridled female imagination. In a brief footnote she observes that this film departs from the usual pattern of the genre in that the imagination is seen in a positive light and affects both the man and the woman. She notes that the woman's ugliness is essential (i.e., congenital), whereas the man's is accidental. I would add two observations. The split nature of Oliver's physical wounds grow out of the need to mark his accident as occurring in the traditional male arena of war and, simultaneously, to differentiate his looks from those of the star in a war film. Equally interesting in this film is the presence of another male character, who is blind.

The film is narrated by a blind pianist (Herbert Marshall) who, in the opening frame, plays and narrates a tone poem he has composed about Oliver and Laura. Blindness, as discussed, is comparable to crippling wounds as a sign of castration in the action film. But it functions in a significantly different manner here. The narrator fits into the sensitive musician mold that Doane notes is another common type in the love story. Artistic sensitivity is a character equivalent of feminized male appearance in the genre, and Herbert Marshall fits both categories. Unlike Hendricks in *Rio Lobo*, whose blindness functions only as a castrating image, the narrator–pianist's blindness, the result of a World War I wound, draws on another convention whereby insight more than compensates for the loss of sight. Since the love story does not present traditional images of powerful patriarchal males, the wounds and scars on their bodies function differently from the way they do in the world of violent male action. These differences reveal the underpinnings of the traditional images and the cultural assumptions that shape them.

Hawks's films, then, because of their focused concern on the world of masculinity and its relationship to femininity, show in a singular, condensed fashion how gender assumptions in the U.S. cinema mark men's and women's bodies differently and unequally. These assumptions are neither unique to Hawks nor to any of the periods during which he made the films discussed here; they thrive very much today, as a final example from *Cyborg* (1989), a futuristic male action film, illustrates.

The central character in *Cyborg* is played by Jean-Claude Van Damme, the muscular star of kickboxing films. In one scene, he and a beautiful young woman come upon a lake. She takes off her clothes and runs into the water. A rear shot of her in the nude is bracketed by the conventional shots of the man looking, which seem to justify the shots as his point of view, although, in keeping with another convention, the camera is much closer to the nude woman than he is. Later, as they sit by a campfire, he is naked except for a blanket wrapped around his waist. She looks at him and remarks, "You're just a walking wound, aren't you?" She pauses and, after seeing his quiet reaction, adds in an erotic tone, "Sorry, I like scars, really." At this point in the film, he is marked by a bruise and severe cuts on his right cheek. Later, his face is deeply scarred with wounds sustained in more fighting. They give him a heroic strength rather than betray an ugly deformation of a once-beautiful face, and the narrative events bear out that he is a man of truly superhuman power.

Cyborg demonstrates that in 1989, many of the classical conventions surrounding the sexual representation of male and female bodies were still in place. The swimming scene makes clear that for both the audience and the male character in the film, visual pleasure resulting from nudity takes place around the woman's body. He and we look; she is the spectacle. Later in the sequence, when his body becomes the focus, he is partially covered and represented in terms of power, the covering of his genitals, as we have seen, helping to ensure that power. The woman's remark, "I like scars, really," is an unusual statement in a film about how scars generally work to empower the male body; his scars come from having survived a real war, not a war with a blonde in a Brooklyn speakeasy, and his final combat with the villain shows such combat in excruciatingly brutal detail. It is perhaps worth remembering that Odysseus, the archetypal hero and warrior in Homer's *Odyssey*, is marked and identified by a scar. There are several references to the scar and how he received it. When he returns home and tells his father who he is, his father asks for proof. Odysseus replies: "The scar then first of all. / Look, here the wild boar's flashing tusk / wounded me on Parnassos; do you see it?" (1963, 419). But, as we see in the next chapter, there is another side to this long-standing tradition of heroes who have survived battles and have the scars to prove it.

"NO NOTHING"

• • • • • •

THE NOTHING MAN

War, where men go to prove and affirm their masculinity, is perhaps not surprisingly also a literary and cinematic site of a great deal of anxiety precisely about losing that masculinity. In the film *Born on the 4th of July* (1989), a dramatic scene takes place when Ron Kovick (Tom Cruise) learns of his paralysis. He immediately asks whether he will be able to father children, and when the doctor answers negatively, he is devastated. In this chapter I want to turn to a more specific wounding of the male body, direct injury to the sexual organs.

Since the war wound holds so much fascination in films and literature, its discussion in popular sex manuals is not surprising. (Chapter 7 discusses how the sexual representation of the male body has changed in the twentieth century in the wake of the sexology movement.) David Reuben's immensely popular book *Everything You Always Wanted to Know about Sex—But Were Afraid to Ask* (1969) goes into the specifics of World War II sexual war wounds in Germany. Reuben discusses the German development of what came to be called a "castration mine," a dual explosive device that first propelled the mine to just below the waist and "then the second charge blew up and so did the testicles" (p. 14). He goes on to describe that in some cases "the testicles were completely destroyed but the penis was relatively undamaged" (p. 15). Reuben discusses this type of war wound in the larger context of his discussion of impotence. Some 50 percent of the wounded men "were capable of normal intercourse" (p. 15). In others: "The *penis decreased in size*, body hair diminished, sexual potency disappeared and of course sterility was absolute. Sexual intercourse was impossible; no erection, no sperm, no orgasm, and no ejaculate. *No nothing*" (p. 15; emphasis added). From the nothing of medicine, I want to turn to the nothing of literature.

Although the best-known novel dealing with this kind of war wound is Ernest Hemingway's *The Sun Also Rises* (1926), Jim Thompson's 1954 pulp novel, *The Nothing Man*, in many ways offers a much more complex treatment of the subject and is the central focus of this chapter. *The Sun Also Rises* serves as a useful contrast.

The Nothing Man is of particular interest for two reasons: It is an unusually explicit treatment of the "war wound" and one given formal as well as thematic complexity within the novel. The novel's form embodies the extreme crisis of masculinity and the male body, signaled by the title and garrishly blurbed on the back cover of the Mysterious Press paperback edition:

> It had started with a mistake of command, a tragic mistake. Leading the suicide patrol across a field of mines, *feeling the exploding metal tear through his flesh, and then, many hours later waking up to realize that his life as a normal man was ended.* (Thompson 1988; emphasis added)

The portion of the jacket copy I have italicized gives the reader a false impression of the wound, since Thompson never describes what Clinton Brown, the book's narrator and central character, feels when he is wounded. Thompson does, however, detail what the accident was and the feelings Clint has as a result of it.

Jim Thompson (1906–1977) is only now achieving the recognition his work deserves. The main reason for his obscurity probably stems from the fact that his novels were never published in hardcover editions. They appeared and disappeared as trash, pulp fiction. Although many can be classified as crime novels, they are somewhat difficult to characterize. They seem to be part of the hard-boiled tradition, but they are not detective novels because the solution to a crime is not their central concern. Few even feature detectives.

The French, who discovered Thompson, refer to his works as *roman noir*. A schizophrenic criminal personality frequently serves as the narrative point of view, a startling strategy that leads the reader to identify with frightening characters.

Prestigious filmmakers have been interested in Thompson's work. Stanley Kubrick not only admired his novels but also used him as a screenwriter on *The Killing* (1956) and *Paths of Glory* (1957). There have also been several major adaptations of his novels. *The Getaway* (1972) was directed by Sam Peckinpah, and Bernard Tavernier adapted *Pop. 1280* as *Coup de Torchon* (1981). The releases of *After Dark, My Sweet* (1990) and, particularly, Martin Scorsese's production of Stephen Frears' *The Grifters* (1991) have brought heightened attention to Thompson's novels. *Noir* writers in general are being rediscovered, and as part of this larger process, Thompson's novels are available for the first time since their original publication. Within this context Mysterious Press republished *The Nothing Man* in 1988.

In the first chapter of the novel, Clint Brown, with his typical cynical humor, says that he has given his "penis for his country" (Thompson 1988, 3). The second chapter describes in harrowing detail one of the consequences:

People laugh about it, privately perhaps, but they laugh. They give you sympathetic smiles and glances, their faces tight with laughter restrained. And even when they do not laugh, you can hear them. . . . *Poor guy! What a hell of a—ha, ha, ha—I wonder what he does when he has to . . .?*

You can't work. You can't live. You can't die. You are afraid to die, afraid of the complete defenselessness to laughter that death will bring. (pp. 8–9)

This is an unusually poignant passage about the fear surrounding the body and the penis, a fear so intense that it looks beyond death. Indeed, far from bringing relief, death becomes the ultimate humiliation. "The truth," as Thompson calls it, becomes Clint's obsession. It is not that he is ruined by having to live a life without the pleasures of genital sexuality but that if others knew about him, he would become the object of their laughter. In a sense, laughter becomes the ultimate dread. While he is alive, he can at least make sure that virtually no one knows the secret that his body will yield up in death. Yet if someone were to find out his secret, living would be as impossible as dying: "How could I live in a world of snickers and whisperings and amused pity?" (p. 29) he asks himself. Similarly, he asks his former wife to put herself in his place when she finally learns the truth: "How long could you live in a world where everyone knew you didn't have a pecker? . . . You could even catch the doctors and nurses in the hospital grinning about it" (p. 38). Thompson creates a nightmare vision wherein Clint can neither live nor die.

Indeed, his fear of doctors and nurses seeing him naked, reminiscent of his fear of his dead body being seen, returns when he has to go to the hospital to be treated for food poisoning. Even though he is deathly ill, he takes the time to put on pajamas:

A pair with all the buttons and no holes. Even then there was a chance that they might see, but—

But I had to risk it. I knew I'd die if I didn't. (p. 127)

On two occasions, Clint goes so far as to characterize himself in terms of the nothingness of the book's title. Looking at himself in the mirror, he wonders why he has been burdened with good looks, since he does not have a penis. "They [women] stretch their goddamned sweet necks to get a peek. And . . . and that's all there is. Only what they can see" (p. 98). Later, he draws a comparison between himself and the newspaper he works for: "The paper resumed its puerile emptiness, a newspaper in name only as I was a man in name only. There was nothing in either of us. We were facades for emptiness" (pp. 173–74).

This extraordinarily explicit account of the wound and the resultant trauma surrounding the sight of the body contrasts markedly with the more conventional manner of representing the war wound. Ernest Hemingway's *The Sun Also Rises*, whose main character suffers such a wound, is an instructive comparison. We learn in Chapter 3 of the novel that Jake Barnes, the narrator, is impotent. A woman expresses sexual desire for him:

She looked up to be kissed. She touched me with one hand and I put her hand away.

"Never mind."

"What's the matter? You sick?"

"Yes." (Hemingway 1954, 15)

Shortly after, he tells her, "I got hurt in the war" (p. 17). A later scene is more ambiguous: "Undressing, I looked at myself in the mirror of the big armoire beside the bed. . . . Of all the ways to be wounded. I suppose it was funny" (p. 30).

The look in the mirror may imply that he sees the damage to his body or may simply suggest that the sight of his dysfunctional penis strikes him as humorous. He may simply be impotent. Such impotence in fiction is generally assumed to result from nerve injury, not literal loss of the penis. The tragedy, presumably, is the inability to have a satisfying sex life. Although this nonspecific account of Jake's wound stands in sharp contrast to the graphic account of Clint's, Jake shares Clint's concern with being the butt of jokes, which is even clearer in an exchange with Brett, an old friend. He tells her, "What happened to me is supposed to be funny" (p. 26). She replies, "I laughed about it too, myself, once. . . . A friend of my brother's came home that way from Mons. It seemed like a hell of a joke" (pp. 26–27). Barnes says, "At one time or another I had probably considered it from most of its various angles, including the one that certain injuries or imperfections are a subject of merriment while remaining quite serious for the person possessing them. 'It's funny, I said. It's very funny'" (p. 27).

Hemingway's treatment of the entire subject is much more muted than Thompson's. Although the specter of being joked about is acknowledged, Jake Barnes understands, appreciates, and even joins in the joking. Much as the wound on his body remains nameless, in contrast to Clint's, his psychological damage is minimal; he is a coping, rational human being, and one for whom life has not lost all its pleasures. Jim Thompson's book is much more insistent on both the physical and psychological damages of the war wound. But what really separates *The Nothing Man* from *The Sun Also Rises* is the formal dimension the novel accords the wound. It is no exaggeration to say that the form of *The Sun Also Rises* bears no relationship to its narrator's condition; in *The Nothing Man* the entire narrative is organized around it.

The first chapter of *The Nothing Man* introduces us to the narrator, who is writing an account of what will become the book we are about to read. Chapter 2 takes us into a flashback that begins a couple of months earlier. The last chapter returns us to the frame story, but with an extraordinary twist. A brief synopsis of the plot is necessary.

Clint works for a small-town newspaper that also employs David Randall, the colonel who ordered the ill-fated mission in which Clint was wounded. Feeling guilty for his error, Dave holds himself responsible for Clint. And, of course, he is the only person who knows Clint's secret—until Clint's wife,

Ellen, from whom he has been separated and expecting a divorce, mysteriously returns to Pacific City. Clint hypothesizes that she has been paid to come back by Lem Stukey, Pacific City's crooked chief of police. Fearing that Ellen will figure out the truth and tell Lem, he kills her.

Although Clint initially appears to be the murderer, he cleverly devises a scheme that not only points to another person as the killer but also gives him blackmail leverage over Lem. He forces Lem into cleaning up the town as part of the search for Ellen's murderer. Complications arise when evidence seems to point toward Tom Judge, a fellow *Courier* employee, whom Clint, thinking himself to be the murderer, does not want convicted of the crime.

The desire to keep his secret, combined with the need to deflect guilt away from Tom, leads Clint to kill two other women. Deborah Chasen, whom he met while on assignment from the paper, has fallen in love with him and presumes that Ellen stands between her and Clint. After reading of Ellen's death, she returns to Clint, expecting to marry him. Since she has expressed herself as a woman with strong sexual desires, Clint presumes that the truth about him will so disappoint her that she will no longer want to marry him and will reveal his secret. He kills her, and leaves behind a poem. Since a poem had been found with Ellen's body, he strengthens the apparent connection between the murderer and the poems, and since Tom was in jail when Deborah was killed, this rules Tom out as the murderer.

Then he kills Constance Wakefield, a book publisher who has approached him about publishing his poems and has copies of them. Unable to discover whether, after reading newspaper coverage of the murders, Constance has connected him with the dead women, he decides to kill her to ensure his safety.

At this point, the narrative returns to the present tense of the first chapter. Clint is in his office typing what we have read when Lem Stukey enters. Suddenly, everything we thought we knew is thrown out of balance. First, Lem reports that Tom Judge, breaking down under the weight of a guilty conscience, has confessed to murdering Ellen. A coroner's report has shown that Deborah was dead before Clint thinks he killed her, and Constance's death has been ruled accidental. We are as surprised as Clint to discover that he has murdered no one.

Unexpected twists are commonplace in detective fiction, but something much different is operating here. First, *The Nothing Man* belongs to a tradition of crime fiction that is separate from the detective mystery. In it, as in many of Thompson's novels, the question is not "Who done it"? His novels usually make the reader identify with a disturbing narrator, one who is criminal, mentally ill, or alcoholic, and frequently a combination of such traits. We know all along what the protagonists have done, though we may be shocked by their actions and intrigued by the dark world they inhabit.

In this regard, Thompson's crime fiction differs not only from the Arthur Conan Doyle and Agatha Christie puzzle-style narrative, but also from the American hard-boiled tradition of Dashiell Hammett and Raymond Chandler, although his style clearly relates to theirs. Thompson's novels do not rely on a strong hermeneutic involving a mystery. But even overlooking this fundamental distinction, I would argue that Thompson's twist in *The Nothing Man* differs significantly from the surprise endings encountered in the other traditions. In Agatha Christie's *The Murder of Roger Ackroyd*, the narrator turns out to be the murderer, and in Alfred Hitchcock's film *Stage Fright* (1950), somewhat similarly, a man who appears framed for the crime he narrates turns out to be the killer. Hitchcock achieves the surprise via the "lying flashback": When we see the murder narrated within a flashback, we simply accept what we have seen as true. Similarly, if the narrator of a novel tells us he is trying to solve murders, we accept that, rather than suspect that he is the perpetrator of the crimes. Such extreme twists can serve many functions, including foregrounding normally unquestioned narrational devices.*

Many less extreme surprise endings than those in *The Murder of Roger Ackroyd* and *Stage Fright* simply give intellectual pleasure to readers who puzzle out the mystery. Searching for clues and trying various hypotheses, readers may feel gratified or even cheated when they learn the truth. But notice that such a process is contingent on the reader's thinking that there is a mystery that needs solving. On the contrary, as readers of *The Nothing Man*, we presume that we know both who committed the murders and why; we may be appalled, but we are not confused. The ending of *The Nothing Man* involves a profound integration of the novel's theme with its form. Far from being a satisfying surprise, the novel's ending is the extreme manifestation of its crisis: Clint could not have committed the murders because he is not a "real" man.

Although Thompson does not position us as readers searching for clues as to "who done it," he does create clues. Clint shows some unusual weaknesses

---

*Kristin Thompson has analyzed *Stage Fright* from precisely that perspective, arguing that the film calls into question a feature of the Hollywood cinema that we normally unthinkingly accept, that all flashbacks reveal the truth.

for a narrator. The first hint of this occurs near the end of Chapter 2 when he confesses that about Deborah "I still couldn't make up my mind whether she was stupid or only appeared to be. As I say, I never could make it up" (1988, 14). This failure to see people for what they are is particularly interesting in light of Clint's attitude of superiority toward those around him—his colleagues at the newspaper, the chief of police, or humanity in general—and his sense of himself as the sharp cynic who sees things for what they are. It is demonstrated several times, by an exchange with Constance and his inability to size her up.

Perhaps most significantly, he totally misjudges Lem Stukey, seeing Lem as little more than a lazy, stupid, sleazy, crooked cop. With great pleasure, Clint forces Lem into the clean-up campaign, and he smugly presumes that Lem is at his mercy. Although Clint has a couple of moments when Lem does not seem quite so stupid, nothing prepares him or us for the full extent of Clint's misunderstanding.

Toward the end of the novel, Clint discovers that Lem had regularly been sending large amounts of money to Ellen and concludes that she has been blackmailing Lem. Confronting Lem, he finds that he has misconstrued both the relationship between Lem and Ellen and that between Lem and himself. The stupid man Clint had been manipulating has known the truth all along and, in a sense, has been manipulating him. Lem says: "I had it doped out right from the beginning almost; that pension, that nothin' wrong showing on you, an' breaking up with your wife when there wasn't another babe, an'—and this place. You wantin' a home—not just a room—and doing your best to have one" (p. 182). Clint is so surprised by the revelation that Lem has been manipulating him, rather than the reverse, that he is speechless.

Clint's predicament not surprisingly leads him to raise the possibility of suicide, but even with ample opportunity he cannot take the step. He lives close by the railroad tracks, and in Chapter 8 he tells us, "I often stand there at night, on the bluff overlooking the tracks, watching the trains go by, wondering if it wouldn't be better to . . ." (p. 61). Breaking off his thought, he simply notes that the last train for the night has passed. Not only is he unable to commit suicide, he is unable either to say the word or to acknowledge that he contemplates it. And once again, Lem perceptively sees this: "Maybe you kidded yourself you was going to do a brodie, but I knew you wouldn't. You couldn't any more'n you could have killed those other people" (p. 190).

It is also worth noting the novel's insistence on the fact that Clint, an extremely heavy drinker, cannot get drunk. In describing his actions on the night he attempts to murder Ellen, he notes, "And while I wasn't drunk, naturally, since I cannot get drunk, I was very far from sober" (p. 32). Other characters remark on his bizarre inability to get drunk. Even the bartender, after watching him down a number of drinks in the morning, exclaims, "I don't know how you do it," he said. "I swear Mr. Brown, if I tried that I'd—" (p. 9). Lem tells him, "The whiz don't do anything at all to you, does it, keed? Just makes you spout a little smoother" (pp. 25–26). When he winds up in the hospital, the doctor warns him, "The amount of alcohol in your bloodstream now would be lethal for the average person" (p. 131).

Usually the ability to drink heavily without getting drunk is a sign of masculine strength and, correspondingly, drunkenness is a sign of weakness. (Recall Dude's drunkenness in *Rio Bravo*.) *The Nothing Man* inverts this logic, making Clint's inability to get drunk just one more failure. If he could get drunk, he would be more like a "normal" man; excessive drinking marks his body as unnatural in a way that the other characters can see and comment on, even if they cannot see the secret of his body. Absolutely everything in *The Nothing Man* points to the impossibility of being a man without a penis; it is literally all or nothing.

Another sign of Clint's weakness throughout the novel is failure of memory. The first instance occurs in relation to the events surrounding Ellen's death: "I tried to remember and, as I had last night, I drew a blank. I was bending over her. Then I was at the boat. And in between there was nothing. . . . I had no recollection of events between my setting the fire and my arrival at the boat" (p. 64).

Similar lapses occur when Deborah calls him in a restaurant and he does not recognize her name; later, when he decides to kill her, his narrative falters—"I am somewhat hazy in spots about the ride to Pacific City" (p. 104). These memory lapses not only signify a weakness in Clint but, combined with the failure to perceive character, suggest something less than the fully omniscient narrative we seem to be getting. Indeed, Chapter 4 opens with Clint prefacing an observation about human nature with the admission, "I may be wrong—I have been wrong about so many things—" (p. 23).

How is it, then, that Clint the character and the narrator has been wrong about the murders he thinks he has committed and narrated in detail? For the answer, we have to look at how Clint sets about murdering his victims. His wife Ellen, the first intended victim, he knocks unconscious with a bottle and sets on fire. He notes, however, that she is semiconscious by the time he covers her with a sheet, soaks it with liquor, and lights it. Moments later, he even describes the spectacle for us: "She had looked very beautiful. She had glowed, oh, but definitely she had glowed. She had been all lit up, burning with a clear-blue flame, and then the mattress had started to smolder and . . ." (p. 41). From such a detailed description of the burning body, we are likely to assume that Clint has accomplished his goal. Very shortly after that, however, Lem informs Clint that Ellen regained consciousness, went to her dresser, and took a poem out of her purse. Her hair had apparently cushioned the blow from the bottle. In other words, she had not been hit with enough force to knock her out. It is not until Chapter 11, however, that it occurs to Clint that he might not have killed Ellen: "I *knew* who had killed Ellen—but did I know?" (p. 91).

He attempts to murder Deborah after bringing her to his house. Yet he does not do so immediately. At one point, he goes out and leaves her alone. On returning, he finds her lying on her stomach, asleep in bed. "I heaved a sigh of relief, and I killed her" (p. 116). He hits her on the back of her neck with his fist. "There was a dull pop, and her neck sagged and her neck bent backward" (p. 116). He disposes of the body by throwing it into a fenced-off area of a dog pound where particularly vicious dogs are kept. As with the way in which he attempts to kill his wife, he chooses the method because of its association with the victim; in this instance, he had taken Deborah to the pound when he first met her and recalls her terror of the dogs. Lem tells him later that the coroner had determined that Deborah was dead from a drug overdose before she was hit. As if this is not enough, Lem adds, "And by the way, you didn't break her neck. . . . huh-uh, you hit her, I guess, but you didn't kill her" (p. 188). Again, the lack of force in the blow is foregrounded; Clint cannot even break the neck of a dead woman.

Constance Wakefield, Clint's third intended victim, is an asthmatic who cares only about money. On a train, Clint attempts to choke her to death with coins. After listening to her strangling sounds, he jumps off. Later, he discovers that she dislodged the coins from her throat, then accidentally fell from the train.

Lem Stukey sees the significance of the pattern that emerges in these attempted murders. Lem maintains that the same person is involved all three cases: "I tell you it's a pattern," Stukey insisted. "I can't lay it out for you like wallpaper, but it's got to be the same guy. He don't carry through, see? He leaves too much to chance. He ain't—well, he don't seem serious about it" (p. 171). The unspoken words indicated by the dash in Lem's last sentence point to the significance of the pattern. The sentence could be completed any number of ways: "He ain't man enough"; "he ain't strong enough"; "he ain't good enough." It all adds up to the same thing, as Clint himself ultimately articulates it. Learning that Lem has known the secret all along, Clint tries to kill him by smashing a liquor bottle down on his head: "Of course, I didn't kill him. I know now that I am incapable of killing anyone. . . . I don't as yet have the answer to certain other questions, I only know that I have not killed and cannot kill, and . . ." (pp. 183–184). The entire novel is precisely about how this man without a penis, this "nothing" man, *could not* have committed murder. He lacks the power, the masculinity—indeed, the phallus.

If Hemingway's *The Sun Also Rises* appears to be a somewhat conventionally inexplicit treatment of the war wound in comparison to Thompson's, we should note the surprisingly explicit discussion of the penis in the posthumously published *A Moveable Feast* (1964), the unique chapter entitled "A Matter of Measurements," where Hemingway tells of F. Scott Fitzgerald's anxiety about the size of his penis.

According to Hemingway, Fitzgerald asked him to lunch to talk about something very important and wanted his honest response. After much delay, Fitzgerald confides, "Zelda said that the way I was built I could never make any woman happy and that was what upset her originally. She said it was a matter of measurements" (Hemingway 1964, 188). Hemingway responds by asking Fitzgerald to step into the bathroom with him. They return to the restaurant where Hemingway pronounces that there is nothing wrong with Fitzgerald: "You look at yourself from above and you look foreshortened. Go over to the Louvre and look at the people in the statues and then go home and look at yourself in the mirror in profile" (p. 188). Fitzgerald replies that the statues may not be accurate. Nevertheless, at Hemingway's insistence, they go to the Louvre and look at statues; Fitzgerald still is unconvinced. Hemingway then takes a different approach: "'It is not basically a question of the size in repose,'" I said. "'It is the size that it becomes. It is also a question of angle.'" I explained to him about using a pillow and a few other things that might be useful for him to know" (p. 189). Hemingway notes, however, that Fitzgerald remained doubtful.

At the simplest level, the chapter is interesting in the way in which it counterposes two alternative ways of responding to penis size. First, Hemingway appeals to art: Look and you will see. As Fitzgerald himself points out, this approach is based on a realist assumption of accuracy. Second, Hemingway starts to talk like a twentieth-century sexologist. His reference to the fact that one cannot judge the size of an erect penis from looking at an unerect penis was to become one of the truisms of the later sexologists and sex-manual authors. Here Hemingway seems to fall into something of a contradiction, first telling Fitzgerald that he looks small only to himself and then saying that even if he is small when unerect, he might not be when erect. (This tension between visual representation and scientific study of the penis is examined in Chapter 7.) Hemingway's response and his narration are important, however, in revealing how the form of "A Matter of Measurements" relates to its subject in a more complex way than the form of *The Sun Also Rises* does.

Throughout the episode, Hemingway presents himself as the unquestioned voice of secure masculine authority; he never wavers for a moment. He glibly responds, "Come out to the office" (i.e., the bathroom) when Fitzgerald states his concern. He "explains" to Fitzgerald such things as the use of a pillow while making love. He speaks with the combined masculine authority of the art historian and the medical doctor. As for the woman, " 'Forget what Zelda said,' I told him. 'Zelda is crazy' " (p. 189). Running parallel to this phallic voice of the truth is Fitzgerald's nagging doubt. Hemingway repeats several times that Fitzgerald remains in doubt. " 'Now do you believe me?' 'I don't know,' he said" (pp. 188–189). After the trip to the Louvre, Hemingway notes: "But he was still doubtful" (p. 189). The polarity between the strong bearer of the truth and the anxious receiver of it is maintained throughout.

But, extraordinarily, the episode is not complete by itself. Hemingway finds a need to jump years ahead in his narrative when he returned to the Ritz and had a conversation with Charles, an employee who had worked there in the 1920s when the event Hemingway described took place. Charles is puzzled by the fact that people keep asking him about Fitzgerald. Once again, the phallic male voice of authority is asked a question: " 'Papa, who was this Monsieur Fitzgerald that everyone asks me about?' " (p. 189). When Hemingway asks whether he did not know him, Charles replies in the negative, observing that he remembers all the other people from that time period. When Hemingway fills in the story, Charles interrupts, " 'But why would I not remember him?' " (p. 190). Hemingway continues and once again Charles breaks in, " 'It is strange that I have no memory of him' " (p. 190). As if in contrast, Charles later notes when Hemingway mentions Baron von Blixen, " 'The Baron was not a *man* that you forget' " (p. 191; emphasis added). The chapter ends with Charles not succeeding in his attempt to recall Fitzgerald. It is Fitzgerald, worried about the size of his penis, rather than Jake Barnes, who is the nothing man of Hemingway's writings. It is no coincidence that the form of the chapter in which this episode is recounted ends with an absolute failure—on the part of one man who has an otherwise picture-perfect memory—to remember who Fitzgerald was—for, from the perspective of masculinity and the male body, he was nothing.

Finally, it is worth noting Hemingway's first description of Fitzgerald in *A Moveable Feast*, in the chapter entitled "Scott Fitzgerald": "Scott was a man who looked like a boy with a face between handsome and pretty. He had very fair wavy hair, a high forehead, excited and friendly eyes and a delicate long-lipped Irish mouth that, on a girl, would have been the mouth of a beauty" (p. 147). The passage is extremely troubled in terms of sexual difference; this is not the description of a man so much as one of a man who occupies a borderline with boys and women. This is perhaps well summed up by the connotations of the description of his face as being between the traditionally masculine "handsome" and the traditionally feminine "pretty." A little later, we get the clincher: "When he sat down on one of the bar stools I saw that he had very short legs. With *normal* legs he would have been perhaps two inches taller" (p. 148; emphasis added). As is so often the case, the crisis of masculinity that we hear about seems to have marked itself visibly on Fitzgerald's body. Even before we learn about the small penis, there is a disturbance of the body. Indeed, the chronology here is interesting. Hemingway's initial impression of seeing Fitzgerald precedes by some time the episode in the Ritz, but one cannot help but suspect that Hemingway has infused the former with the hindsight of the latter—the body speaks too much and too loudly.

ANOTHER NOTHING MAN

• • • • • •

· EDWARD G. ROBINSON AND *SCARLET STREET*

If Clint Brown in Jim Thompson's *The Nothing Man* is literally what the title calls him, Little Bigger, in Thompson's 1953 novel, *Savage Night*, is a metaphorical version of the same thing. Such interplay between the literal and the metaphorical determines a great deal about the sexual representation of the male body. Little Bigger is five feet tall, obsessively worried about his size and the laughter he thinks his appearance provokes in others. He dreads being called "Sonny," a form of address that emphasizes how his size makes many assume he is a "kid," rather than a man. Significantly, the powerful criminal who forces Bigger into his service and ultimately becomes his adversary is known as "The Man." Near the end of the novel, as he loses control of events, Bigger's narration stresses how less and less of him is left. This quantifiable notion of diminishing masculinity receives remarkable formal development at the novel's conclusion when Bigger is hacked to death by a woman, and his narration describes the loss of parts of his body. Before he dies, his metaphorically diminished masculinity becomes literal.

The paradox of *The Nothing Man* is that by being almost singularly literal, it becomes curiously metaphorical: Clint's terrifying fear about not having a penis, about the "truth" being discovered, and about becoming the object of laughter speaks to a much more generalized male anxiety. Clint's fear of dying lest he be laughed at in death, for example, is a wildly illogical, though perfectly understandable, extension of male fear about not measuring up, about not being a true man. Nevertheless, *The Nothing Man* does not displace its fears about male sexual adequacy to other sites of the body. Like *Savage Night*, Fritz Lang's *Scarlet Street* (1947) does so exclusively.

Lang's film belongs to the postwar *film noir* genre and thus is related to the *noir* tradition in the novel to which *The Nothing Man* belongs. It is critical commonplace that the representation of women in *film noir* breaks with Hollywood tradition with the appearance of dangerous women who are outside the home and family. Such women are frequently marked as very sexual and are punished for that sexuality during the course of the film. Among the few critics to comment on the male body and male sexuality in *film noir*, E. Ann Kaplan, in an article on Lang's *While the City Sleeps*, perceptively notes: "In the Fifties, representations of violence become more complicated because of a shift in the image of men. In noir films the investigator was still tough, virile, and traditionally masculine, but increasingly in the Fifties images of weak, feminized men appear" (1980, 55).

Kaplan argues that Lang's films are particularly interesting because they deal with male authority within both the family and the public sphere, and because they link weakened male authority to violence against women. For Lang, a decline in masculine authority poses a serious threat to independent women, who become the victims of what Kaplan calls these "feminized" men. In a later article on *Scarlet Street*, Kaplan discusses Chris, the film's central character, as one such feminized man. Before taking up these issues in detail, a brief synopsis is in order.

Chris Cross (Edward G. Robinson) is the clerk in a successful business headed by J. J. Hogarth (Russell Hicks). Chris is dominated at home by his wife Adele (Rosalind Ivan), who unfavorably compares him to her first husband Homer, a police officer presumed killed in the line of duty. One day, Chris comes to the rescue of Kitty (Joan Bennett), a woman being beaten on the street by Johnny (Dan Duryea), her male companion. Chris falls in love with Kitty, who mistakenly thinks that he, a Sunday painter, is an extremely successful artist. Johnny then devises a plan to trick Chris out of some of the money they presume Chris earns from the sale of his "famous" paintings. Chris is so attracted to Kitty that he falls easy prey to their scheme, first using his own hard-earned money to set her up in a Greenwich Village apartment and then stealing from his employer in order to continue meeting the expenses.

Two events upset the equilibrium. Unknown to Chris, Johnny has taken some of Chris's paintings to an art dealer and learns that Chris is an unknown amateur. Several of the paintings are displayed on a Greenwich Village sidewalk when Janeway (Hess Barker), an influential art critic, discovers them; searching for the artist, he mistakenly thinks Kitty painted them. Once again, Johnny figures that they can cash in by selling Chris's (unsigned) paintings as Kitty's. But Adele, seeing the paintings in an art dealer's window and mistakenly concluding that Chris is hiding something from her, angrily confronts him. Kitty convinces Chris that she should continue to play the role of the artist and leads him to believe that only his marriage prevents them from marrying.

Adele's first husband Homer, suddenly appears, revealing to Chris that his "death" was a ruse and threatens to nullify Chris's marriage to Adele. Chris will not be blackmailed and tricks Homer into revealing his identity to Adele. Free at last to marry Kitty, he is jubilantly happy, but when he tells her of Homer's return, he learns how she and Johnny have cruelly manipulated him. In a rage, he kills Kitty. Circumstantial evidence points to Johnny, who is convicted and executed for the crime. Chris, driven by a guilty conscience, tries to commit suicide and to confess his guilt, but no one believes him. He has lost everything—his job, his wife, and even his paintings, which circulate under Kitty's name. He is left a broken man, wandering the streets as a bum.

Kaplan's reading of *Scarlet Street* stresses the way in which Lang's film typically provides invisible and smooth transitions between scenes in a way that naturalizes the distinction between the private sphere (the home) and the public sphere (the workplace). Only once, in her view, is the classical style upset: a series of jarring, expressionistic cuts that occur in the brief courtroom scene during Johnny's trial. This stylistic departure, Kaplan argues, causes a momentary break in bourgeois ideology. She sees Chris as a feminized character both at home, where he is contrasted with Homer, and at work, where he is contrasted with J. J. Hogarth. His motivation for taking up with Kitty is threefold: He is dissatisfied with his home life, he must prove he is a man because of Adele's unpleasant domination of him, and he must compensate for his low position at work by taking a mistress like the one his boss has.

Kaplan's argument does not go far enough in critical areas. Her generalizations are too broad. Obviously the film belongs to the classical style of invisible editing, but paying careful attention to the cutting reveals complex moments that do not simply conform to the classical style. I would also question the significance Kaplan attributes to the trial montage. It is perfectly in keeping with the 1940s classical style to have brief montage episodes, and their noticeability should not be too quickly associated with a break from bourgeois ideology. Perhaps of most immediate significance, Kaplan does not pay any attention to how the feminization of Chris is inscribed on the body. This in turn reveals a major oversight: Kaplan simply presents Homer as a real man who, like J. J., offers a marked contrast to Chris, overlooking the fact that through much of the film Homer is seen only in a painting. When he appears, he is unexpectedly different from his represented image. I regard these omissions about the two men's bodies and how they are represented as critical because *Scarlet Street* is centrally preoccupied with the question of the representation of the male body.

The film opens at a businessmen's dinner where Chris Cross is honored for twenty-five years of devoted service to the firm. In an economical fashion characteristic of classical texts, this scene establishes two important antitheses: one between men and women and one between "real" men and a man deficient in masculinity. The exterior establishing shot shows women on the street, and an interior establishing shot shows a female employee sitting outside the room where the men are having their dinner. J. J. Hogarth, the powerful boss, sitting at the head of the table as the men sing "For He's a Jolly Good Fellow," receives a message. He calls for attention and announces, "Well, boys, I hate to break up a good party but you can't keep a woman waiting, can you? You know how it is." They all quickly agree, and J. J. happily adds, "I can see you all understand all right." He then gives a short speech about Chris's years of service and rewards him with the traditional watch before taking leave of the party.

Suddenly, the powerful man is repositioned as subservient to a woman. Again in fairly typical fashion, the man both posseses the woman because of his power (she is represented as the beautiful mistress of a richly successful executive) and is potentially threatened by her (she breaks up the all-male gathering and determines when he should leave).

Throughout the scene, there are connotations of diminished masculinity attached to Chris. His indecisive speech and stammering mark him as lacking control of language; he initially turns down his boss's offer of a cigar and then, as if in a rare moment of daring, accepts one, only to superstitiously cross his fingers behind his back when he is the "third on a match." Finally, he sneaks out of the party early with a colleague to whom he confesses with adolescent innocence that he wonders what it would be like to have a young, beautiful mistress as J. J. has.

A summary of events does not mention what is visually obvious: Edward G. Robinson, an actor of diminutive stature, is cast as Chris Cross. From the outset, then, the film's replication of bodies, to use Roland Barthes's term, fixes our dominant cultural assumption of a relationship between masculinity and the body: To be a real man is to look like one, to be tall, strong, powerful. Moreover, this notion of masculinity is obviously quantifiable; one can be more or less of a man, and Chris is clearly less. He neither acts nor looks like a "real" man.

The next two sequences confirm this. As Chris walks to his train, he comes upon a man beating a woman. Although he rushes to the rescue, the manner in which he intervenes marks him as childlike and effeminate in a way I examine in detail later. He succeeds in the rescue, however, and rather than go home directly, takes the woman, Kitty, out. The next day we first see Chris at home, and the colleague with whom he left the party the night before visits. Out of fear of Adele's disapproval, Chris whispers to his friend a fabrication about what time the party ended so that he will not have to account for the late hour at which he arrived home. Chris meekly attempts to appease the domineering Adele by clearing the dishes and refusing the offer of a cigar. When he shows off his paintings, we find that even this hobby has to be carried out in cramped quarters, out of Adele's way. In short, Chris is the stereotype of the henpecked husband whose domineering wife is predictably represented within the codes of the star system as an unattractive woman.

An important new element of the replication of male bodies is introduced in this scene. A large portrait of Adele's first husband, hangs on the wall in the apartment. Higgins is represented as a large, powerful man with a body in sharp contrast to Chris's. As if this were not enough, he is a policeman in uniform. And to cap it off, his medal of honor is affixed to the portrait; if the realist representation might not be 100 percent proof of the real man, the medal he earned while dying in the line of duty seals the deal. Throughout the film, the portrait of this "real" man looms over Chris's groveling behavior in front of Adele. Homer presumably was everything that Chris can never be.

Having set up these simple representations of power, *Scarlet Street* proceeds to call them into question. As is inevitably true in the classical cinema, when fundamental assumptions about such things as masculinity and realism are critiqued, stylistic fissures occur within the text. Before fully charting the troubled ideology of masculinity and the body in the film, I want to detail the sequence of the previous night, where Chris says good-bye to his colleague and walks to the train station, for it contains a particularly revealing stylistic rupture.

First, Chris encounters a policeman whom he asks for directions, blaming his confusion on the irregularities of Greenwich Village streets, which we, of course, are asked to read via a cultural reference code as a signifier of other, more profound irregularities within the exotic art world. Chris's reliance on the Law is straightforward and simple. Continuing on his way, he spots a domestic dispute between a couple (Kitty and Johnny), rushes over to stop the escalating violence, and knocks the man down. The representation of the last part of the action is troubled. Chris uses an umbrella to strike out at Johnny. Neither we nor he, however, see how he has accomplished this. In an action coded to suggest feminine movements, Chris strikes out at Johnny, who just begins to fall back (9) as we cut to Chris, who coweringly covers his eyes (10). When we next see Johnny, he is lying flat on his back, unconscious in the street (11).

How did he end up that way? He has not been struck hard enough to be knocked out or even knocked down. The speed of the action leads us to presume that Johnny has stumbled, fallen, and knocked himself unconscious. Yet such a scenario is all but impossible. There is nothing for him to hit his head on, and the discrepancy between the angle at which he starts to fall and the way he is lying on his back further blocks a reasonable account of what happened. The film's plot requires that Chris perform this action, but the film's gender ideology blocks it from showing us how he accomplished it. A central premise of *Scarlet Street* is that Chris lacks the phallic power his culture says a "real" man should have, and this informs casting Robinson as Chris. To show Chris even momentarily possessing the power to overcome a man would create a severe ideological problem. Thus the editing pattern diverts the spectator's attention away from this dilemma; by using an extended-reaction shot in place of the action in which Chris accomplishes what he must, for the sake of the narrative, but the action is represented

9

10

11

in a way that denies what it shows. It somehow just happened; neither we nor he know how. Even Chris's reaction shot is followed by a shot of Kitty before the camera moves and we see Johnny on the ground. This further delays and sidetracks the logical completion of the action sequence. When we finally do see Johnny, Chris's symbolic powerlessness is still intact. As if to emphasize this, he immediately rushes off looking and sounding like a child as he yells, "Officer, Officer!"

Chris's trajectory throughout the film confirms the lack of masculine power that so obsessively marks him at the film's outset. He easily falls into the trap that Johnny and Kitty set for him, never for a moment suspecting Kitty's story or her sincerity. When Kitty is falsely "discovered" as the talented artist of Chris's paintings, he plays along. He directly acknowledges how this arrangement reverses that of the usual marriage whereby the man's possession of the woman is marked by her taking his name. "Why, its just like we're married, only I took your name," Chris tells Kitty as she signs Chris's works, something he himself never had the confidence or assertiveness to do. He is the invisible man behind the woman. Not surprisingly, he characterizes his weakness as a painter to Johnny by remarking, "Yes, that's the one thing I never could master—perspective." This is the worst sin of all within realist styles and one that betrays yet another weakness with feminine connotations.

At the end of the film, when Chris kills Kitty, even this action is represented as totally nonmasculine. First, he confronts her without the faintest notion of killing her. She laughs and taunts him for being stupid enough to believe that she could love someone as old and ugly as he is. She laughs in the face of his threat that he had thought about killing Johnny and, like Adele, she ridicules his masculinity by comparing him to another man: "You, kill Johnny. I'd like to see you try. Why, he'd break every bone in your body. He's a man." Chris recoils in terror and accidentally knocks over an ice pick. He intends to put it back, but when Kitty continues her verbal abuse, he advances toward her with the ice pick in hand. She misperceives this (as earlier Adele has sarcastically pretended to misperceive Chris's advance on her with a kitchen knife in his hand), and fearing that he intends to kill her, she actually motivates him to do so by yelling, "Get away from me," and pulling the blankets over her head. He then loses all control and repeatedly plunges the pick into the shape beneath the blanket.

At the moment Chris murders, everything conspires to undercut the action as one of masculine power. Rather than effectively execute a plan of action, he hysterically loses control of himself and acts so emotionally that he seems unaware of what it is he is doing. Kitty's excessive laughter and cowering beneath the blankets combine to give him a power he did not know he had and allow him to use it by literally covering up what it is he does. Just as he could only accidentally knock out Johnny at the beginning of the film, surprised by what he has done, so he can kill Kitty only without knowing and seeing what he is doing. Once again, neither do we see what Chris has done. Finally, when Johnny is falsely convicted of murdering Kitty and executed for the crime, Chris, driven by guilt, hangs himself, but fails to die. He is left pathetically wandering the streets, unable to kill himself or even convince the law that he is guilty of murder. This powerless little man has failed at everything and lost everything.

Given Chris's consistent narrative trajectory of powerlessness and loss of control, the film's ideology of masculinity and the body seems both simple and banal. Where does the aforementioned critique of masculinity and its representation enter? The first and most obvious instance occurs with Adele's former husband. Even more surprising than his reappearance are the circumstances behind it. In trouble because of his illegal activities on the force, Homer took an unexpected opportunity to fake his death and returns in hopes of blackmailing Chris.

Two major consequences in the film's sexual ideology result from this plot development. First and foremost, representation of the male body is seen to lie. Everything about the portrait of the decorated police officer led us to presume that, in contrast to Chris, Homer was a strong, powerful man and an ideal embodiment of the Law. In short, a "real" man. Throughout the earlier domestic scenes in the film, we constantly see Homer's portrait looming over Chris as he servilely fulfills traditionally feminine domestic chores such as cooking and cleaning. This little man, frequently wearing an apron, seems the exact opposite of the big man with a uniform and a medal. But now we find that this big man is a crooked coward, afraid of both the Law and his former wife.

When Chris refers to his fear of Adele's wrath ("You know what she's like"), Higgins waves his hand in recognition; he apparently did not control her any more than Chris does. And although he threatens Chris by saying, "She'd kick you out in a minute for a man like me," this bum looks nothing like the man in the portrait. Chris does not even recognize him at first. Only when Homer removes an eyepatch, a disguise that links him to Chris's artistic failure to master perspective, does Chris know who Homer is. When Chris lures him back to the house, Homer momentarily stands in front of the portrait. The contrast is startling. And here is where the second consequence arises—Chris easily manipulates Homer into falling for a scheme whereby Adele will discover that he is still alive. Thus Chris is more powerful than this looming image of the Law. Indeed, this is the one point in the film where Chris successfully wields power, though it is marked as a form of feminine trickery.

We are suddenly asked to rethink our assumptions about power and the representation of the body. We are asked not only to question the fixed relationship between the body and masculine power (i.e., our culture's constant identification of true phallic power with body size) but also the means of representing bodies. The relation between the signifier and the signified is doubly questioned, and the conventions of realist representation of male bodies are revealed as just that—*conventions*.

The second plot development bears on a directly related issue. Janeway, a well-known art critic, discovers Chris's paintings in a Greenwich Village street display where Johnny has left them with another artist in the hopes of making some money. The artist and Janeway search for the unknown painter and find Chris's other paintings in Kitty's apartment. Johnny perceives the value of duping Janeway into thinking that Kitty is the artist. On hearing this, the Village artist exclaims, "I never would have guessed it was a woman." "Nor I," Janeway responds, "Your work is very strong, Miss March." Later in the scene, he remarks to Kitty, "I can usually tell whether a canvas has been painted by a man or a woman, but you fooled me completely, Miss March. Your work is not only original but has a masculine force." Nevertheless, Janeway falls for the scam and simultaneously "falls" for Kitty. He immediately courts her in romantic tones, arranges lunch with her, and sets himself up as the man who will give her work the attention it deserves.

Janeway's response to the paintings again presumes a fixed relationship between force, masculinity, and representation—to look at the strokes of a painting is to know whether they were made by a man or a woman. Yet Janeway thinks he is mistaken, just as earlier we *were* mistaken about our response to the representation of Adele's first husband. Thus Janeway implicitly acknowledges that the relationship between masculinity and "force" in painting is not as fixed as he presumes—a woman can paint like a man.

This potential critique is contained immediately in two ways. Most obviously, Janeway's intuitive grasp is correct—the painting was done by a man. (This, incidentally, creates an unresolved contradiction because Chris has in all other regards been represented as lacking true masculine force. Why, then, should such force show in his paintings?) Thus, while Janeway is temporarily fooled, the audience never is. The situation is somewhat analogous to that of James Garner in *Victor/Victoria* (1982), who is certain that "Victor" is a woman. Even though the film severely critiques Garner's insecure, homophobic sexuality, the fact remains that by the film's end his initial confidence in a natural difference between men and women is confirmed. He may have been scared, but he was also right. Though Janeway is a minor character, his "mistake" seems to confirm for us the very thing that it obscures for him, namely, that there is a difference between the hand of a male and female artist.

Of equal interest is Janeway's romantic response to Kitty; his discovery of her masculine power is synonymous with his desire for her. He moves to contain the woman whom he perceives as powerful. Laura Mulvey and Peter Wollen in their film *Amy!* (1980) analyze the public response in England to the feats of a woman who flew around the world. The country fell in love with her, and she became the object of desire in popular songs. Mulvey and Wollen point out that this response contains the threat posed by a woman who has succeeded in what is presumed to be a masculine domain. In his own way, this is precisely what Janeway does, but since he is wrong and since Kitty will be contained in quite a different way, he is dropped from the narrative, and we hardly notice his absence.

Scarlet Street is built on a wildly contradictory impulse. In the subplot dealing with Homer, the film unequivocally implies that looking at a man cannot tell you about the extent of that man's phallic power, nor can a realist representation of that man simply and truthfully convey the information. Yet everything about the casting of Edward G. Robinson in the central role and the troubled scene in which he knocks Johnny down works to confirm the most commonplace assumptions about masculinity, power, and the representation of the body. To believe that Chris is so childish, naive, and subservient to his domineering wife, he must be presented as a small man. And to keep that powerless image intact, we cannot see him knock Johnny out.

Janeway's assertion that certain techniques in painting are masculine seems absurd, and his mere articulation of that idea seems to open it up to criticism. Why should certain brush strokes be masculine and powerful, any more than certain bodies should? And we have all just seen how easy it is to be mistaken about the latter. But Janeway is right; he looked, and he knew. Finally, the romantic subplot that is set in motion with Janeway's discovery of Kitty's work is never itself critiqued. It seems natural that this powerful critic who finds unexpected masculine power in the paintings of this beautiful woman should fall in love with her.

Not only the central male character is weak in *Scarlet Street*; masculinity and the Law do not fare well in general in this film. Higgins, a decorated policeman, is a deceitful coward. Johnny, the "real" man, who acts as a foil to Chris, breaks down and screams with terror as the guards drag him to his execution. And his cries of innocence are true. The Law fails to convict the guilty man. Even in the film's final scene, the Law proves inadequate when two policemen dismiss Chris's confession as the confused ramblings of a pathetic bum. Janeway, the art critic whose name even connotes feminity (as does Chris's), is easily duped into believing that Kitty is the artist and that she is interested in him. The official art world, the police, the courts, and even the hoodlum all suffer a symbolic loss of phallic power. Only the relatively minor character of J. J. Hogarth seems significantly untouched by this virtual epidemic of failed masculinity, though in the opening scene his mistress commands his attentions.

Since *Scarlet Street* is a remake of Jean Renoir's 1931 French film, *La*

Chienne, it is revealing to look at the original regarding these issues of masculinity and the male body. The narratives of the two films are remarkably similar. Once again, Ann Kaplan's work supplies a useful starting point. She argues that whereas Lang's film is primarily preoccupied with sexual difference, Renoir's film is primarily concerned with economic class and the relationship of the individual to the community. Of the central character in the film, Kaplan notes: "Legrand's main problem is not seen as being one of inadequate maleness; rather, he is set up as a condescending man who considers himself above his peers" (1983, 38). In this view, Legrand's (Michel Simon) problems stem from his bourgeois class notions; once freed from those, he attains a new vitality. Within this framework, I want to compare the scene where Legrand comes to Lulu's (Janie Mareze) aid and the scene where he kills her with their counterparts in *Scarlet Street*.

Since lack of traditional masculinity is not a central part of Legrand's characterization, his body is not marked as symbolically powerless; Michel Simon's body and the way in which he is costumed and directed have none of the connotations of childishness, weakness, and femininity so evident with Edward G. Robinson's Chris Cross. Nevertheless, the film does not entirely avoid a discourse on the male body and sexuality, although it is marginalized and different from that in *Scarlet Street*. Several times in the film, Adele (Madeline Berubet) speaks about her former husband, a decorated war hero presumed killed in the line of duty and a "real" man in contrast to Legrand. His portrait hangs on the living room wall, and after one of her derogatory comparisons, Legrand remarks, "Obviously I'm not built like Alexis Godard." Yet the issue is one of looks, not strength. She remarks how "handsome" he looked in his uniform. Legrand appears as a man too preoccupied to concern himself with his appearance; his dressing, grooming, and posture all suggest indifference. On one occasion when Adele berates Legrand for not being a "real" man, she refers to Godard as "a regular lady killer." Clearly, Legrand is not that; when Lulu confronts him with the truth about their relationship and her connection with Dede (Georges Flammand), she tells a puzzled Legrand to look into a mirror if he wants to know why. As Adele has previously done, Lulu tells Legrand that he is not handsome; with the sole exception of a single reference Lulu makes to his age (forty-two), this seems to be the central feature of Legrand's masculinity that the film foregrounds. Still the fact remains that it comes up several times, and, as in *Scarlet Street*, both Adele and Lulu reject Legrand in comparison to other men in their lives.

The issue of masculinity is perhaps somewhat more present in the film than Kaplan acknowledges. What, then, makes it so different from the discourse on masculinity in *Scarlet Street*?

First, there is no issue of masculinity in the scene where Legrand discovers Dede and Lulu fighting, and thus there is no problem with representing the rescue. Lulu is lying on the ground; we see Legrand simply and easily push Dede, who appears drunk, down next to her. He does not cower from what he does, nor does he blindly strike out only to be surprised by the results. He competently and calmly accomplishes his goal. Having done so, he does not rush off calling for an officer in a childish voice. This is critical, since neither the characters in the film nor we in the audience perceive him as lacking masculinity. He may be a somewhat unusual man, but he is a man.

Not surprisingly, the scene where he kills Lulu is also structured in an entirely different way from its counterpart in *Scarlet Street*. Like Kitty, Lulu laughs at the man the moment of the revelation, but, unlike Chris, Legrand does not become hysterical and lose control; on the contrary, he kills Lulu in a calculated way. She in turn does not provoke him by cowering and then covering herself with a blanket. The scene is cross-cut with a scene of people gathered in the street outside the apartment singing and listening to a street musician. Lulu is fully visible before the cut to the exterior scene, and her body lies sprawled over the bed when we return to the interior scene. Indeed, Legrand caresses the body, fully looking at what he has done. This supplies quite a contrast with the final image of the scene in which Chris kills Kitty.

Neither the rescue scene nor the murder scene, therefore, betrays any concerns with Legrand's masculinity. The stylistic awkwardness that results from the unusual way in which Chris knocks Johnny down is totally absent from the corresponding scene between Legrand and Dede because Renoir does not deny power to Legrand and has no difficulty showing the complete action. Lang's dilemma was that to show the action in a conventional way would confer the very power onto Chris's body that the film constantly denies him.

Scenes of this sort point to the danger of making broad stylistic generalizations when analyzing sexual ideology. For instance, Kaplan's essay on these films asserts the commonly held views that films in the classical Hollywood style work within an invisible mode of smooth transitions and that Renoir's French films of the 1930s work within extreme depth of field. While these films certainly bear out these generalizations, significant moments do not conform to larger patterns. The scene where Chris knocks Johnny down does not represent a stylistic departure from the film's norms in the way in which the trial scene montage analyzed by Kaplan does. It is not, in short, part of a stylistic strategy operative throughout the film, but a momentary rupture within the film's style that reveals a great deal about the film's ideological assumptions about masculinity and the male body.

We see in Chapter 9 that a similar moment with similar significance in terms of understanding the ideology of the representation of the male body occurs in Nagisa Oshima's *In the Realm of the Senses*. The fact that that film is a far cry from classical Hollywood cinema should underline that the need to explore style at very specific local levels does not arise only when dealing with the invisible style of classical Hollywood cinema.

It is by now a commonplace of film criticism that films of the late 1940s are marked with many sexual tensions resulting in part from the consequences of World War II. *Scarlet Street* certainly seems to confirm Kaplan's analysis about the weakening of masculinity in such a context. Everything bad that happens in the film can be traced back to Chris's inadequacies. But Kaplan also points out that this fear of weakened male figures is not unique to Lang's postwar American films; it can be traced all the way back to his important German films. Although *Scarlet Street*'s epidemic of symbolic castration may very well relate to a historically specific late 1940s anxiety, much of how it is represented cuts across time periods and nationalities. Kaplan hints at this in her discussion of *While the City Sleeps* and its relationship to *M*, one of Lang's German films of the 1930s, of which she notes: "Beckert, the sick hero of the film, lonely and alienated, clearly represents the 'feminized' male in his stance and appearance, although there is no explicit analysis of this in *M*. He has a soft round face, large sensitive eyes and a high whining voice" (1980, 56). I would add to this list that Peter Lorre, who plays Beckert, is a small man whose stature and rounded body recall that of Edward G. Robinson. My point, as I show momentarily, is not one of auteurism. Furthermore, Lang shows "no explicit awareness" of the underlying assumptions of this casting in either *M* or *Scarlet Street*. Put quite simply, Lang presumes that a male character who does not embody traditional male qualities of strength and power will have that deficiency marked on his body—in the characters of Cross and Beckert by casting actors with small, rounded bodies and faces.

This unexamined and ideologically loaded assumption is remarkable in view of the fact that *Scarlet Street* is, in part, about representation and the body. Although both *La Chienne* and *Scarlet Street* deal with central characters who are artists, *La Chienne* develops a much more marginal and different discourse about art than does *Scarlet Street*, and this bears a direct relationship to its much more marginalized and different discourse on masculinity. Legrand does not have a defect as a painter equivalent to Cross's inability to master perspective, nor is "masculine force" an issue when the art critic discovers the paintings. Nor, for that matter, is Legrand wandering the streets lost and confused when he comes on Lulu and Dede. Nothing in the film's discourse about art or artists is linked to sexuality.

Even more significantly, *La Chienne* does not contain a discourse on realist representation, as *Scarlet Street* does. Lang makes a point of the actual medal that hangs on Higgins's portrait, and this is the absolute clincher. As if the realist portrait style (which Chris contemptuously dismisses) does not guarantee the accuracy of its representation, the real medal does. Chris's paintings are, by contrast, noted for their lack of realism. When a colleague looks at them, he notes with astonishment the gap between the actual flower that sits before Chris and the painting of it that Chris is just completing. A panning shot emphasizes the disparity between the two, as it moves from the "real" flower to its representation.

On one level, then, *Scarlet Street* critiques both the notion of a fixed relationship between the body and masculinity and between realist representation of the body and its actual referent. Our culture asserts: "Just look at a man, and you can tell how powerful and masculine he is." Realist representation simply claims to reproduce that first order of fixed, visual truth: "Just look at this portrait, and you can tell what kind of man is pictured in it." One of the themes of *Scarlet Street* is that this is not true.

The problem is that the film participates in perpetuating the very assumptions of realist representation it seeks to critique. This is most clear in its use of the star system and casting conventions. Casting Edward G. Robinson as Chris makes the character of this "henpecked" man "believable." Similarly, casting the part of Adele with a woman who is unattractive within cultural and star-system codes is a common way of punishing her for her unpleasant wielding of power (Kitty's fate points to the other common strategy of physically punishing or killing the powerful beautiful woman).

Would, for example, the film work with John Wayne playing Chris? There is no reason why it should not, except that our culture asserts and realist representation participates in reinforcing the belief of a fixed relation between the male body and connotations of masculinity—to be a strong man is to look like a strong man, and to be a weak man is to look like a weak man. A large man, obviously, can be dominated just as much by his wife as a small man.

The way in which the star system fixes the relation between the body and personality is a strong component of this ideology. The star system implies a fit between the body and the part for which the actor is being cast. At times this fit is generic. The point here is that *Scarlet Street* simultaneously fools us into believing that we know what kind of man Homer is by looking at the picture of him at the same time that it confirms for us what kind of man Chris is by looking at the realist image of him. And it is here that the panning shot from the flower to Chris's painting of it is revealing. We never see the real flower. We see a representation of a real flower within the classical style. What we as spectators are really doing is comparing a representation with a representation within a representation. But since the Hollywood invisible style supresses the first order of representation, the panning shot positions us to compare within one shot the "real" flower with the painting of it.

The casting of Edward G. Robinson also has historically specific connotations. Starting with *Little Caesar* (1930), Robinson was strongly identified with gangster films. Traditional genre criticism has long noted the obvious difference in body types between Western heroes and gangsters. Invariably the Western hero is associated with large, strong-looking men like Gary Cooper and John Wayne and the gangster genre with short men like James Cagney and Edward G. Robinson. The tricks used to make Alan Ladd look taller than he was in *Shane* (1953) and many of his other films are widely known. There would have been no need for boxes for him to stand on and trenches for the leading lady to walk in alongside him in the gangster films of the 1930s. The other side of the coin can be seen in Cagney's Westerns. Although several of them were made with well-known directors (Raoul Walsh and Nicholas Ray), he did not become identified with them in the way he did with his gangster and musical-comedy roles. The generic fit was not right.

I would suggest that we need to complicate our perceptions of these genres; traditional wisdom about Western and gangster stars is revealing and inadequate. The Western hero, we are told, is a larger-than-life mythic figure. The gangster is frequently compared to the tragic hero of the theater. The films follow the pattern of a hero's rise to power and his consequent fall from it, along with his death, all as the result of a flaw. Moreover, we are reminded that the urban gangster of the 1930s was an Everyman figure, identifiable by the audience. Unlike the cowboy, who inhabited the West of wide open spaces and the historical past, the gangster was a contemporary urban figure with whom those in the audience could identify.

Unless we are willing to elevate smallness and shortness to the level of a tragic flaw, I suggest we reformulate the foregoing account. Nothing in current theories of identification would support the notion that we will identify more closely with an actor who looks more like us by not seeming "larger than life." On the contrary, our identification will be strengthened via the more ideal image on the large screen in the darkened theater. I think there is something less rational and more disturbing that lies within these generic casting assumptions. The fact is that the mythic Western hero seldom dies, and the gangster frequently does. The gangster lacks the phallic power manifested by the Western hero. Whether we call it his "flaw" or blame it on the economic circumstances of the depression, the central male figure in this genre is weak by cultural standards. He fails where the Western hero succeeds. It is precisely the assumption that this weakness must be marked on the body of the actor that accounts for the casting conventions. Thus the Western and the gangster film conform to dominant cultural assumptions about both the fixed relationship between power and the body and between symbolic power and the replication of bodies. Although on the surface the meek, naive character of Chris seems far removed from the tough, blustery figure of Rico in *Little Caeser*, beneath the surface both characters share a failed masculinity that leads to their ruin. These characters are two sides of the same coin.

It is particularly interesting to consider Howard Hawks's *Tiger Shark* (1932), starring Edward G. Robinson, within this context, since, as we saw in Chapter 3, Hawks's films frequently and systematically foreground the representation of the body. Set in San Diego, the film deals with tuna fishing. Robinson plays the central character, Mike Mascerena, a Portuguese fisherman whose masculinity is marked as lacking in several areas. At the beginning of the film, Mascerena collapses in a lifeboat, his arm dangling over the side. He loses the arm to a shark, and the next time we see him, he wears a prosthesis. He is immediately marked as lacking in his ability with women. His girl friend makes an excuse not to meet him at the dock. When Mascerena's friend observes, "Mike don't do so good with these girls," another woman remarks, "They get rid of him in ten minutes." Even one of his crew remarks to Mascerena that he does not have any girls. When an older member of his crew is killed, Mascerena marries the man's daughter, even though she tells him she does not love him and is marrying him solely because of the kindness he has shown following her father's death. When he spruces up for the wedding, in a direct reference to *Scarface*, made earlier that year, a friend tells Mascerena of his scent, "A little effeminate, eh?" Not understanding, Mascerena replies, "Yeah." His best friend and best man at the wedding falls in love with his wife. Their relationship starts at the wedding, but Mike cannot see what is going on directly before his eyes. His bride asks him to dance, but he says he does not dance, yet another sign of lack, and tells her to ask his best friend. He then passes out from drinking too much, an act that recalls his collapse from exhaustion at the beginning of the film.

At one point, the wife breaks down and tells the best friend that she cannot go on with her marriage and that she is in love with him. The friend then has a fishing accident and is nursed to health by Mascerena's wife. The three are on a fishing trip when Mascerena discovers the affair, becomes hysterical, and throws his unconscious friend into a sinking lifeboat. In yet another act of incompetence, Mascerena accidentally falls overboard and is saved by the friend, who regains consciousness just in the nick of time. After being brought back on board, Mike lies between his friend and his wife. Looking at his wife, he acknowledges the obvious: "With the women I don't do so good." Then, referring to his mutilated body, he says, "First they got my hand, but now . . . ." The way in which he breaks off implies that, like Clint Brown in *The Nothing Man*, the wounded part of the body is now literally the genitals and thus his masculinity. The last shot of the film shows him dying with his arm around, not his wife, but his best friend.

Even in this brief account of the film, Mascerena's entire narrative trajectory is one of loss, and every aspect of his character is marked as inadequately masculine. Although the films are totally dissimilar in all other ways, in terms of the central drama of inadequate masculinity and loss, the characters played by Edward G. Robinson in *Scarlet Street* and *Tiger Shark* are remarkably similar. Separated by fifteen years and by genre, the films make similar use of Robinson's short, rounded body as a sign of a pervasive, failed masculinity.

Thus, as we later see with other aspects of the male body, the casting assumptions surrounding the small, rounded man are not historically limited to one brief time period, though certainly other major examples spring to mind from the time in which *Scarlet Street* was made. Consider John Ford's casting of Donald Meek as the whiskey drummer in *Stagecoach* (1939) and as the prosecutor in *Young Mr. Lincoln* (1940). In the former film, he plays a timid Easterner who wishes to return to the "bosom of his family" rather than risk the dangers of a journey through the wild West. His masculinity becomes the subject of several scenes in the film, and at one point he even nervously jumbles his words and expresses a desire to return to the "bosom" when he means the family. Even the hat he wears marks him as comically out of place in the West. He presents quite a contrast to John Wayne's Ringo, the quintessential Western hero. In *Young Mr. Lincoln*, Meek contrasts similarly with the imposing tall figure of Henry Fonda, playing Lincoln. In this film, a limp and a cane replace the ridiculous hat as a further mark of masculine deficiency. Lincoln's superiority in the courtroom is prefigured in his body; this imposing figure will surely defeat the little man with the limp—which is, of course, exactly what happens.

It is instructive to compare the casting in *Young Mister Lincoln* with that in Alfred Hitchcock's *Marnie* (1964). Sean Connery plays Mark Rutland, the film's central male character. In addition to Connery's imposing physique, the actor already had connotations of extreme masculine power from playing James Bond. In the course of the film he comes into dramatic conflict with Strutt (Martin Gabel). Gabel is an extreme example of the short man with a very rounded body and face. He also wears thick glasses that, like Meek's hat and cane, further mark his appearance. Once again, the little man is no match for the powerful figure, who easily contains his potential threat. It is unimaginable to reverse the casting by having Connery play Strutt and Gabel play Rutland. The point is not simply one of Connery's box-office draw. If he were as unknown an actor as Gabel, it would still be unimaginable precisely because of cultural assumptions about the relation between the male body and certain attributes of masculinity. Logically, again, there is no reason why a short, rounded man with thick glasses could not outwit an imposing, tall man. This recurring casting of actors like Meek and Gabel in opposition to actors like Fonda and Connery works to reinforce the cultural assumptions about the already fixed relationship between the body and phallic power. A number of years ago, Danny DeVito announced his desire to remake *Scarlet Street* with himself in the Edward G. Robinson role. Whether or not he ever makes the movie, the mere prospect of it shows that the more things change, the more they stay the same. His "twin" from *Twins* (1988), Arnold Schwarzenegger, would obviously not be believable as a weak man who cannot control his wife, his mistress, or his actions. Or as a painter who has not mastered perspective.

"I'LL SEE YOU IN SMALL CLAIMS COURT"

● ● ● ● ● ●

PENIS-SIZE JOKES AND THEIR RELATION TO

HOLLYWOOD'S UNCONSCIOUS

In *The Nothing Man* and *Scarlet Street*, central male figures who literally and symbolically lack phallic power fear ridicule; laughter plays an important part in their actions. Recall that Brown's constant fear extends even beyond his death and that when Kitty breaks into uncontrollable laughter at the prospect of marrying Chris, he loses control of himself and kills her. Similarly, Jake Barnes in *The Sun Also Rises* remarks several times about the funny nature of his wound.

Indeed, the linkage of humor and lack of masculinity might even account for some central elements of the comedy film genre tradition. Male domination of the slapstick tradition, for example, has nothing to do, of course, with any difference in physical ability between men and women; women can and have performed physical comedy as adroitly as men. In the silent cinema, when the slapstick tradition was at its height, cultural assumptions about the active–passive, masculine–feminine split were even more pronounced than they were in the United States in the 1980s. Because men were supposed to be powerful and active—that is, in absolute control of their bodies— images of male bodies out of control, physically marked as powerless, or both, sharply contrasted with cultural expectations. But because femininity was not defined in terms of activeness or control, women performing the same feats as men would not have had the same comic impact (nor would children). Blake Edwards's *Switch* (1991) is interesting in this context because most of the slapstick action centers on the female lead (played by Ellen Barkin), whom the narrative defines as a man trapped inside a woman's body. In all his other slapstick comedies, including the Pink Panther films, the slap-stick revolves around male characters. In order to center female slapstick, Edwards required a narrative that qualified the female character as one with a man inside her body.

Women, as we saw in Chapter 3, are powerful by virtue of their beauty, and unattractive women become the object of jokes. (Indeed, a comedienne like Joan Rivers creates a great deal of humor at the expense of her own body by telling jokes about being flat-chested and the like.) Because comedy is often developed in situations where both male and female characters do not measure up to cultural expectations for their gender, many of the stars of the slapstick tradition are short or slight men, whose feats seem more amazing and their bumblings more pathetic. So Harry Langdon, a small man with a rounded face and body, stars in *The Strong Man* (1926), accomplishing un-expected feats of strength. In much the same way Peter Sellers (in the Pink Panther films) and Dudley Moore (*"10,"* 1979, and *Micki & Maude,* 1984) star in Blake Edwards's comedies that derive a great deal of humor from male characters who do not satisfy cultural expectations of masculinity.*

Buster Keaton is particularly interesting in this regard; despite his slight and unimposing appearance, his films reveal an extraordinary mastery of physical control (seemingly the opposite of, say, Peter Sellers playing Inspec-tor Clouseau). But Keaton's characters are usually oblivious to their environ-ment and what is happening to them; blind luck gets them through, and they remain blissfully unaware of narrowly escaping even mortal injury. Thus they never fully shape or comprehend their victory. But on a different level, the

*For a discussion of this aspect of Blake Edwards's films, see Lehman and Luhr (1981, 1989).

actor seems fully in control, a disparity heightened in Keaton's case because of publicity circulated widely about how the actor did his own stunts, risking his life and injuring himself in the process. So Keaton himself satisfies cultural expectations about masculinity, allowing us to admire his physical dexterity as we laugh at the character's shortcomings or near misses.*

John Wayne would be an unlikely candidate for a successful slapstick comedian, not because of any acting inability, but because of his height and powerful appearance. In other words, he looks too much like a real man to become primarily associated with a tradition that derives laughs from masculine failure or unexpected success. *True Grit* (1969) is a clear exception, for Wayne's self-parody requires a gap between his appearance and his performance. It is funny to see John Wayne fall off a horse, for example, precisely because we have seen him handle horses masterfully many times in Western after Western, not because, as in the case of an actor like Harry Langdon falling off a horse, he looks as if he cannot control it. Parody is one form of comedy that requires departing from expectation; casting against type is another. Such exceptions merely prove the rule. We laugh at men when they do not measure up to looking or behaving like real men. What is quite extraordinary about much Hollywood filmmaking in the 1970s and 1980s is how often this laughter occurs with explicit reference to male sexuality and the male body.

"I hope his dick is bigger than his IQ," a woman remarks to her friends near the beginning of *The Witches of Eastwick* (1987), and the joke inaugurates a whole series of penis-size discussions. Later in the same sequence, the three central female characters talk about their ideal man. One (Michelle Pfeiffer), referring to penis size, says he should be "huge." Another (Susan Sarandon) likes "small" better aesthetically and says she was physically uncomfortable with her former husband, who was large. Completing this democratic survey, the woman in the middle (Cher) says that she is in the middle on this issue. When the central male character (Jack Nicholson) invites Cher to his estate in the hope of seducing her, he tells her that his servant has a huge penis, adding that he has heard that women do not care about that. Later,

*Patricia Mellencamp has developed a related argument in her analysis of "I Love Lucy" (1986). Lucille Ball played Lucy Ricardo; week after week, she failed in her attempt to escape domesticity, in the process paradoxically performing brilliant physical comedy and upstaging both Desi Arnaz and the male guest stars.

when Cher is with Susan Sarandon, she says that she was sore for days after making love with Nicholson and goes on to describe the unusual curvature of his penis.

Although *The Witches of Eastwick* is obsessively laced with this kind of talk, such chatter about the penis was a common characteristic of films in these decades. Indeed, the end of the 1980s witnessed *Me and Him* (1989), Doris Dorrie's film about a man with a talking penis, which only he and we hear. Now, instead of the chatter being about the penis, the penis does the chatting (and indeed the narrating), although it remains off-screen. In a party scene, we hear a room full of talking penises. And, as we might expect, we have the inevitable penis-size joke when the main character (Griffin Dunne) stands at a urinal surrounded by his colleagues, and his penis informs him that 75 percent of American men think their penis is smaller than average. This trend continues in the 1990s, for instance, in *Truth or Dare* (1991), a documentary in which Madonna's preoccupation with penis size surfaces repeatedly.

Critics have not commented on this compulsion to talk about the penis because so little attention has been given to the representation of the male body in the cinema, and because this talk frequently takes the form of penis-size jokes, which are generally dismissed as not worthy of serious attention. Moreover, many of the films in which these jokes occur are not prestige films, and the phenomenon may have been dismissed as an uninteresting feature of films aimed at the teen market; such jokes may simply seem to exploit adolescent anxiety about changing bodies and sexual discovery. But, as the examples of *The Witches of Eastwick*, *Me and Him*, and *Truth or Dare* should make clear, penis-size jokes and related chatter occur in a wide variety of films, appearing in virtually every type of film in the last decade. In *The Decline of the American Empire* (1986), two women in a sauna talk about their sexual experiences. The scene is structured around the woman who tells of the time she picked up a handsome man only to discover that he had a very small penis; both women break out in laughter and concur that her discovery is the worst possible thing. In *Flashdance* (1983), a man in a bar propositions the central female character, who replies by citing to him the size of the smallest penis on record. In *A Nightmare on Elm Street* (1984), a high school boy tells a girl that he woke up with an erection with her name written on it, to which she replies that this is impossible because his penis is not big enough for the number of letters in her name; in Part 4 of the same series (1988) a high school girl calls a boy "needle dick" and tells him that he is the only boy in school who suffers from penis envy. *Porky's* (1981) contains numerous penis-size jokes, beginning at the outset of the film when we see Pee Wee (guess where the character gets his name) measuring his penis. In *The Godfather* (1972) and *The Cotton Club* (1984), women speak in awe of someone's large penis. In *Bloodbrothers* (1978), when a character urinates on the street, another says, "Looks like a penis, only smaller." And so it goes.

In a survey of the usual terms in which our culture constructs sexual difference, Stephen Heath notes the emphasis placed on the visible. Psychoanalysis stresses the significance of the penis, the sight of it, and the concomitant concept of the female "lack." In Freud's terms, "little girls . . . notice the penis of a brother or playmate, *strikingly visible* and of *large* proportions, at once recognize it as the superior counterpart of their own *small* and inconspicuous organ" (quoted in Heath 1978, 53; emphasis added). Such an account of sexual difference can only be called dramatic, and where we have drama, comedy cannot be far away—if only because one source of comedy is the failure of drama.

Freud's assumptions and language clearly establish the basis for such comedy with his emphasis on visibility and size. The two, of course, are connected; if one is going to stress the visible, then the larger something is, the more visible it is, especially if one presumes the spectacle is *strikingly* visible. As Dr. Freud might well have known, not all penises are strikingly visible, and certainly not all the time. If we believe that the sight of the penis is the basis for the ultimate psychoanalytic drama, it is no wonder that we are anxious about the collapse of this dramatic spectacle, something that emerges in the "peniscope" cartoon (12).* During the early 1970s, Paul Harvey, a conservative radio news commentator, reported with relish a story about two women who "streaked" a public event. They were caught, taken to the police station, and booked, whereupon it was discovered that only one of them was a woman. In his unique style, Harvey told the story as a joke that spoke for itself, the assumption being that any long-haired man who would engage in such disgusting behavior would turn out to be inadequately marked as a man. Similarly, when a man "streaked" the Academy Awards while David Niven was speaking on live television, Niven joked about the size of the man's penis. These jokes reveal a paradoxical nervousness. On the one hand, the penis should not be shown and seen. On the other hand, if it is, it had better be a "strikingly visible" drama. What better way to put down a

*I found the drawing in a tourist shop in Tombstone, Arizona.

THE PENISCOPE

man who breaks the taboo and threatens the awe and mystique surrounding the organ than to joke about his inadequacy?

Ironically, then, the awe we attribute to the striking visibility of the penis is best served by keeping it covered up. The relationship of hard-core pornography to Hollywood cinema perfectly illustrates this. Hard-core porn is the one place in our culture where the penis is always on display, and as we see in Chapter 9, the conventions of the genre work to guarantee the supposed drama of the event. Actors are chosen because they are well endowed, they are usually shown erect, and close-ups emphasize the thrusting of the penis or the feat of women who, performing oral sex, can take the huge organ into their mouths. Small, unerect penises are seldom shown. If we see the male get undressed, he is frequently partially erect; if he is not, we glimpse him only briefly as a precursor to the ensuing drama, which may even be heightened by the comparison. The striking visibility of male sexuality— right down to the obligatory climax when the man withdraws and ejaculates on the body of the woman—is at the center of the genre. In Hollywood the situation is reversed. The penis is almost always covered, but, as I have indicated, there is endless fascination in talking about it: Now you see it, now you hear about it. Not surprisingly, jokes and comedy emerge within the sphere of what we hear, rather than what we see. This also structures the Tootsie Roll joke (13) that appeared on a greeting card. If hard-core pornography tries desperately to assert the visual drama, Hollywood jokes incessantly about its failure. Between the two, the mystique is left intact.

Talk about the male body in general and penises in particular quickly leads to joking. In her book *The Nude Male*, Margaret Walters notes, "I found men sometimes reacted defensively and sarcastically when told I was writing about the male nude; comments ranged from the crude joke—'What a lot of old cock!'—to sophisticated analyses of my penis envy" (1978, 17). In his treatment of jokes and humor, Freud spends a good deal of time analyzing dirty jokes, what he calls "smut." He argues that "smut is . . . originally directed towards women and may be equated with attempts at seduction" (1960, 97). According to Freud, men who tell such jokes to other men derive pleasure from imagining what they are socially inhibited from doing, and men who laugh at those jokes do so as if they were spectators of an aggressive sexual act.

Freud's analysis has to be positioned historically. If, in Vienna in 1905, men always told dirty jokes and women were always the object of those jokes,

the same is certainly not true in the present-day United States. A few examples will suffice. The first two are jokes recently told to me by women in social situations. The first, in fact, the joke teller introduced as "my feminist joke." "Why are women such bad mathematicians?" she asked. Placing her thumb and forefinger a few inches apart, she continued, "Because for years they've been told that's eight inches." (A version of this joke occurs in a 1988 film, *Gotham*.) The second joke involves Freud. His daughter, who has never seen a penis, asks him what one looks like. He drops his pants and shows her. "Oh," she responds, "like a phallus, only smaller." A third example comes from the early 1960s and was told me by a girl in high school. "What are the three most ego-deflating words a man can hear?" she asked. The not very reassuring answer to an adolescent boy was, "Is it in?"

It is beyond the scope of this discussion to detail what may be transpiring when these jokes are told in actual social situations, but a few useful points can be made before returning to films. Most obviously, Freud's generalizations about smut are no longer accurate, if they ever were; women tell jokes with the male body as the object of those jokes. Nor is seduction the goal of these jokes. This is important because Freud attributes a great deal of significance to men displaying hostility toward women through jokes after being turned down by them in actual social situations. In fact, he theorizes that a man initially desiring a woman at a party, for example, would tell a dirty joke in her presence to embarrass her or in her absence to share a bond with other men at her expense. The hostility, in other words, came from frustrated desire. There is obvious hostility in the aforementioned jokes, but it is hostility of a different kind.

Freud distinguishes two kinds of jokes that are not "innocent" jokes told as an end in themselves but serve another purpose: "It is either a *hostile* joke (serving the purpose of aggressiveness, satire, or defence) or an *obscene* joke (serving the purpose of exposure)" (1960, 97). Women's jokes about men seem to be a combination of the two, rather than the one or the other suggested by Freud. Women's jokes are certainly based on "obscene exposure," and they are motivated by aggressiveness and satire. Women revel in the fact that the male body is not what it is cracked up to be. They do so not out of frustrated desire for that body but out of revenge. These jokes speak more of a desire to get back at men than a desire for them. As such, they take their place alongside *Playgirl* and male stripping. Some women may derive a pleasure from *Playgirl* that stems from feeling that if men look at women that way, turnabout is fair play. Such pleasure, which is conceptual and involves getting back at men, is far removed from the intensely erotic, masturbatory response that men may have when looking at pictures of nude women or strippers. We cannot simply fit women's telling penis-size jokes into the categories Freud developed for men telling dirty jokes about women. More important for my purposes, we cannot presume that the function such jokes serve when told by women in social situations is the same in films. Films entirely recontextualize such jokes because even if a woman is telling a penis-size joke in a film, in the overwhelming number of cases she is telling a joke written and directed by (and for) men.

In *Rationale of the Dirty Joke*, G. Legman offers some additional perspectives on sexual jokes. He argues that one important function of sexual humor is to aid in controlling intense anxieties that are shared by the teller and the listener. In contemporary Western society these culturally determined anxieties deal primarily with venereal disease, homosexuality, and castration. Many penis-size jokes in films do, in fact, seem partially explainable in relation to this concept of controlling anxiety and may be classified as castration jokes.

In his exhaustive collection, categorization, and analysis of sexual humor (which does not include films), Legman has several categories that bear upon the kinds of jokes I have identified in so many recent films. In a section devoted to jokes about the penis, Legman begins by linking jokes about long penises to sadism and the desire to harm the woman. Sadism, according to Legman, is a defense against castration anxiety wherein "the sadist reassures himself that *he* does not deserve the punishment of castration and, that, in fact, his own body remains physically and phallically unharmed" (1968, 285). Jokes concentrating on large penis size are "a simpler and, fortunately, a more common neurotic method of self-reassurance against the fear of castration" (p. 285). Legman also calls jokes dealing with erection a reassurance against castration.

Legman calls one group of jokes about the penis phallic brags, and he makes clear the connection between such jokes and castration: "Brags about the length of the penis are intended to reassure everyone concerned—in the story and listening to it—that his penis is not really as small as he fears: that is to say cut off!" (1968, 292). But such attention to the penis, according to Legman, is linked to homosexuality and therefore jokes that deal with measuring penises or brag about exaggerated sizes exclude women from them. Legman also identifies a group of antibrag jokes that he claims attempt the same reassurance as the brag—they protect us from our fears by having us articulate them about ourselves before someone else does. Legman compares this to the old joke, "You can't fire me—I quit." Within this joking structure, we do to ourselves what we fear others will say or do to us. In the case of antibrag jokes, this amounts to self-castration, though Legman points out that frequently in such jokes the castration threat is posed by a male father figure rather than a woman.

The jokes I am dealing with in this chapter do not easily fit into Legman's categories or his analysis, but his work is nevertheless helpful. The jokes that interest me are unrelated to both aspects of Legman's analysis of phallic brags because they involve a man being put down for his small penis instead of bragging about his big one, and the joke context involves women. Nevertheless, I argue that there is a connection and that jokes about small penises in cinema that utilize women still involve both castration anxiety and elements of homosexuality. Nor do cinema jokes easily fit into the anti-brag grouping. Many of them involve women and are not at all reassuring. Furthermore, for the male spectator, they certainly cannot fulfill the function of doing to himself what one fears will be done to him.

Like Freud, Legman presumes that sexual jokes are the province of men, who are the creators and tellers of them. From this perspective, the attributes of women are merely the projections of men. In relation to penis jokes, this means that men project their desire for the importance of large penises onto women, who, according to Legman, do not desire large penises that actually hurt them physically. Since it bears so directly on material in the next chapter, it is worth noting that Legman actually uses medical statistics to argue that thick penises of 5 to 5.5 inches in length are much more pleasurable for women. Such an "ideal" penis never appears in penis-size jokes, except in a contemptuous manner. Long-penis jokes, then, seek to attribute to women a masochistic desire to be hurt that is, in fact, the man's desire to hurt her. What Legman terms the real hostility that women may feel toward the penis is thus absent from jokes:

> What jokes express is, therefore, more often a mere projection upon the woman of the male fantasy of the desirability of a very long penis. Instead of being expressed as brags, it is expressed in the form of insults, which also subserves the uses of sex hate, which seems to be the basic emotion in most jokes about sexual relations. (1968, 331)

This observation about insults and hate perhaps relates most directly to film jokes, though it is important to reiterate that this is complicated by the fact that the women who utter the insults are extremely desirable.

We must be cautious not only about associating penis-size jokes with certain types of films but also about presuming that we can always learn more from "serious" films than from "disreputable" films. This need to talk about penises is complicated in cinema by its central aspect of visual representation. When novels such as *The Godfather* and *Gardens of Stone* assert that a character has a large penis, that assertion is uncomplicated by further questions of representation. In the cinema, one has either to see the large penis or to be denied its view. Hard-core pornography graphically displays the penis, whereas the mainstream cinema almost always covers it.

In *Once Bitten* (1985), a film aimed at the teen market, we see high school boys taking showers. Every shot carefully covers the view of all the penises. One shot is particularly noticeable in that it is a long shot with a thin shelf in the foreground that just happens to be both in the right place and thick enough to cover the groins of the boys who stand behind it. *Opposing Force* (1986), an adult action film, has a scene of prisoners undressing and being deloused. The scene includes long shots of groups of men as well as various closer shots, but in all cases either the physical positioning of the camera, the set design, or the gesture of the men holding their hands over their groins covers the view of their genitals. Once again, this structure is very evident in *Escape from Alcatraz* (1979) when Clint Eastwood strips in a prison and walks to his cell; he is either shot from behind, or only his lower legs or upper torso are shown in frontal views. Similarly, in *O Lucky Man* (1973) a table top is in the right place and of the right thickness to block most of the view when Malcolm McDowell strips in a police station. In the many sex scenes in *Last Tango in Paris* (1973), Marlon Brando's body is spared the full exposure given to Maria Schneider's.

The Last Temptation of Christ (1988) is significant in this regard because the film places repeated emphasis on the naked male body being looked at by characters within the diegesis, while always denying the view of that body to the spectators of the film. Near the beginning of the film, a man is prepared for crucifixion. A startling close-up shows his loincloth being ripped off immediately before the cross is raised up. Although we see those who have gathered to watch the crucifixion stare at the man who has just been stripped, we see the man only from behind. Later, a group of men gather around a bed on which lies a naked male corpse. Although they look directly down at the body, we see it only from a long shot, side view. Before Christ is crucified, we see him naked while he is being beaten. Although his body is in motion, the way he moves and the position of the camera totally obscure his genitals. Similarly, the position of his legs when he is nailed to the cross allows frontal shots of the crucifixion and simultaneously blocks our view of his genitals. What makes this film somewhat unusual is the startling emphasis on others looking at the naked bodies that we do not see. Indeed, the scene with the viewing of the corpse is particularly extreme because most viewers are likely to be surprised that the groin is not at least covered.

Robocop (1987) supplies another extreme example of this structure. A male police officer and his female partner close in on a group of armed and dangerous criminals. The police officers split up, and she comes across one of the men as he urinates. She tells him to put his hands up, and he immediately turns around and follows her command, asking if he can complete dressing himself. She glances at his penis, and this allows him to disarm her. Because of her look, she cannot carry out her part in the mission, which leads to her partner's being sadistically mutilated and left to die. As a result, his body is transformed into the robot of the title. Thus it is no exaggeration to say that the woman's glance at the penis sets the entire narrative in motion. Yet we never see what she sees. Nothing that we might see, it seems, could justify the impact this moment has on the narrative.

Moreover, the moment contradicts an earlier scene in the police station dressing room. In a remarkable tracking shot, we see men putting on their uniforms when a woman unexpectedly appears. Her shirt is open, and her breasts are momentarily visible as the camera moves by. Moments later, we see other women and conclude that in this futuristic film men and women share the same locker room with no sense of embarrassment or vulgarity. Dressing together is a simple fact of being on a police force composed of men and women. Even more astonishingly, the woman who is briefly glimpsed is not eroticized in any of the usual ways. The camera does not dwell on her, there is no shot from the point of view of a man looking at her, and the lighting and positioning of her body do not create an erotic spectacle. Visually, we spectators are in the same position as the characters. The nudity has no erotic interest for us.

At the simplest level, we might wonder why a woman used to sharing a locker room with men would be unable to resist looking at a man's penis in a life-threatening situation. Furthermore, the locker-room scene treats the representation of the woman's body maturely and without embarrassment. Yet when the sight of a man's penis becomes the object of a woman's look and sets the narrative in motion, we are denied the sight of it. If the entire motivation of the plot by such a moment seems extreme in *Robocop*, it is virtually repeated in *Hard to Kill* (1990). In this action film, the hero (Steven Seagal) lies in a coma for years. One day, his attractive young nurse (Kelly Lebrock) looks under the sheets and remarks in a near swoon on the large size of his penis. This remark brings him out of his coma and sets the narrative in motion. At the end of the film, when he finally confronts the villain, he points his gun directly at the man's groin and fires, remarking that, since he seldom misses, "They must have been smaller than I thought."

In Clint Eastwood's *Unforgiven* (1992), once again the narrative is set in motion when, in the opening scene, a prostitute laughs at a cowboy's small penis. Unlike *Hard to Kill*, however, in *Unforgiven* this incident receives complex development in an examination of many genre assumptions about the male body including wounding and scarring.

When reviewing *Tango and Cash* (1989), the newspaper critic Robert Cauthorn remarks about "the repeated jokes about penis and gun size. OK, what say we all chip in and buy Sly a ruler for Christmas. I mean, this guy has a complex" (1989, F14). Cauthorn's response is revealing because it presumes that the film's preoccupation with size jokes is unique and, facetiously, that it is Sylvester Stallone's problem. Even if we were to displace the obsession from the film's star to its writers and director, we would be obscuring the point. Its true significance lies not with one or two individuals "who have a complex" but with a large community of filmmakers and spectators who seemingly cannot get enough of this joking and chatter. Nor is it confined entirely to theatrical films. Recent television episodes of "Designing Women" and "Murphy Brown," and the 1990 made-for-TV movie *Blue Bayou*, all contain similar moments. Nor has radio been spared Howard Stern's obsessive talk in New York about penis size or "Pirate Radio" in Los Angeles with its parody of "New Kids on the Block." In this parody, we hear two women's voices as they talk about looking at the nude Kids on the Block. One of them says that she does not see anything. Finally she remarks that it is so small that it may explain why he has such a high voice.

Although I want to make clear the wide variety of films wherein the penis is spoken of but not seen, a final example comes from a comedy and returns us to our main concern. In *Bull Durham* (1988), a woman goes to bed with a baseball player she has selected as a partner. As he undresses in anticipation of having sex with her, she tells him to stop and begin again, undressing slowly while she watches. He does, but he stops with his underpants on. Although the scene is structured around her both controlling the situation and deriving pleasure from watching him, the logic of the scene is entirely broken when he simply leaves his underpants on and she does not remark about it. Later in the film, we see a locker-room scene that exactly fits the pattern in *Once Bitten* and *Opposing Force*. In another scene, a player has a classic anxiety dream about pitching without his clothes on—except that he happens to be wearing a jockstrap and garter. The garter makes perfect narrative sense because we know that the player has been wearing one under his uniform, and the jockstrap allows the visual humor of the scene to take place without exposing the genitals. As with *The Last Temptation of Christ*, the pattern in *Bull Durham* is significantly paradoxical; these scenes all openly raise the spectacle of others looking at the naked male (especially the undressing scene and the anxiety dream) but then awkwardly circumvent the view for the film spectator. Like so many recent films, *Bull Durham* simultaneously foregrounds the display of the male body and protects it from the spectacle it circles around.

These awkward visual structures that deny the view of the genitals are compounded when we hear characters talk about the penis, but we are denied the view of it. This combination opens a potentially interesting ideological space that is likely to be foregrounded even in the conscious perceptions of the viewer: What is at stake in so carefully and systematically denying us the view of what we are hearing about?

We should also wonder why so much of the talk about penises in mainstream cinema takes the form of penis-size jokes. In many instances, the joke structure involves women who make men the object of their jokes. But as in *Flashdance* and *The Witches of Eastwick*, the films were written and directed by men. Although the women in these films may appear to threaten men, is there another structure at work wherein the threat becomes pleasurable for the male spectator?

Robert Altman's films provide a good starting point for a close examination of penis-size jokes in films. His films are laced with references to penis size, at least since *That Cold Day in the Park* (1969) in which we overhear a conversation between women in which one is surprised to discover that penises are not all the same. This quintessential reference is to a particular male anxiety that lies beneath one structure of penis-size jokes. As Phyllis Chesler notes, if women become aware that penises vary, they may become discriminating and judgmental. The moment at which the woman becomes aware is thus particularly charged. In *California Split* (1974), a male employee in a bar asks the woman behind the cash register if he can borrow some money because he is a "little short." She contemptuously replies that he was born short. In a similarly displaced reference in *Popeye* (1980), Olive Oyl dreamily sings a song with the repeated lyrics, "He's large." The film, which seems to many a curiosity in Altman's work, is actually consistent with his other films if one perceives Altman's concerns with body types and sexuality. Its cartoon source allows Altman to represent a world peopled with a startling array of unusual body types.

McCabe and Mrs. Miller (1971) most significantly raises and addresses this Altman preoccupation. The penis-size joke is centered, direct, and comparatively graphic. An unnamed cowboy (Keith Carradine) has come to town to visit a whorehouse. Addressing the prostitutes, he asks with relish, "Who wants to be next?" We see a prostitute laughingly whisper in another's ear. The cowboy looks on with interest, and as they continue to laugh, one of them holds two fingers together to indicate they are laughing at the small size of his penis. When he realizes what they are laughing about, a look of dismay crosses his face. On the surface, this seems to be just one more Altman penis-size reference and one that again betrays the fear that knowledgeable women will become judgmental. What makes the joke different is that it is carefully woven into the structure and theme of the film.

In a later scene, we see Mrs. Miller (Julie Christie), the madam of the whorehouse, dressing Ida (Shelley Duvall), one of her new young prostitutes. The scene begins with Ida saying, "Well, it just hurts so much. Maybe I'm small." Her emphasis is on the last word. Moments later, while looking at her body, Mrs. Miller remarks, "Oh yeah, you really are small, aren't you? Just like me." Aside from linking sexual smallness to both sexes, the scene unexpectedly links the young prostitute to Mrs. Miller. In a much more indirect and complex way, it also links the small cowboy to McCabe (Warren Beatty).

McCabe makes his initial appearance in the film as a powerful, mysterious figure. His riveting charisma establishes him as a "man among men." We soon learn, however, that all this is an elaborate con job; he is not the man he appears to be. When he becomes involved in political conflict over his business enterprise (the whorehouse), he fears for his life and watches for a gunfighter who might be sent to kill him. When the cowboy rides into town, he looks like that powerful gunfighter. McCabe readies his gun for a fast draw and cautiously approaches the stranger. Only after the man looks at him with a puzzled expression does McCabe suspect his error. He asks what the man wants and learns that he has simply come to visit the whorehouse.

The cowboy's entrance into town rhymes with McCabe's. Just as the men in the town presume McCabe to be a gunfighter and a powerful figure, McCabe presumes the cowboy to be one. We quickly learn otherwise. Neither is what he appears to be, but in the case of the cowboy, the misperception is specifically linked to his penis—he is not a big man. But the comparison between McCabe and the cowboy extends from their initial appearances in the town to their deaths.

Although we do not see any further scenes with the cowboy in the whorehouse, Altman lingers on the scene when the cowboy leaves. Several of the prostitutes, including Ida, come to the door with him, wish him well, and see him off. Ida, who is cheerful and smiling, is particularly emotional. "Be careful," she says warmly. The other prostitutes go back into the house with a new customer ("Here's Shorty," one of them says), while Ida stays outside watching and wistfully saying, " 'Bye cowboy."

This brief scene is crucial. Now the cowboy and Ida—the small man and the small woman—are linked together. Clearly in her intercourse with him she has enjoyed sex for the first time, and we have not seen her in the film since the scene in which she talks about her smallness and the pain of sexual intercourse. The scene also includes the throwaway joke, "Here's Shorty." There is a virtual epidemic of shortness of every kind in Altman's films. Most important, the scene sets up the cowboy's death.

Walking away from the whorehouse, the cowboy starts to cross a bridge when he is confronted by a gunfighter who bullies him in the hope of getting him to draw his gun. The cowboy is scared and blurts out that he cannot shoot well. The gunfighter tricks him into showing his gun and uses this as a pretext to draw his own gun and shoot the cowboy. Altman cuts to a slow-motion shot of the cowboy as his body crashes through the ice into the water below. The scene moves from the literal to the symbolic; the cowboy has a small penis and does not know how to use a gun. His death has even further sexual connotations because cold water can cause genitals to retract and become smaller. The cowboy's death reveals him as a total failure; he is lacking literally in the sexual realm and symbolically in the realm of masculinity.

McCabe dies similarly. He pursues his gunfighter opponents through the heavy winter snows of the town. He begins with a rifle that he carelessly puts down in a church so that he may more easily climb a ladder to survey the surroundings. He returns and begins to look for his rifle, only to discover that someone has taken it. Aiming McCabe's rifle at him, the man orders him out of the church. McCabe leaves the church and continues his mission with a pistol, the latter all the more emphasized by the incompetent manner in which McCabe has lost his rifle. Finally, he is mortally wounded. His assailant approaches, thinking McCabe is dead, but he feigns death until the man is close. McCabe then pulls a derringer from under his hat and kills the man. McCabe is left to die in the snow, holding the small handgun. The final images we see of him are of his frozen, snow-covered body. As the cowboy is literally small, so McCabe is symbolically small. And both men die amid the shriveling connotations of coldness, visual images that recall the common male expression, "I'm freezing my balls off."

In *McCabe and Mrs. Miller*, Altman draws complex parallels between the literal and the symbolic, making clear that the representation of the male body involves the problematic relationship between the penis and the phallus. It has long been a commonplace of genre criticism that guns in Westerns are phallic symbols (I noted how such symbolism functions in *Rio Bravo* in Chapter 3). Moreover, *McCabe and Mrs. Miller* belongs to a group of films made in the late 1960s and 1970s that attempt to reformulate genre films, often commenting on their conventions in the process. This is precisely what Altman has accomplished with the sexual smallness motif in the film.

Penis jokes are usually throwaways with unattractive male characters as their object. This is true even when a woman speaks the line, as in *Flashdance*. This structure is very clear in *Where the Boys Are '84* (1984). A college girl tries throughout the film to get her dream hunk, whom she sees on the beach during spring break. Finally, she meets him and goes back to his apartment with him. She is shocked to discover that he wants her to pay him for making love to her. Taken aback, she asks him to undress for her so that she can see what she is buying. He does so. She looks him up and down and contemptuously jokes, "So where's the rest of it? . . . I'll see you in Small Claims Court." She later tells her girl friend about the experience, remarking that the man "turned out to be just another jerk in a leopard bikini." "Something's got to hold him together," her friend responds, upon which we hear the predictable reply, "There wasn't much to hold." In this film and in *Flashdance*, the audience identifies with the women who utter the remarks and laughs at the men who are disparaged. This structure reinforces dominant presumptions that to be a man is to have a big penis.

In *McCabe and Mrs. Miller*, something entirely different happens. The audience identifies with the cowboy and Ida. Because each is marked as small, the characteristic is not just attributed to men. More significantly, each of the "small" characters is linked to the central character of his or her own sex—the hero and heroine of the film, each of whom is cast within the established codes of the star system. Mrs. Miller tells Ida that she is built like her, and McCabe is revealed to be like the cowboy. Thus, smallness is not a simple sign of inadequacy; on the contrary, it comments on our presumptions about masculinity and femininity. This is something rarely achieved in any of the countless penis-size jokes that characterize current cinema.

Comedy is an important part of many films, if only via traditional comic subplots or moments of humor isolated or scattered throughout the film. A *Variety* film review asks, *"Thinkin' Big* is a B movie that poses the pointless question: can a full-length feature be constructed from jokes about penis size?" (Lor 1988, 24). Given the topic of this chapter, *Thinkin' Big* might seem a better example than *McCabe and Mrs. Miller*. But notice what results from that assumption. The B comedy is dismissed as tasteless, and the presence of related jokes in such critically acclaimed films as *The Decline of the American Empire* and *The Witches of Eastwick* goes unnoticed. But the wording of the *Variety* review unwittingly raises another question: Might some comedy be more suited to isolated moments than to feature-length treatment? Rather than minimize the significance of the brevity of penis-size jokes in films such as *McCabe and Mrs. Miller*, I find them all the more significant in that such jokes need to be told but require a structure wherein they will not be emphasized or, perhaps, even noticed. Many people who have seen the films discussed in this chapter will not remember or have thought about the penis-size jokes because the films in which they occur are not about penises (as *Thinkin' Big* apparently is). Paradoxically, then, penis-size jokes must fill an important need because so many films contain them, but they are not important enough for a film to be about them. Jokes, comedy, and humor of this kind should be carefully scrutinized rather than dismissed.

Paying attention to this kind of comedy also has theoretical significance for other areas of film studies. When these jokes are told by women, but the male body is not shown, they are part of a structure that denies both objectification of the male body and female subjectivity. This denial can be situated at many textual levels including that of eyeline glances and point-of-view shots. It is common in Hollywood films that when a man looks desiringly at a woman, a point-of-view shot that shows what he desires follows. The woman's body is not just shown but is shown through a particular circuit of desire. I suggest that something more extreme than denying female subjectivity happens with the missing point-of-view shot in penis-size jokes in Hollywood films. In place of the logical objectification of the male body, we have the fetishistic objectification of the woman who looks. Her very desire or contempt for what we never see becomes fetishized. This in part explains the attraction of the structure to men and links penis-size jokes to nonjoking dominant structure in the Hollywood cinema—a woman looks with desire at (rather than speaks her desire for) the naked male body (see Jacqueline Bisset in *Rich and Famous*, 1981).

Even when no nudity is involved, posing the male body as spectacle has always been a problem within the classical cinema. Richard Dyer notes that "*Rebecca*, for instance, a film whose first half hour is entirely constructed around the never named female protagonist's desire for Maxim/Laurence

Olivier, nonetheless, entirely denies this character any point of view shots of him" (1986, 184). In *Rich and Famous*, Jacqueline Bisset picks up a young man, and they make love. As she sits on a bed watching, he undresses standing up. We see only a shot of him naked from behind; although logically she is the desiring subject in the scene, her face as she looks at him is the erotic focus of the scene.

It is no coincidence that this scene is structured around the look of an actress such as Jacqueline Bisset. Women marked in the narrative as beautiful and sexually desirable are almost always the ones who utter penis-size jokes (as in *The Witches of Eastwick* and *Flashdance*) or who are the center of the desiring look at the man's body. Their beauty and desirability are crucial to the fetishization of the woman's desire for and talk about the man's body. Counter to logic, these women become eroticized for the male gaze exactly at the moment when they seem to be eroticizing the man or, in the case of penis-size jokes, putting down the man for failing to live up to their erotic expectations. Thus, watching Jacqueline Bisset's face as she looks at the penis we do not see may be erotically charged. If within the codes of the star system and the narrative structure, the scene were shot and edited the same way with an actress marked as unattractive, the effect would be entirely different. Indeed, in all the examples I have gathered of penis-size jokes and the woman's desiring look at the penis, none involves unattractive actresses. The structure only seems to "work" if the woman can be fetishized. This suggests another possible area of investigation, namely, masochism.

Much recent work has emphasized masochism as an important structure of male pleasure in the cinema. Gaylynn Studlar, for example, argues that Von Sternberg's Dietrich cycle turns on a structure whereby the man's pleasure is determined by his subordination to and loss of the woman he desires. Similarly, I would argue that when beautiful, desirable women erotically look at and make evaluative judgments about the penis, the structure may be masochistically pleasurable for men. If this is true, joking about a man with a small penis would be an extremely erotic possibility, although the structure is very similar to that in which the woman quietly looks with serious desire. In the latter case, her look makes clear that she is in the powerful position of seeing, knowing, and evaluating, and the filmic structure makes clear that we would rather watch her see, know, and evaluate then observe what she sees. That most of these films are written and directed by men certainly makes sense from this perspective. What is seemingly women's desire becomes masochistic male pleasure.

Legman's analysis of penis-size jokes entirely omits male masochism, per-haps rightly, when one considers that the verbal jokes he analyzes frequently exclude women or, when they are included, make them unattractively hos-tile. His hypothesis that such jokes work to contain castration anxiety is well supported. What complicates these film jokes is precisely the fact that they are uttered by beautiful women with whom men in the audience are likely to identify. Rather than contain castration anxiety, these jokes may very well revel in the possible pleasures of such anxiety. To be thus judged and found physically lacking by a desirable woman inscribes on the male body the loss and pain experienced as pleasure within the masochist aesthetic. If, as Leg-man argues, large-penis jokes are sadistically hostile to women, on whom such penises inflict pain, even to the extent of symbolically killing them, the cinematic small-penis jokes I have been analyzing reveal a male masochistic pleasure in the penis's absolute loss of even its presumed normal (as opposed to exaggerated) power.

From this perspective, penis-size jokes may also relate to the rise of rape-revenge films during the 1970s and 1980s.* In these films, a beautiful woman hunts down the men who raped her and kills them one by one, frequently reveling in the pleasure of their agony when they realize who she is and what she is about to do. Although these films have appeared in a number of genres, several B-movie cult classics, such as *I Spit on Your Grave* (1977), *Ms. 45* (1981), and *Alley Cat* (1982), are the best examples. This structure has, however, entered the mainstream cinema. *Hannie Caulder* (1972), a Western starring Raquel Welch and directed by Burt Kennedy, is the earliest such film I have identified, and Clint Eastwood's *Sudden Impact* (1983), starring Sondra Locke, is a later example.

Men in these films are victims of violent women. This reverses the usual pattern of suspense and horror films in which a dangerous man systematically terrorizes and victimizes women. Moreover, these films, which are nearly always made by and for men, revel in the spectacle of a woman killing a man in a gruesome and protracted fashion. Sometimes the contexts are even overtly erotic, as in *I Spit on Your Grave*, when the avenging woman leads a victim to believe that she is about to make love to him but instead slips a noose around his neck and hangs him, or, in a similar scene, when she cuts off her victim's penis. Both scenes are followed by shockingly graphic images of the

*For a detailed discussion of female rape-revenge films in general and *Steel and Lace* in particular, see Lehman (1993).

partially naked body swinging at the end of rope and the naked man scream-
ing hysterically as blood gushes from his wound. Not surprisingly, there are
even hard-core porn rape-revenge films, such as *Naked Vengeance* (1985).

Most of these films are either so exploitational or so clearly within entertainment genre traditions that they do not even masquerade as seriously concerned with women and rape. As is true with small-penis jokes, the women in
these films are nearly always beautiful (e.g., Locke and Welch), something
that once again suggests that their sexual desirability is crucial to the pleasure that men get from watching them exact retribution. But, unlike films
with penis-size jokes in which the penis is never shown, here it is not just the
women who are watched, it is also the men in their horror and pain. These
films position their target male audience to enjoy the gruesome spectacle of
a woman wreaking havoc on the male body. Her rape is merely a narrative
pretext for setting this bizarrely pleasurable pattern in motion. These films,
made by and marketed for men, make male characters victims and their punishment a matter of pleasure for male viewers. The pleasure that men get
from watching the destruction of the male body by the sexually desirable
woman is the dramatic equivalent of her joking about the male body in the
films surveyed earlier.

If, on the one hand, this use of beautiful and desirable women allows for
a masochistic heterosexual reading, on the other hand the presence of the
women may serve to mask homosexuality. Concern with penis size is predominantly a male anxiety and one that specifically arises from boys and
young men looking at and comparing themselves with one another. Such activity may give rise to conscious desire for, or homophobic fear of, other male
bodies. Legman sees a similar structure in the phallic brag jokes, where
attention to the size of the penis is foregrounded within an all-male context. He even notes that such jokes and talk can be a preliminary part of
homosexual encounters. Legman pays no attention to homophobia or the specific consequences of heterosexual males who do not consciously desire the
joking context to become openly sexual. From this perspective, the jokes,
looks, and even sadistic actions of the beautiful women in these films may
create a successful heterosexual veneer for what may much of the time be
unconscious homoeroticism.

Within this context it is interesting to analyze several films directed by
Pedro Almodóvar and Rainer Werner Fassbinder, both self-acknowledged
gay filmmakers whose work consciously acknowledges how women may be
used in such a manner. The first scene comes from Almodóvar's *What Have*

I Done to Deserve This? discussed in detail in Chapter 1. There my concern was to show how the shower scene and the sequence in which it appears create a unique cinematic dramatization of the penis–phallus distinction and relationship. I want to look at the scene again from a different perspective. Diegetically, the desiring look of a woman authors the view of the nude male body, but, of course, Almodóvar the director authors it. The scene, in other words, seems to be one of heterosexual desire for and display of the male body. The remarkable opening credit scene of Almodóvar's *Labyrinth of Passions* (1983) foregrounds the entire situation. A woman walking down the street looks with desire at men's bodies followed by close-ups, the majority of which are crotches. Almodóvar intercuts this with similar shots of a gay man looking at men's bodies followed by point-of-view close-ups, one of which is an exact repetition of a previous crotch shot that represented the woman's point of view. As if this were not enough, the scene is edited so that several of the cuts confuse the spectator as to whose point of view the crotch shots represent, since they initially seem motivated by the look of either the man or the woman. But after the close-up, the film cuts to a shot of the other looking. Thus the initial look may have been abandoned in a manner that retroactively turns the close-up into the other's point of view. Since the man and woman do not walk and look from the same place, the shots cannot be read as simultaneously representing both points of view. The alternating shots present the same sexually desiring look at the male body through male and female gazes, at times not even clearly allowing us to distinguish one from the other. Almodóvar's directorial, homosexual gaze, however, structures all the shots that look similar and, in one instance, are identical.

Fassbinder's *Ali, Fear Eats the Soul* (1974) and *Fox and His Friends* (1975) supply other examples. In *Ali*, we see a woman open a bathroom door to discover her lover taking a shower. She looks desiringly at his fully displayed body and remarks how beautiful he is. A later scene shows him undressing and standing completely naked and facing the camera as he awaits a woman who is about to make love with him. These scenes in *Ali* contrast with several scenes in *Fox and His Friends*, a film that centers on gay male sexuality. In one scene, Fox (played by Fassbinder, a foregrounding of his directorial presence) and a friend take a mudbath at a health club. Several naked men walk by, and conventional point-of-view shots present clear, full shots of their bodies; there are no obstructions, nor is the view a hurried, peekaboo glimpse. Later, the scene continues in the locker room with shots carefully composed so that genitals are fully on display during a dialogue scene involving shot–reverse shot and even mirrors to accentuate the display of the male body. This film also contains a great deal of talk about penis size, and as with the visuals, it is all part of an acknowledged desire.

Although the subject matter is gay in *Fox* and heterosexual in *Ali*, what is striking is that the male body is similarly presented in both. It makes little difference if a heterosexual woman or a gay man authorizes the desiring look at the male body. What these films make clear is that a simple heterosexual content or surface structure should not blind us to homosexual elements— elements that Almodóvar and Fassbinder do not attempt to cover up in the way Hollywood mainstream filmmakers do. These common elements also indicate that we should not be too quick to assume a simple alternative to male sexual representation in the work of gay filmmakers, a point to which I return in Chapter 9 in relation to Robert Mapplethorpe's photography. Women who look at or joke about the male body may well be stand-ins for men who either hide or unconsciously block the homosexual element. Thus, it may be men who want to look at or joke about the penis, but who need to disavow that desire by the diegetic use of women.

Steel and Lace (1990), an unusual hybrid cyborg/rape–revenge film, makes this clear. A brother creates an avenging cyborg after his sister commits suicide when the men guilty of raping her and conspiring to cover up the truth are acquitted in a trial. The film features the usual eroticized revenge murders with graphic destruction of the male body. The major difference is that it is the brother who seeks the revenge and derives deep satisfaction when it is exacted; the female (the cyborg that only appears to be female) simply carries out his desires. Furthermore, scenes in which the brother watches video replays of the grisly deaths foreground the way in which male spectators of this film and others like it do the same thing. One extraordinary scene even has the cyborg disguised as a man who changes into a woman in front of her victim's (and our) eyes. Clearly, the inclusion of a woman and the attendant heterosexual veneer can cover complex, disturbing sexual structures including male homosexuality and even, perhaps, radically alter gender positions.

Legman, like Freud, assumes that the sexual joking in our culture has been exclusively the domain of the male. Although women's sexual jokes may have gone unnoted and unrecorded by these men, it is not surprising that jokes about the size of the vagina, which Legman analyzes, are mere variations on penis-size jokes. Such jokes reveal male anxiety about, for example, the penis getting lost in the vagina and are not really about women's bodies. Even when told by men to men in contexts that clearly articulate male anxiety, penis-size jokes affirm the importance and centrality of the very thing they question. In the movies, men frequently draft women into their service with these jokes. Contrary to appearances, women who look, evaluate, and joke about penises in most films pose no threat to male pleasure; these women simply tell men what men have always told themselves about the importance of the penis.

Freud analyzed dirty jokes exclusively from the point of view of men telling them with women as the hostile object of them. The penis-size jokes analyzed in this chapter only seem to reverse that structure by having women tell hostile jokes about men; because nearly all of these films are made by men, the Freudian perspective is extremely helpful in understanding how that apparent reversal may in fact involve disavowal and homosexuality. The men who create and enjoy such jokes may be denying their vulnerability by positioning themselves as superior to the objects of the joke. Or, in heterosexual, masochistic desire, they may be identifying with the male judged inadequate by the desired woman and thus enjoying that vulnerability. Or, in a disavowal of homosexual desire, they may be using the woman to deny their own homoerotic desires to look at and evaluate other men's penises. In accordance with my earlier argument about multiple and contradictory male subject positioning, all three perspectives may be simultaneously occupied and all or any combination of them is amenable to Freudian analysis.

It is fitting to close by returning to Freud's work on jokes from another perspective. As with dreams and slips of the tongue, Freud found a much greater significance in jokes than did most of his contemporaries. Even today, as if it were a contradiction in terms, we have trouble taking comedy seriously. We should expect, therefore, that our initial response to fleeting moments of isolated joking might be to dismiss them without much consideration. Can we not learn more by studying films that have extended and centered treatments of their subjects than we can from analyzing jokes that take less than a minute in a two-hour film? On the contrary, one of the most important functions of comedy in cinema is to sneak in a joke almost unnoticed, make us laugh, and then allow us to forget that we ever thought something was funny. In the next chapter, we turn to another cultural discourse about penis size, one that takes its subject very seriously and asks us to believe that the subject is of the greatest importance.

"THE QUESTION OF THE CENTURY"

● ● ● ● ● ●

SEXOLOGY AND THE MEDICAL REPRESENTATION

OF MALE SEXUALITY

After a brief introduction, David R. Reuben's 1969 best-selling sex manual, *Everything You Always Wanted to Know about Sex—But Were Afraid to Ask*, adopts a question-and-answer format that is retained throughout the rest of the book. What is the first question? "How big is the normal penis?" And the first sentence of the answer is, "That is the question of the century" (Reuben 1969, 5). The widespread attempt to measure and document the size of the penis is an invention of the mid-twentieth century. If the twentieth century's respectable arts and media, as well as the evolutionary sciences, have been reluctant to deal explicitly with the penis, the same cannot be said of sexology and popular medicine. Here, the penis becomes a focal point, a virtual obsession. The penis-size jokes so prevalent in films and social discourse of the 1970s and 1980s also point to the medicinal and sexological discourse about the penis and their popularization through mass-market books and magazines. The popularity of penis-size jokes in society and the movies, in other words, can be understood only within a larger cultural discourse that has centered on penis size.

Reuben's starting point is, then, understandable, perhaps even predictable. The chapter in which his initial question is raised is entitled "Male Sexual Organs" (p. 5). The entire book, like the first chapter and the first question, assumes a centrality for male sexuality. If, as Reuben asserts, every man worries about the size of his penis, then this anxiety logically for him becomes the crux of the question of the century, but he does nothing to question the ideology behind privileging this question.

Why has this become so important a question? When and why did we start measuring penises and distributing the data? Nineteenth-century "marriage manuals," as they were called before the modern separation of sex and marriage, place the penis within a different discourse from that of the twentieth century. Some marriage manuals, such as J. H. Kellogg's 1888 *Plain Facts for Old and Young: Embracing the Natural History and Hygiene of Organic Life*, Eugene Becklard's 1859 *Know Thyself: The Physiologist; Or Sexual Physiology Revealed*, Jean DuBois's 1839 *Marriage Physiologically Discussed*, and, at the beginning of the twentieth century, William H. Walling's 1904 *Sexology* give no details about the physiology of sex and thus contain no discussion at all of penises. In a section entitled "A Chapter for Boys," Kellogg devotes only one paragraph to what he terms "The Reproductive Apparatus" (1974, 337); he never mentions the penis and only cautions that the reproductive organs were not meant to be used until the body is fully mature. Instead of being the question of the century, for these writers the matter of size seemed to be no question at all. This silence does not necessarily mean that the topic was of no importance but that, in certain books, it was inappropriate to speak about it.

If the penis is an unspeakable subject in these books, other aspects of the male body do receive emphasis in sometimes bizarre fashion. Becklard goes into great detail about the male body as a whole, describing "a fine-looking man" in terms of height, shape of forehead, hair texture, placement and color of eyes, placement and density of eyebrows, shape of nose, prominence of cheekbones, size of mouth and shape of lips, pattern of facial hair, complexion, and shape of face. He lavishes on other parts of the body the same detailed attention he gives to the head. The neck, throat, breast, shoulders, hips, arms, waist, back, posterior, thighs, knees, calves, shins, ankles, and foot are carefully described in terms of proper size, shape, and placement.

Virtually everything but the toes come in for attention. What strikes the contemporary reader of this cataloguing of the male body is the narrow range of acceptability of the features described. For example, "the neck should be of moderate length and incline to thickness; his throat free from that protuberance commonly called the apple of Eve" (Becklard 1974, 91). Interestingly, DuBois devotes a great deal of attention to body size, arguing that it is very important for men to marry women appropriate for their size. "Little men" should not marry "very large women," tall men should not marry short women (1974, 58–59). The exception lies with unusually proportioned men and women, who are advised not to seek partners like themselves: "Tall men should, therefore, marry females of respectable proportions; and very small men should seek partners approximating towards the middle height" (p. 59). Becklard prescriptively catalogues every part of the body but the genitals, and DuBois similarly limits his highly prescriptive account of the proper match between bodies to general stature.

When nineteenth-century marriage manuals do discuss and describe the genitals, they do so in ways quite different from twentieth-century manuals. R. T. Trall's 1881 edition of *Sexual Physiology: A Scientific and Popular Exposition of Fundamental Problems in Sociology* devotes seven pages to "The Male Organs of Generation" (p. 15); nowhere does he describe size or mention statistics. Significantly, the issue does come up in a later chapter on "Sexual Generation" (p. 47) during a discussion of hermaphrodism. The issue, as in the case of Herculine Barbin, brought to attention recently by Michel Foucault, is how to determine whether "deformed" individuals are men or women, whether they possess an abnormally large clitoris or an abnormally small penis. Trall refers to a highly publicized 1847 account of a Connecticut man charged with being a woman, a charge that reminds us of the political significance of establishing and maintaining sexual difference because a man declared a woman would lose the right to vote. Upon examination, the man was found to have "an imperforate *penis* subject to erection, about two inches and a half long. . . . The *scrotum* was not more than half the usual size" (p. 54). As the sole reference in the entire volume to the size of the male genitals, it points to the way in which, for the nineteenth century, size was of importance only in cases of extreme "deformity" resulting from birth defects, disease, or accidents.

Frederick Hollick's 1850 *The Marriage Guide, or Natural History of Generation; A Private Instructor for Married Persons and Those About to Marry Both Male and Female; in Every Thing Concerning the Physiology and Rela-*

tions of the Sexual System and the Production or Prevention of Off Spring—Including All the Discoveries Never Before Given in the English Language devotes an entire chapter to the male sexual organs. After a six-page detailed discussion of the penis in which size is, once again, neither described nor statistically noted, Hollick devotes twenty-one pages to sections entitled "Absence and Malformation of the Penis" and "Want of Development, or Congenital Small Size of the Penis" (1974). Hollick devotes nearly four times as much time and attention to the abnormalities of the penis as he does to the normal organ. Once again, although size is never mentioned in the discussion of the normal organ, it plays an important role in the discussion of the abnormal. Without a sense of irony, Hollick actually comments on this paradox: "It is sometimes difficult to say whether the Penis is too short or not, because there is no precise standard of limitation and in different people the development varies very much" (p. 144). Stated simply, at this point in the nineteenth century the medical profession took measurements only in extreme cases of deformation but had no statistical base to which findings could be compared, a problem that the twentieth century has corrected with a vengeance. Two sentences after noting the lack of data about the normal penis, Hollick observes, "I have seen a man of forty years of age in whom the Penis was only two inches long and about as thick as the little finger" (p. 145). Hollick goes into detail about another of his patients: "On examination the Penis was found about *two inches and a half* in length and about as thick as the forefinger" (p. 148). After describing a treatment, Hollick concludes, "This system was rigidly pursued for six months under my own inspection, at the end of which time the Penis was four inches long when erect, and quite firm, so that coition was possible" (p. 150). After describing a device called a "Congestor," Hollick claims: "I have known patients, in whom the whole organ was not *half an inch long,* and without the slightest tendency to erection, and yet the Congestor has caused it to grow, and has given it power, until perfectly capable for the purposes it was intended for" (p. 151). Penis size, then, is referred to only to document extreme deformation, and the norm is the one that in Sheets-Johnstone's terms we could call reproductive competency.

In these manuals I have found only one reference to the relation of pleasure-giving competence and penis size. In a discussion of the womb placement of women who have more than one child at a birth, DuBois argues that their husbands also probably "had large *virile* members":

If however, a couple under those circumstances have any drawbacks upon their conubial desires, they also have much pleasure to balance them, as the size of the penis, and the consequent pressure of the vagina, which is usually not very expansive in those cases, excite the rapture of copulation to a pitch of perfect beatitude. Indeed, there are instances where the parties can rarely perform the operation without a shout of mutual delight at the climax. (1974, 98)

DuBois denies, however, that "very large genital organs are more potent than others, as those of moderate dimensions have a decided advantage in the mysteries of re-production, and also in producing voluptuous sensations" (p. 99). A very large penis introduces pain, which offsets the pleasurable stimulation. DuBois concludes: "I do say, that, where an effort is necessary for effecting an entrance, and when the vagina presses elastically upon the penis, that the benefit of nuptial intercourse is augmented, and the chances of procreation advanced" (p. 99).

Although retaining the concept of the adequate penis as one that functions well reproductively, DuBois also at least raises here the concept of the penis as a pleasure-giving organ for the woman. He was able to reconcile these two positions because he believed that the size of the penis was critical to the fertilization process, since a large organ would penetrate beyond the womb and deposit the semen too far up and a small organ would not penetrate far enough and deposit the semen too far away from the womb: "The evil here, lies in the difficulty of propelling the semen with sufficient power to impregnate, and dislodge an ovulum—together with the usual want of an immediate union at the climactic shock" (p. 100). The woman's orgasmic pleasure was, for DuBois, part of the reproductive process. Thus, when he talks of men "whose copulative members scarcely measured an inch" (p. 100) but who have impregnated women, he concludes that this is highly unlikely, since "the chances are greatly against fruitfulness, as the excitement of the clitoris, by so unimportant a body, is hardly sufficient to inspire the female with corresponding sentiments" (p. 100). Notice once again, that precise measurements are referred to only with reference to what is regarded as extreme abnormality and that the reason for the concern with the penis as an organ for giving women pleasure is totally bound up with a reproductive argument that impregnation is much more likely to occur if the woman is excited and brought to a climax.

Whereas Hollick remedies the problems of abnormally small organs with the prescription of a penis-size enlarger (which incidentally sounds like a forerunner of those currently advertised in men's magazines and denounced in contemporary sex manuals as harmful), DuBois does so with the prescription of an artificial penis extender made of leather and cotton:

> With this instrument the clitoris can be excited almost as potently as by the natural genital organ, by which the semen will be ejected with more concentration and precision toward the uterus; and it may also have the effect of producing an immediate response on the part of the female, at the moment of emission; without which, by the way, it is impossible to accomplish a healthy impregnation. (1974, 101)

Female pleasure is thus tied to reproductive efficiency in a way that actually makes the issue of the pleasure-giving competence of the penis (or even its substitute) a part of reproductive competence. Nevertheless, in contrast to many other manuals, DuBois acknowledges a pleasure-giving function for the penis.

During the twentieth century, the medical and popular sex-manual discourse about the penis has shifted markedly from that of the nineteenth century. Two principal reversals took place: The emphasis shifted almost exclusively to the size of the normal, rather than the abnormal, penis; and reproductive competence gave way to pleasure-giving competence. Central to these shifts was the preoccupation with extensive documentation of penis size. If Hollick complained in 1850 that there were no established parameters for defining the normal penis, no doctor could make a similar complaint in the twentieth century. Alex Comfort's 1972 best-selling manual *The Joy of Sex* neatly summarizes both shifts. Whereas Reuben organized his manual around a question-and-answer format, Comfort uses a dictionary format with entries arranged alphabetically. Under the category "Starters," we find an entry for "Penis" and one for "Size." That size should be an issue of such importance that it warrants a separate entry parallels Reuben's privileging it as the first question. This is all the more remarkable in view of the fact that a major portion of the entry under "Penis" deals precisely with size.

Comfort remarks, "that the human penis is much bigger relatively than in other primates is probably due to . . . complex psychological functions; it's an aesthetic as well as a functional object" (1972, 79). Like Sheets-Johnstone, Comfort draws attention to the evolutionary significance of the size of the human penis, but unlike her, he makes a distinction between the aesthetic and the functional. Indeed, a few sentences later, after terming male preoccupation with size "irrational," Comfort claims: "Size has absolutely nothing to do with their [penises'] physical serviceability in intercourse, or—since female orgasm doesn't depend on getting deeply into the pelvis—with capacity to satisfy a partner, though many women are turned on by the idea of a large one, and a few say that they feel more (pp. 79–80)."

This single sentence summarizes the paradoxical position of all mid- to late twentieth-century sex manuals on the pleasure-giving competence of the penis: The question whether size is important to women's pleasure is always directly raised, and the answer is always that it is of no great importance. In her newspaper column, Dr. Ruth Westheimer confidently states: "You have probably heard me say this before, but I will repeat it. The size of a man's penis does not affect the enjoyment a woman receives from sex" (1990a, B5). Or: "Penis size is not the important thing. . . . Why don't you read books about female sexuality so you will understand what women do want" (1990b, 4).

In much the same way as all nineteenth-century marriage manuals dwell on the dangerous evils of masturbation, twentieth-century sex manuals dwell on penis size only to dismiss the issue as of no importance for female sexual pleasure. Indeed, if size is the question of this century, masturbation was the question of the last century. And if the contemporary reader is surprised by the unquestioning tone of certainty with which nineteenth-century writers proclaimed the evils of masturbation, consider the remarkable reassurance that Comfort offers his readers on our century's preoccupation with penis size: "If you have anxious preconceptions, get rid of them. All the preceding statements are true" (1972, 80). We need not remind ourselves that writers in the nineteenth century were equally certain that the statements about the physical and psychological problems they attributed to masturbation were true. But the use of the word *anxious* is as revealing as the use of the word *true*, for it betrays the way in which twentieth-century manuals have deployed a discourse of reassurance for men. This discourse in the service of relieving male anxiety far exceeds a mere presentation of "true" facts. Twentieth-century manuals assert the importance of male pleasure-giving competence for females but then assert that penis size has nothing to do with that competence. In part, this is accomplished by the split between the psychological (what Comfort calls the aesthetic) and the physiological. Stated bluntly, if size matters to a woman, it is for psychological reasons, not physical ones.

After all this discussion of size takes place in the alphabetized heading

of "Penis," it comes as something of a surprise to encounter "Size" in the
S portion of *The Joy of Sex*. What could be left to say? First, in a manner
once again reminiscent of Sheets-Johnstone, we learn that the male preoccupation with size is "built-in biologically to men" as "a 'dominance signal,'
like a deer's antlers" (Comfort 1972, 89). In a way also typical of all mid- to
late twentieth-century manuals, Comfort cites six inches as the average size
of the erect penis. Most other writers include a range, usually five to seven
inches, or occasionally, as Reuben does, four-and-a-half to eight inches.

Comfort dismisses all claims such as those made by Hollick in 1850 that
various remedies exist that will increase penis size. Then, devoting only one
sentence to the subject, he notes: "The few cases where male genitalia are
really infantile go with major gland disturbances and are treatable but rare"
(1972, 89). Notice how this virtually reverses the nineteenth-century emphasis on the "abnormal" penis. Ever since R. L. Dickinson's 1949 documentation of penis size in *Human Sex Anatomy*, the twentieth century established
and forever repeated the range of normative penis size. Most manuals pro-
claim that 90 percent of all men fall between five and seven inches, a few
extend the range by a half inch on one or both sides. Indeed, the years between the first edition of Dickinson's book in 1933 and the second in 1949
show how this documentation was a phenomenon of the mid-twentieth century. The subject is singled out in the Preface to the second edition: "Very
exact measurements on 1,500 American white males . . . yields an average
penis length of 6¼ inches or 16 cm . . . and it corresponds with the 3500
self measurements obtained by Kinsey" (Dickinson 1949, vi-a). In the 1933
text, which is unchanged in the second edition, Dickinson notes: "Elaborate search of medical and other literature has brought to light no published
series of measurements of the erect penis; nor, with one exception, do the few
writers who give figures state their sources of information" (p. 73). Dickinson
describes how he looked for such data both in the United States and abroad
before assigning the task to one of his top researchers, who concluded, much
like Sheets-Johnstone, that "this silence seems to mean that these organs are
not recognized as belonging to anthropology at all" (Dickinson 1949, 73).
An 1899 study by Heinrich Loeb, a German physician, is the only one that
is documented; significantly, Loeb gives only the size of the flaccid penis,
since his research dealt with the urethra for the purposes of administering
medicine in gonorrhea cases. His measurements are thus not even part of
the later discourse of sexual normality that would define such studies. In the

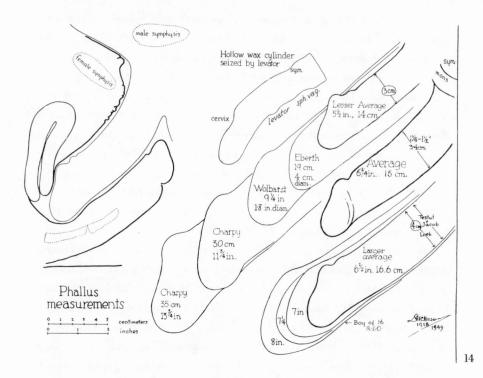

Phallus
measurements

0 1 2 3 4 5 centimeters
0 1 2 inches

14

absence of documentation, Dickinson nevertheless used nine studies (dated between 1879 and 1931) that reported measurements and averaged the figures to conclude that the flaccid penis was four inches long and the erection six inches long with the circumferences being three and three-eighths and four and three-eighths inches. Furthermore, he augmented the data with drawings categorizing and illustrating size differences (14).

Because Kinsey did not publish his penis-size data in his 1948 volume *Sexual Behavior in the Human Male*, the next significant contribution came in 1969 from William H. Masters and Virginia E. Johnson's *Human Sexual Response*, in which they argue against the notions that a larger penis is more effective in coitus and that larger, unerect penises are significantly larger in erection than are smaller, flaccid penises. Both of their major conclusions have been accepted with near unanimity by later medical professionals and authors of sex manuals and are frequently cited in such a way as to imply further proof is unnecessary. Although Masters and Johnson do not present their full data on penis size (saying that it confirms the dimensions given by Dickinson and Loeb), they do give data on their investigation of the relationship between unerect and erect size (noting that on three different occasions the same person measured all eighty penises in both flaccid and erect states). Their study involved eighty men, forty of whom were in the smaller end and forty in the larger end of the range of normal dimensions. They conclude that larger flaccid penises do not increase to a significantly greater erect size than do smaller ones, but size differences do remain in the erect state. Nevertheless, in their sample the largest increase occurred in a man with a smaller flaccid penis that more than doubled in length, while the smallest increase occurred in a man with one of the largest flaccid organs; their erections were exactly the same length. Still, Masters and Johnson dismiss any potential concern about the general constancy of small penis size by referring readers to the chapter that discusses the way the vagina involuntarily adjusts itself to the size of any penis during penetration.

The Kinsey Data, released in 1979, a decade after Masters and Johnson's *Human Sexual Response*, is the first publication of massive documentation on penis size. The Kinsey Institute data are presented in five tables: measured circumference of the flaccid and erect penis; the subjects' estimate of erect penis length; the measured length of the penis erect and flaccid. The respondents are categorized as white college, white noncollege, and black college subjects. The data are given as a percentage for each demographic and size category; measurement segments differ by quarter inches. For example, 4.2 percent of white college males report an erect penis of five inches in length and 23.9 percent report an erect penis six inches in length. This volume presents data but does not interpret or discuss them.

Following on Masters and Johnson's work, Comfort writes in *The Joy of Sex*: "Non-erect size in the male is equally unimportant—some men before erection show no penile shaft at all, but extend to full size equally" (1972, 90–91). This claim is typical of modern manuals, but such observations play no part in the nineteenth-century literature because there were no empirical data on the subject. Indeed, I have found no evidence regarding commonly held beliefs about penis size; the manuals I have seen do not address the issue, except to document abnormally small genitals, comparing them against an unknown standard. Comfort's claim unwittingly points to yet another significant absence in the modern sexual representation of the male body: the image of penises that "show no shaft before erection." Although there are many illustrations of the penis in *The Joy of Sex*, none approximates this verbal description. One looks almost in vain through the history of photography, art, cinema, and medicine for this allegedly "normal" sight, and this absence of imagery points to the role of diagrams and drawings in the normative representation of the penis in medical texts.

The common profile diagram, for example, shows a great deal of the shaft in a penis that hangs down. Only in recent years have some texts, such as the 1988 edition of *Human Sexuality* by William H. Masters, Virginia E. Johnson, and Robert C. Kolodny, designed for introductory college-level courses, begun to modify this homogeneous image of the penis, and then usually by showing two or three sketches or photographs. The images usually differ only slightly in size and contrast a circumsized penis with an uncircumsized one. The history of this shift can be seen in the four different editions of the college textbook *Our Sexuality* by Robert Crooks and Karla Baur. The original edition (published in 1980) shows sketches of three penises to illustrate normal variations. In the second edition (1983), the sketches are replaced with three photos. The third edition (1987) also uses three photos, though one is significantly different from those in the previous edition. The fourth edition (1990) uses color photos that emphasize that one of the models is black. Interestingly, in all four editions, on the same page as the illustrations, the authors quote someone they call an "extremely tall, husky male" describing his penis in the following manner: "When I'm flaccid it looks like all I have is testicles and a glans. My shaft is practically invisible" (Crooks and Baur 1990, 168). None of their sketches or photographs approximates a penis of this sort. Like Comfort in *The Joy of Sex*, the authors assume that they must acknowledge this physiological type, but they seem reluctant to represent it visually.

Even the slight pictorial variations of the penises found in recent college textbooks, however, highlight the monolithic traditional medical representation of the penis. Predictably enough, even in the realm of medicine, the penis is expected to perform a highly specular function. Justine Hill makes this abundantly clear in her *Plain and Fancy Penises* (1979), a series of eighty slides that shows a range of penises, varying in size, shape, and color. Intended for college courses and adult groups, the slide presentation's accompanying written commentary stresses that seeing such variation is important for relieving men of their anxieties regarding their penises. Hill's project might be the harbinger of an expanded range of visual representations of the penis.

This brief account of medical representations of the penis serves to show how such representations are part of discourses that dramatically shift and change. The nineteenth century knew nothing of the massive medical measurements that became standard in the twentieth century. Paradoxically, the twentieth century measurement of the male genitals can only be understood in the larger context of the nineteenth-century development of measuring nearly all other parts of male and female bodies—heads, brains, feet, and just about everything else. In fact, Dickinson's (1949) *Human Sex Anatomy*, presents full-length views of a naked male with average measurements for all parts of the body, the penis included (15). Dickinson notes that several late nineteenth- and early twentieth-century manuals did publish measurements for the average penis in flaccid and erect states; although the authors of those studies do not give any information about how many men were measured or by whom and under what circumstances, the circulation of such data points to how the penis was being drawn into the nineteenth-century discourse of scientific measurement of the body. Given the apparent lack of scientific method, it is also interesting to note that the measurements given in those studies are remarkably similar to those of twentieth-century sexology.

If the medical documentation of penis size did not occur until the mid-twentieth century, such measuring was occurring elsewhere in Western culture. Large penises have nearly always played a role in pornography and erotic representations (a point that is central to the next two chapters), and the Marquis de Sade's writings are significant in this respect. In *The 120 Days of Sodom*, written in 1785, Sade describes each of the male participants by giving detailed measurements of their penises, at times even down to a sixteenth of an inch, a fraction much smaller than would be employed by modern sexology (1967, 232). Within the context of the late eighteenth century, such statistics would function somewhat differently than they do in the present, since there was no widely circulated standard against which to compare them. Much like Hollick's lament in 1850 that the medical profession had no data to which he could relate his measurements, Sade's work anticipates this sexological development, as indeed it anticipates many others, such as describing and categorizing sexual aberrations. Sade, however, clearly did not share medical science's reluctance to place the penis on the measuring stick of "pleasure-giving competence."

Stephen Jay Gould has shown how the nineteenth-century practice of measuring parts of the body relates to IQ testing; I suggest that there are some parallels between IQ testing and the sexological practice of measuring penises. Much as IQ testing leads to the normative number of 100, penis measuring leads to the normative number of six inches. Similarly, normal

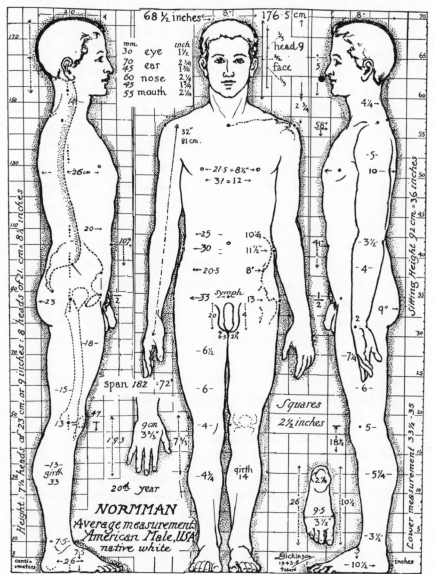

15

ranges are established numerically so that five to seven inches is the normal erect penis range, just as 90–110 is the normal intelligence range. Just as IQ testing created new ways of trying to define and categorize intelligence, penis measuring did the same for male sexuality. Indeed, Gould's title *The Mismeasure of Man* is uncannily apt when applied to sexology.

A common observation is that IQ scores accurately measure only the ability to take IQ tests. To equate such abilities with a total concept of intelligence is questionable, to say the least. But such testing has other consequences. The very notion that intelligence can be measured and represented by one number marks a profound shift in our cultural understanding of intelligence. It also gives extreme significance to a comparatively small numerical range (e.g., 10 points of approximately 100). Measuring penis size has similar consequences; an inch becomes extremely important. Yet many women who have read or heard earlier versions of this research have told me that the difference of an inch in an erect penis is imperceptible to them. Although statistically a five-inch erection is at the bottom of the normal range and a six-inch erection is at the center, this statistically significant variation is for them irrelevant and meaningless. In the film *Dick* (1989) (see the concluding chapter), a woman interviewed about penis size remarks, "You know, that's one thing I've always wanted to do. . . . I never have a ruler handy, so I've never really measured. I don't know—six to eight inches [laughter from the interviewer and interviewee], somewhere in between." The woman conducting the interview says, "That's pretty big," to which the interviewee responds, "Is it?" If we simply credit the medical definition of size as accurate, we miss the important point that such measurement marks a significant shift in perception of penis size; it does not simply supply accurate data. Much as one might wonder about mental abilities not tested by IQ testing, one can readily think of perceptual issues of size that are ignored by medical measurement. The sight of the penis on an actual body may involve such perceptions as proportion to other bodily parts or even to such other variables as thickness of the same organ. Thus, simply to isolate and measure one dimension at a time and equate that measurement with "size" may be to simplify the notion of size in a manner similar to the way in which IQ testing simplifies the notion of intelligence. This point is particularly important in view of the fact that such measuring was undertaken and the results widely distributed precisely in relation to questions of female satisfaction during heterosexual intercourse. Yet, as the film's interview demonstrates, the medical documentation of penis size implies that women do not know about size unless they have measured and that their perceptions may be "wrong."

In *The Modernization of Sex*, Paul Robinson surveys the ideological assumptions operative in the work of the major twentieth-century sex researchers. His chapter on Masters and Johnson characterizes their thought as more conservative than that of Kinsey because they were medical professionals who sought to help people adjust to a socially acceptable and enshrined system of sexual expression. Therefore they did not radically challenge that

system by positing a superior alternative. Robinson argues that their con-
servatism manifests itself in their reliance on a model of long-term heterosexual relationships with emotional involvement, an emphasis on procreative
aspects of sex as opposed to pleasure-giving aspects, and a positive pop-
psychologizing about sex. Their work is informed by feminism and a democratic desire to level differences both between the sexes and within each sex.
It is in this context that Robinson takes up the issue of penis size.

He refers to Masters and Johnson's "patronizing discussion" of the penis,
which is intended "to relieve men of any anxieties they might have about the
adequacy of their sexual equipment" (Robinson 1989, 154). With a tone of
incredulity, he concludes that the argument "suggests that not merely penile
size but the penis itself is irrelevant to a woman's pleasure" (p. 154). The first
part of Robinson's observation coincides with what I have termed a discourse
of reassurance, but my conclusions are different from those of Robinson, and
the differences are revealing.

Although Robinson acknowledges Masters and Johnson's claim that since
the vagina is a virtual rather than an actual space, it will accommodate itself
to whatever size penis is introduced into it, he notes that Masters and Johnson never asked women how they felt about penis size. Here we are reminded
of Maxine Sheets-Johnstone's observation (see Chapter 1) about Symons,
Crook, and Hite. Once again, the observation is a pertinent one. But note
Robinson's underlying assumption: "Of course, they could always argue that
any increment in gratification derived from a *large* penis was purely psychological" (1989, 155; emphasis added). Robinson assumes that, if asked, any
preference women expressed would naturally favor large penises. Robinson
returns to this topic in his conclusion when he argues that the egalitarian
world of the clitoral orgasm is being replaced by the aristocratic world of the
vaginal orgasm: "It is a world in which large penises make a difference."
Masters and Johnson's sexology, which refuses to acknowledge such a world,
is compared to "the virtues of a low-priced compact against the wasteful lux-
ury of a Cadillac or a Lincoln" (p. 190). Putting aside the issue of whether
or not 1975 marked such a comeback for the vaginal orgasm, Robinson once
again assumes that such an orgasm necessarily favors the large penis.

If Robinson is correct that Masters and Johnson too readily assert the lack
of importance of penis size in the name of egalitarianism, he is unaware that
he leaps to the assertion that the only alternative is the superiority of the
large penis and fails even to imagine that some women could psychologically
or physiologically prefer smaller penises. Thus, his analysis of Masters and

Johnson is caught up in a phallic discourse that he himself does not understand. For this reason, he is upset by the notion that Masters and Johnson undervalue the penis: "Men, then, are to think neither well nor ill of themselves because of the size of their penises. In fact, as far as sexual matters are concerned, it hardly matters whether they have penises at all" (Robinson 1989, 155). Once again, Robinson links his critique of Masters and Johnson's egalitarianism regarding penis size to the unthinkable notion that penises might not matter. In fact, for some women they do not matter, but what is particularly revealing is Robinson's need to exaggerate this aspect of Masters and Johnson's research and to make the same point twice in almost the same language.

The clitoral versus vaginal orgasm debate has been a political issue for many feminists, who consider the vaginal orgasm a myth that creates a fetish out of the penis while ignoring or devaluing women's clitoral pleasure. The concept of the vaginal orgasm shifts attention in intercourse away from clitoral friction and implies the superiority of the large penis with its powers of penetration. In other words, women might be indifferent to size, not because small and large penises are equally effective during penetration, but because women do not derive their pleasure primarily from penetration. To banish the horrible thought that penis size might not matter, Robinson asserts that it does, and that bigger is better. Thus, the penis is saved from its feared irrelevancy and placed within a phallocentric patriarchal discourse. We see in the next chapter that Robinson has unexpected female allies in this fight for the supremacy of the penis–phallus.

AN ANSWER TO THE QUESTION OF THE CENTURY

● ● ● ● ● ●

DICK TALK

Several years ago, I was critiquing in class the representation of homosexuality in a popular movie when a student noted that she had several gay male friends who liked the movie very much. The fact that they liked it alone seemed to her to undermine my argument that the film was disturbing in its representation of gay men. Her assumption points to the necessity of questioning our reactions to film. Although artistic and theoretical practice have diversified during the last decade, moving away from heterosexual male domination toward a plurality of voices, all of us—speakers and listeners alike—have to be careful. Recent work has shown how many marginalized groups and subcultures produce their own textual meanings, but we cannot assume that members of any group are vested with especially keen insight simply because they have been silenced too long. Such notions are appealing but are undermined by the recognition that all of us are caught up in dominant ideologies; none of us stands outside them.

So, even if some gay men like a certain film, their reaction does not seal it off from criticism, nor does it give us much insight into the film. This is not to say that the responses of gay men to a film are uninteresting, invalid, or unjustifiable, but only that to maintain a truly critical perspective, we have to know more than what someone's responses are. We must analyze *why* someone has such a response, then consider whether the response is politically and socially progressive. If ideologies structure us unconsciously to want and desire what is in the best interests of the dominant culture, we cannot speak of our authentic responses because they are neither ours nor authentic. Still, it is important to speak and to listen.

Dick Talk (1986) gives us a unique opportunity to do some listening.* A videotape produced anonymously by women in the Houston area and exhibited at the Houston Center for Photography, it presents five women talking about what the title suggests they will discuss. The moderator asks women questions that investigators such as Crook, Symons, Hite, and Masters and Johnson do not ask. Indeed, a central question is what, as we saw in the last chapter, David Reuben has dubbed "the question of the century."

The tape is divided into sections with the following titles: "the first," "images," "size," "best/worst," and "mystery." All participants are anonymous. As we hear them talk, the camera shows their bodies and part of their faces, but never above the mouth. Thus, we see how they are dressed and how they gesture while they speak, but we never see the complete person. They are seated in a living room around a coffee table on which there are coffee cups, glasses, and a bottle of nail polish.

The tape begins with the sound of laughter before the title appears. We then hear one participant ask if it is all right to use personal anecdotes, and another encourages her to do so. In the opening section, "the first," the moderator asks the women about the first time they thought about a penis and what they thought about it. One relates how she thought penises were like rockets that detached themselves from men, entered women's bodies, and transformed themselves into babies. She had seen diagrams in a book, and since she had seen her father walking around the house in his shorts without a visible erection like that in the diagram, she assumed that his had become

*Information on *Dick Talk* is available from the Houston Center for Photography, 1441 West Alabama, Houston, TX 77006. Some of the points I make in this chapter originally appeared in "Talk Show" (1986) and an anonymous response by the director ("**x**") appeared in a letter in the following issue of *SPOT* (1987).

detached. She then relates a dream about men in suits with attaché cases in which they keep their penises. The other women laugh and enjoy this anecdote; we hear these sounds of pleasurable bonding before the opening title, and throughout they form an important part of the tape. For these women, talking about these topics is fun. They also talk about their first orgasms, recalling memories of being stimulated as little girls by such things as a warm bath or by the sight of a neighborhood boy and likening the sensations to sitting in the grass.

In "images," the women talk about using magazines and Sears catalogues to look at images of men. Again, there is the same kind of friendly laughter. They then talk about their fascination when, as little girls, they first saw a penis. Several of the women agree about how beautiful penises are, and one remarks that the penises shown in porn magazines are never beautiful. The conversation segues into a discussion of such pictures. The moderator then passes out magazines, and the pictures are shown to the camera as the women give their responses.

In "size," the moderator talks about how important penis size is to her and asks the others if she is the only one who feels that way. Another agrees with her that she prefers not having small ones and that she does not return for sex with a small man. Another remarks that she feels the "chemistry" is the most important thing, not size, and one woman adds that she has had very good sex with men who were not well endowed. The moderator then asks the women about the worst sex they have ever had, and one recounts an experience with a man who had the smallest penis she had ever encountered.

The tape then segues into the "best/worst" section. One of the women talks about the manner in which she likes to be picked up by a man while having sex, and another says she likes "a man who can eat good pussy." The moderator replies that she has never found any men who adequately performed oral sex; they simply seem to be fulfilling an obligation. The women agree that good kissing is important. Several express a preference for bodies that are not too hairy, one for bodies with good muscles, one for "a good set of balls." One looks at the way a man eats; she feels that if he really loves food, he will be sensual. Several agree that they hate the manner in which many men put a hand on the back of a woman's head, forcing her down. The section concludes with the women discussing the distinction between "fucking to fuck" and "fucking to come." During this section, one of the women is applying fingernail polish during the conversation.

Building on the differences between men's and women's pleasure that emerge from relating their best and worst experiences, the final section, "mystery," continues with one of the women's comments made at the beginning. "I believe there is a mismatch . . . she's going to outlast him and there's going to be a lot left over." The women seem to agree at this point that "our picture is bigger. It's a lot bigger. It includes a lot more." Several also agree that they cannot even let men know the scope of their desire because the men could not handle it. They talk about sex as a power struggle they want to reject, including the struggle between denial of desire and affirmation of it. They agree that women have much more "sexual energy" than men, and they return to the theme of reticence: "I hesitate to let a man know about how I feel about my sexuality or how much of it there is," one remarks. Another adds, "You can't tell them you'd love . . . to fuck for a couple days, not a couple times." The women feel "sad" about this "mismatch" between men and women. The tape ends with one of the participants suggesting that it would be interesting to do a similar tape with men talking about sexuality and then one with men and women talking together.

Borrowing a term used by Richard Dyer in his analysis of gay and lesbian cinema (1990), *Dick Talk* can be called an affirmation video as it affirms the uniqueness and validity of female sexuality. Indeed, its existence is a testimonial to women who defy the silence that patriarchy attempts to impose on them regarding their sexuality. For these women, simply talking about men, the male body, and sex in this manner is a liberating experience. The sense of sharing through the use of personal anecdotes and bonding through laughter that permeates the tape is a constant reminder of the value that this process holds for the women.

In spite of its liberatory process, however, the tape's discourse may actually silence criticism: If affirming their sexuality in this manner is valuable for these women, who has the right to criticize them? I think that the tape's discourse must be respected but that it is equally important to retain a critical perspective on it; if the value of affirmation filmmaking lies in positively asserting the validity of a group's experiences, its limitations lie in enthusiastically embracing experience at the expense of analysis and understanding. With no disrespect to the tape's discourse, I now want to turn attention to the complexities and contradictions of the experiences represented in *Dick Talk*.

According to the producer, the reason for the participants' anonymity was to protect them both personally and professionally. The anonymity, however, at the simplest level creates an unusually voyeuristic atmosphere. The way the camera scans parts of the women's bodies may create a desire to see the whole. It invites the spectator to fantasize about these women to complete the picture. The sound works similarly; in clinical terms, there is an aural equivalent to voyeurism that gives an erotic pleasure to someone who overhears or listens in. *Dick Talk* creates more of this atmosphere than it would have done had it been less secretive in its mode of presentation. In fact, over the opening credit we can barely understand the women we hear talking and laughing. This immediately eroticizes the tape as we strain to hear what they are talking and laughing about. We hear one of the women ask if they should talk about width and circumference or whether they should tell personal stories. The answer is personal stories, and the stage is thus set for us to "listen in" on a private conversation to which we would normally not have access. This is a pleasurable invitation.

I do not wish to challenge the use of personal stories. Anyone who teaches gender studies knows that personal stories are indispensable to discussing these topics. As men and women, we fall back on our personal experiences in order to articulate our feelings about our struggles with cultural notions of masculinity, femininity, and sexuality. For heterosexual men and women, as well as gay men, talking about penises is certainly highly charged in personal ways. Such personal experience can be incorporated into larger perspectives, which make use of the anecdotal material. *Dick Talk*, however, sustains the personal, anecdotal mode almost exclusively. We simply enjoy hearing more and more about these women's personal lives; contrary to some assumptions, this talk is neither challenging, threatening, or disturbing to men. The tone of the conversation much of the time is closer to gossip than serious discussion, although two of the women frequently avoid dwelling on personal details and articulate issues.

The women's choice to remain anonymous does not require that they remain mysterious. Information about their backgrounds in terms of age, class, race, ethnicity, or education could have been provided without compromising their privacy, and I think it is revealing that the videomaker chose not to offer this information. All our responses are shaped and formed by the cultural, historical moment we live in, as well as by our unique psychoanalytic histories. Certainly, age, class, race, and education are important parts of our histories. That does not mean that if we knew, for example, that one of the women held a Ph.D. and another never went to college, we should privilege the former over the latter, but we might learn something about how class and education help structure sexual response. There is, as the five women in this tape make clear, no such thing as *a* woman's response to penises. There are many responses, none of which can be isolated from history, both cultural and personal.

Dick Talk could have acquired a critical perspective in at least two ways. The moderator could have encouraged the women to examine their responses, rather than merely report them. The woman at the far right of the room, dressed in a white blouse and brightly patterned slacks, fulfills a moderating function. She gets things going and at one point even says that she has a friend who is a "great dick talker." She relishes the personal stories and urges the speakers on with more details. But except for expressing enthusiastic agreement or surprise, she never probes any of the responses. Thus, neither the women nor the viewer have to think about the implications and significances of the stories; they are simply offered up as personal truths.

The videomaker–moderator (presumably the same person) could also have introduced a critical perspective by intercutting an analytical narration with the documentary footage. The 1986 uncredited *SPOT* article entitled "Bringing Up Dick and Jane," which presents four anonymous women responding to the anonymous women in the tape, supplies precisely what *Dick Talk* lacks. Among other things, the women in the article analyze and object to the way the women in the tape zero in on one part of the male body, unquestioningly accept stereotypes, talk like men, and sound like something out of a porn magazine. The videomaker could have intercut such critical commentary by women with her original footage. Either the use of an analytical narrator or a group of analytical respondents would have broken the voyeuristic, personal eavesdropping tone of the piece and would have openly articulated questions about the individual responses, preventing a simple reification of them as authentic expressions of personal truth. As the tape is structured, only those spectators who bring an active critical framework with them will get beyond the very real fascination of listening to these women talk about their intimate lives.

During the first section, the woman in the striped blouse tells of her ignorance at imagining an erection, since clearly she had pictured a penis as something that hangs down. Furthermore, the notion of the penis thrusting during intercourse was unimaginable to her. "I wasn't born all knowing," she says of her early sexual performances. "But basically you were, don't you think?" the moderator responds. She adds: "I'm not talking expertise, I'm talking a real good response." "Well, I waited a long time for actually—now that I think about it, for the—not even knowing what the word was about what my fulfillment was supposed to be. And what the experience was. I knew there was something more to the whole thing than just watching the skilled person go in and out." The moderator's glib remark about being born with a "good response" blocks the insightful comments made by the woman in the striped blouse. A more analytical moderator may have picked up on the phrase "what my fulfillment was supposed to be" as revealing how a great deal of our sexual responses are learned. When analyzed symptomatically, the first section of the tape reveals just how significant the penis is in determining sexual difference in our culture. All the women remember and speak about it with near awe. The tracings of patriarchal culture's "successful" emphasis on the phallus are evident. These reminiscences about penises do not tell us something "essential" about women; they tell us something about how women are formed within our culture. *Dick Talk* never makes that clear.

The section "images" is equally revealing. Of her early childhood interest in the penis, the woman in the turquoise dress remarks, "It was just a visual fascination. We didn't touch each other." "Why did you want to look at it?" the moderator asks. "It was just fascinating. That little, bitty, tiny pink penis was sticking out there was fascinating." The moderator's question presumes the speaker should be able to answer *why* she was fascinated. Not surprisingly, all she can do is add more personal anecdote to what she has already told us. It should be the moderator's job or the videomaker's job to address that question. The "why," which should be the most important part of this tape, is simply thrown back to the speaker.

When the moderator produces the pornographic magazines with images of penises, she mentions that she is not aroused by these images; she finds them full of oppression, force, and aggression. But then she wonders why pornographic pictures and movies always show the male ejaculating: "But see the little drop right here. . . . Apparently there's something to do with watching the cum come out. In all the fuck movies I've seen, every time they start sucking, he never comes in her mouth. You have to see the squirt of the semen. Is that for men or for women?" We need something more than a personal response to answer those questions. Obviously, it is for men, since they are the market for the pornography in question.

Paul Willemen (1980) has argued that this development in pornography (like all images, these are in part historically determined, though no one in the tape ever reminds us of that) stems from a desperate need to make the "truth" of male sexuality visible. I return to this point later because I think it is not unrelated to porn's emphasis on big penises, though none of the women make that connection, either here or later, when they speak about size. Richard Dyer's (1982) analysis of male pin-ups carefully explicates why they so notoriously "fail" to arouse viewers. Whereas female models either acknowledge the male look by shyly looking away or by offering a come-hither look of their own, males typically stare aggressively out of the frame at the spectator or else avert their eyes in a way that suggests they are distracted by profound thoughts. In either case, they are not available to the viewer, as the female is. Dyer also notes that the image of the penis awkwardly fails, since the literal organ collapses under the symbolic weight imposed on it by the phallus. The gap between the literal and the symbolic is too great. For this reason, the myth of the phallus benefits from keeping the penis hidden.

If no one adequately examines why pornographic images fail to satisfy any of the women, the same is true of the images that apparently do please several of them. "This arouses me," one of the women remarks (voices of approval are heard), "Calvin Klein has the best touch. Where does he get this stuff?" "Real life," the moderator replies, and someone adds, "Yeah." When another woman observes that the other images are from "real life too," someone responds by adding, "But it isn't our real life." If Calvin Klein ads provoke an erotic response in some of these women, it cannot be understood by reference to naive realism, nor is such a response necessarily positive. We need to find out not only how the ad's images and the pornographic images differ, but we also need to place the ad's images within the same phallic mode that structures the pornography. One of the dangers of dismissing por-nography without understanding it is that presumably other kinds of images (in this case advertising) then appear entirely different, when, in fact, they have a great deal in common.

Both Willemen's and Dyer's points are crucial to understanding "size," the next section of *Dick Talk*. The moderator sets the tone by stressing that size is important to her. "If you get a grown man with a little Vienna sausage, that's a sad day because he's so proud of himself." Someone says, "I know," and adds, "but what can you do?" "Well, you should send him home," the moderator replies. "They're the ones that say size doesn't matter because obviously the guy who wrote the book, the guy who said that, has a real little dick." Later, the woman in the turquoise dress refers to a study that indicates that although women have been saying that size does not matter, they have not been telling the truth.

As I argued in the previous chapter, the representation of the male body and the penis in medical and scientific discourse should receive the same critical scrutiny that artistic representations receive. The standard representation of the penis in medical texts cannot be understood as a neutral, objective image. Penises vary greatly, but not in medical texts. Similarly, the way in which books on sex quickly and confidently assert that size does not matter, clearly betrays a male anxiety. It is comforting for men to "know" that they have nothing to worry about.

But instead of using this as a starting point for further inquiry, the moderator uses it as an excuse to revel in her love of big penises. She never questions why big penises are so attractive to her. She says, "The first time I saw a pornographic movie and I saw this enormous dick, I said, that's for me. Why shouldn't they be big?" Although she consciously traces her desire back to pornography, a form produced for male pleasure, she is not troubled by the connection, nor does she link it to the earlier discussion of pornography. I would suggest that the large penises in pornography are an integral part of the domination and aggression she finds so repulsive in those pictures. They are also closely linked to the emphasis on male ejaculation she finds so puzzling and unerotic. Size is linked with power. As I argued in Chapter 3, this is symbolically displaced onto the whole male body in a culture that values height in men as a sign of attractiveness. It explains why many people find incongruous the sight of a tall woman and a short man together. The man "should be" taller than the woman precisely because he should dominate her. Indeed, pornography's large penises are in this regard like the large, powerful men associated with Westerns.

Large penises in pornography are also part of the need to make the "truth" of male sexuality visible and to affirm the serious visual drama of sexual difference that revolves around the penis as phallus. Our culture has so much invested in the construction of sexual difference around the sight of the penis that the penis must be hidden or dramatically exaggerated. Hard-core pornography ensures this drama with its star system of men with large penises. Information even circulates on how large the penises of some of the stars are, down to the fraction of an inch. Scenes of undressing are frequently elided as the actors get down to business, or, if undressing is shown, the penis is frequently blocked from view or only glimpsed. In other examples, the men have been aroused before they undress, are very large when flaccid, or both. Seeing these large penises ejaculate is a double affirmation of the visual drama of sexual difference. Logic might dictate that the men in the audience would find these films anxiety producing because their penises do not match those on the screen, but another logic takes over. They identify with the symbolic notion of the powerful phallus that, the films assert, women need for their satisfaction. The women frequently express their desire for the "big cock" and even the supposed lesbian lovemaking scenes sometimes include a dildo, which stands in for the absent penis. This is a desperate male fantasy about the central importance of the big, highly visible penis to woman's sexual satisfaction.

The moderator's expressed desire for possessing big penises like those in porn films, just because it contradicts the reassuring assertions of the medical discourse that size does not matter, cannot be accepted simply as an expression of female desire that escapes male domination. There are more male myths than one. If it is true that men have attempted to block women from contemplating penises and from expressing any sexual desire for them, it is equally true that they have, in other ways, told them to be impressed with big penises. These are, after all, the same men who like to tell penis-size jokes. It is possible to move from one oppressive myth to another, equally oppressive one.

Like one of the women quoted in the article "Bringing Up Dick and Jane" (1986), I am reminded of "Saturday Night Live." There were two hilarious skits where Jane Curtin, Gilda Radner, and some other women sat around talking about men's problems (including, of course, worrying about size) and another where John Belushi, Dan Ackroyd, and some other men sat around talking about women's problems (including, of course, their periods). Imagine for a moment the all-male session proposed by one of the women at the end of *Dick Talk*. If five men sat around talking about sex in this fashion, undoubtedly various fetishes would come out. Some would talk about how much big breasts turn them on (if they spoke like the women in this tape, they would call them "tits"), and others about how much long legs and high-heeled shoes turn them on. If the moderator of that session were like the moderator of this one, he would chime in with comments like, "Oh yeah, don't you just love big tits," or, "Really?" if someone said they preferred small ones. No knowledge about *why* men fetishize women's bodies would emerge. None of us would hail such talk as insightful. Knowing that some women need big penises to get aroused, by itself, is no more interesting than knowing that some men need big breasts to get aroused. The interest derives from the fact that many spectators may never have heard women talking about these things, at least not in such an open and direct manner.

These obvious contradictions build in the "best/worst" section. As they talk about oral sex, one woman tells of a man who said of cunnilingus, "If you can get past the smell, you've got it licked." Several of the others voice displeasure as the woman continues, "I thought that was real crude and I don't want to be talked about like that." But many of these women have been speaking crudely about men and, no doubt, few men would like being spoken about that way either. Nor can one defend such talk by saying that turnabout is fair play. The turnabout may give some women pleasure, but such pleasure does not promote insight.

The last section of the tape, "mystery," is one of the most interesting. The women express their feelings about their sexuality in ways that, they suggest, lie beyond men's understanding. And some feel there is a mystery to women's sexuality. They are afraid to tell men about the scope of their desires and what they do want because they feel the men will react negatively. They express deep desires for longer, less goal-directed sexual experiences. Many feminists have discussed how the male linear notion of foreplay, build-up, and climax imposes a masculine structure of pleasure on women. Much of what we hear in this conversation makes that poignantly clear.

In this context, the moderator remarks, "I would like somebody to get hard, stay hard and fuck until I am unconscious. That's what I like, until I just am totally unconscious—and then keep going." This image recalls an earlier one where the woman in the turquoise dress, much to the surprise of the moderator, says that her best sexual experience was with a man with a small penis. She goes on to explain, "But one time I came too and the bed which had been up against the wall was in the middle of the room ["God!" the moderator interjects in awe], and I knew we had fucked." In both cases, the women's pleasure results from an extremely active male sexuality that reduces them to a state of unconsciousness. In the latter instance, the fact that the bed has moved becomes a sign of the way in which the man with the small penis successfully overcompensated for his physical shortcomings. Not surprisingly, at an earlier point, the moderator remarks that hard thrusting during intercourse is always superior for the woman's pleasure. Throughout the tape, good sex is nearly always described in quantifiable ways: bigger penises, harder thrusting, and longer lasting. What emerges is an image of a sort of sexual olympics with men as the superactive, pleasure-giving phallic power. There are virtually no descriptions of anything gentle or slow to be heard in the tape. My point is not to criticize any practices or preferences that give these women pleasure but to reveal a pervasive discourse about masculinity and the male body that, in this case, structures many of these pleasures. In other contexts, any of these preferences could be interpreted differently.

In part because of the way in which the moderator minimizes and brushes over exceptions, there is a strong sense of homogeneity underlying the sexual discourse in *Dick Talk*. When the woman whose worst sexual experience was with the man with the smallest penis returns to the subject, she notes that many of her best experiences were with men who were not particularly well endowed; the moderator simply responds in surprise and does not pursue the topic.

Anaïs Nin, in her remarkable and intimate journal of her sexual growth and experiences, writes of Henry Miller:

> The first time Henry made love to me, I realized a terrible fact—that Hugo was sexually too large for me, so that my pleasure has not been unmixed, always somewhat painful. Has that been the secret of my dissatisfaction? I tremble as I write it. I don't want to dwell on it, on its effects on my life, on my hunger. My hunger is not abnormal. With Henry I am content. (1990, 76)

In the film *Henry and June* (1990), Nin lies in bed with Henry after making love and tells him that Hugo is too large for her. He winces in embarrassment, and the moment is turned into a penis-size joke that typically elicits laughter from the audience. The scene is bizarrely contradictory, however, because even in the film it is clear that Nin prefers his smaller size and is not insulting him. With the exception of this one moment, *Henry and June* always treats its sexually explicit material in a remarkably mature manner, though it is also interesting to note that the film minimizes the importance of Nin's discovery about size. It comes as nothing less than a central revelation in the book, but is merely a throwaway moment in the film. This brief, jocular treatment is perhaps predictable in light of my analysis in Chapter 6 of penis-size jokes in films.

Nin also singles out Miller's slow thrusting as something that gives her an exquisite pleasure she has never known before. Nin's diary is in part remarkable precisely in how it chronicles a woman's growing awareness of her erotic pleasure. Central to that process is the discovery that she strongly prefers the smaller penis. When describing an erotic dream she has about June, Nin writes, "I felt a penis touching me. I questioned her and she answered triumphantly, 'Yes, I have a little one; aren't you glad?'" (1990, 91).

Not surprisingly, what little data have been published on women's preferences about penis size reveals that some women prefer smaller penises. Indeed, June M. Reinisch, the director of the Kinsey Institute, observes that

when size is a problem, it is because of big penises, not small ones (1991).
Similarly, Robert Crooks and Karla Baur in their college textbook *Our Sexuality* quote a woman who remarks: "You asked if size was important to my
pleasure. Yes, but not in the way you might imagine. If a man is quite large,
I worry that he might hurt me. Actually, I prefer that he be average or even
to the smaller side" (1990, 167).

It is precisely such voices that are either absent from or nearly silenced
in *Dick Talk*. Unless one holds an extraordinarily reductionist or essentialist
notion of female sexual pleasure, one would expect a variety of preferences
in regard to penis size, including small and large and indifference to size.
Thus, generalizations to the effect that women do not care about size (many
women who have responded to earlier versions of my research have told me
that with absolute certainty) are similar to assumptions that bigger is always
better. Yet many men and women in our culture, including scholars (see the
discussion of Robinson in Chapter 7), make such generalizations.

If most of the time the discourse in *Dick Talk* sounds overly homogeneous
and uncritical, there are exceptions. In the final section, the woman in the
white suit introduces the one attempt at theoretical analysis into the discussion. Unfortunately, she gives a highly inaccurate summary of Jacques
Lacan's psychoanalytic account of sexual difference and of its application
in film theory. She describes a cultural myth of a love–hate relationship between men and women based on a male principle and a female principle:
"And in fact, it got to the point that a few years ago, that intellectuals were
going to movies and they were saying, 'Oh boy, this is gonna be a really great
movie. Let's see the good woman die.' Anytime the hero, the man, would
accomplish something, he would fall in love with this woman and she would
sacrifice herself for him and to move the story along, she would die. And this
was the scriptwriter's unconscious, touching down beneath into this myth
that one of them is going to have to die in this struggle. And that because
men were producing and making all the movies—unconsciously or not, they
were killing all the good women in the movies."

It is true that Lacanian-based psychoanalytic film theory has attempted to
analyze the structural place of women in narratives, but in a different way
from the one she describes. First, not the good woman, but women who are
outside the control of men are the problem. They may be physically punished, killed, dropped from the narrative, or brought under control through
marriage to the hero by the film's end. The problem of forward narrative
movement usually has nothing to do with killing the good woman. Narra-

tive momentum is threatened by the desire to fetishize the woman's body. It is this desire that, linked in Freudian–Lacanian film theory to castration anxiety, turns the woman's body into a spectacle. Some movies virtually come to a grinding halt to dwell on the fetishized spectacle, and the demands of Hollywood pacing require the containment of these tendencies as much as possible. Nor is Lacanian film theory primarily used as a means of aesthetic evaluation. Aside from a dangerous appeal to anti-intellectualism, nothing is gained by claiming that "intellectuals" love movies because the good woman is killed. Psychoanalytic theory is used to explain structures of pleasure that traditional aesthetics simply ascribe to "good form." We can, in other words, explain *why* certain structures which recur in films are pleasurable. This is quite different from making them pleasurable simply because they conform to a pattern that joyfully confirms our alleged notions of the regrettable state of affairs between men and women in our culture. But neither the moderator nor the videomaker ever challenges or puts in perspective anything that anyone says. So we simply hear agreement of how appalling it is that "intellectuals" go to movies to enjoy watching the good woman killed in order to forward the narrative.

Nevertheless, *Dick Talk* is part of an important development in both art practice and theory. As I note in Chapter 1, Rosalind Coward has observed that men have managed to keep their bodies out of the glare of sexual scrutiny. It is important for both artists and theorists to turn the light back on men who have for so long stood in the darkness directing the light on women. Although it is important that men not "escape," it is equally important that they not become the object of simple notions of getting even. The critical purpose of turning attention to men's bodies has nothing to do with the current liberal notion in popular magazines and newspapers that men should have equal time with women. As long as we leave men and their bodies out of the picture, we simply cannot continue the important gender work of the past decade. The many contradictions and difficult positions that we hear from the women in *Dick Talk* significantly underline the need to address the issue of heterosexual female desire for the male body. Placing *Dick Talk* in relation to works by other women artists and scholars who have openly dealt with this issue is illuminating.

Sarah Kent, who has addressed issues of female desire and the male body as both a photographer and a critic, analyzes women's representations of men, arguing that men are shown as either "beasts that need restraining" or "placid castrati" (1985, 102). In her photographs of male nudes, she claims: "The body is neither invested with lustful potency nor shameful impotence. The genitals are seen not as symbols of dominance nor as evidence of vulnerability, but more matter of factly as a known source of intimacy and pleasure" (Kent and Morreau 1985, 106). Kent's language recalls Rozsika Parker's analysis of Helen White's *Man in Bath* (16), which Parker describes as "a man in his bath, limp, vulnerable, eyes closed" (1985, 48). But the man is more than limp; because of the camera's position and his being submerged in water, his penis appears small. Contrast this with Robert Mapplethorpe's *Patrice* (18), a photograph that Kent interprets as "confirming rather than questioning the myth of masculine virility" (1985, 86). In her view, her own photographs avoid this dichotomy, but in many ways they reinforce it by linking certain connotations to certain body types. It is no coincidence that Kent's model (17) has an average-size penis that falls between the stereotype of the small, vulnerable man and the large, virile man. She claims that the photograph neither valorizes virility nor suggests vulnerability; I contend that the image can be read against her claim, not because of the formal features of the photograph but the model's body type. Were the Mapplethorpe model with a large penis to be photographed in the same way, the viewer might very well conclude that the photographer was addressing virile masculinity.

The unacknowledged assumption that emerges in Kent's work is that the "gentle" male body has nothing to be proud or ashamed of and is equated with an average penis—exactly between the large, virile penis (which she acknowledges repeatedly as a feature of Mapplethorpe's work) and the small penis (which she never acknowledges as a feature of male nudes who would fall into the placid castrati category). Thus, some central cultural assumptions about masculinity and the body are fixed rather than truly questioned. Moreover, Kent does not show the face of her model in an attempt to block the traditional female response of identifying with the person rather than looking at the body. The tactic has the effect of centering the spectacle of the penis. She also poses her model like Michelangelo's David and places him in nature (in another photograph in the series, we see the ocean behind his body). The high-art tradition and the natural setting work to aestheticize and naturalize the context and weaken the sexual interest in the body.

Kent's discussion of Mapplethorpe's work raises the important issue of heterosexual female response to photographs that depict male homosexual desire, in contrast to photographs that address an implied heterosexual female viewer. While critiquing conventional notions of masculinity in Mapplethorpe's male nudes, Kent describes how they nevertheless allow for plea-

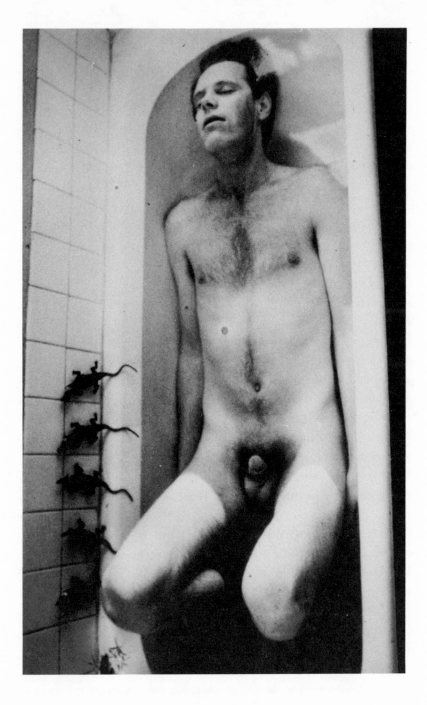

16

surable viewing by a heterosexual female. Even though they are part of a homoerotic structure with men talking to men, they allow the female viewer to listen in on the conversation and overcome the conventional embarrassment that would accompany looking with desire on the nude male body, a body that in Mapplethorpe's work presents mythic male potency as something available in the real world. Ironically, for Kent, male pin-ups such as those in *Playgirl*, directed at female viewers, do not afford a similar erotic pleasure. Somewhat similarly, Suzanne Moore, arguing against Mark Finch's claim that women do not objectify men's bodies and that such objectification in television shows such as "Dynasty" allows a gay male erotic gaze, says that *"the codification of men via male gay discourse enables a female erotic gaze"* (1989, 53). Thus, instead of being an exclusively male province of erotic pleasure, certain male homosexual structures allow women access to an erotic gaze otherwise denied them.

Kobena Mercer (1986) has convincingly argued that the emphasis on large penises in Mapplethorpe's black nudes involves a fetish structure whereby the white photographer–spectator balances knowledge (not all black men have big penises) with denial (in these photographs they all do). Jane Gaines (1990) notes that in this formula castration anxiety is not merely a matter of

18

having a penis or not having one, as is the case in the classical Freudian formulation, but of having enough or not having enough of one. The latter structure, of course, is based on size comparisons that Gaines points out use the white male as the standard of measure.

Even when it does not involve a racial fetish, penis size relates to castration anxiety because it evidences that the mere possession of a penis may not fulfill the function of adequately marking the male body. There is a constant fear, not only in individuals, but in representation and discourse, that the penis fails to fulfill this awesome function. For this reason, as noted in the previous chapter, the sight of the small, retracted penis is perhaps the most taboo image of all. Alex Comfort can write about it, but none of his many illustrations can show it, any more than *Playgirl* can. This link between the fear of small penises and castration anxiety also relates to jokes like the one recounted in Chapter 6, where one of two female streakers was found to be a male. The medical need to determine the clear and distinct difference between a small penis and a large clitoris makes this connection clear. As I have argued throughout this study, in most cases, whether the penis is shown or not and how it is shown has nothing to do with erotic pleasure but with the fundamental assumption about the male body that maleness is defined by the mere possession of the penis.

As interesting as Gaines's reading of this aspect of Mapplethorpe's photography is, her discussion of the penis is limited solely to the white male's perceptions. Although she puts forward several fascinating accounts of how white middle-class women and black women variously read these photographs in terms of desire for the black male body, she never takes up the question of how large black penises function for these female spectators. This silence forms an elision that is all the more noticeable because the topic is insightfully discussed in relation to the white male viewer.

Melody Davis raises some of these same issues in her analysis of Mapplethorpe's photographs of black men. Like Kent and Gaines, Davis asserts that although these photographs are clearly homoerotic and their market is primarily male homosexuals, "this also appeals strongly to women" (1991, 69). For Davis, Mapplethorpe's male nudes illustrate what she terms the metonymic fantasy whereby the powerful, muscled body becomes a metaphor for the erection that is never shown. She forms a negative assessment of Mapplethorpe's representation of black subjects: "By making black men into the embodiment of the metonymic fantasy, Mapplethorpe denied them identity, sadistically objectifying them, and simultaneously he reinforced their difficulties by masking them with idealization" (1991, 85). Justine Hill's commentary on slide 7 of her "Plain and Fancy Penises" sequence (1979) supports Davis's observation. The slide shows the genitals of a black man who grew up oppressed by the myth that blacks are larger than whites. He was so happy to see himself represented in Hill's program in a way that he could help dispel the myth and save other black men from suffering as he had.

Davis's analysis also touches on the subject of fetishism in a manner that relates to that of Mercer and Gaines. Summarizing the traditional Freudian account of how the male child constructs the fetish to deny that women are not men, she concludes: "From Freud, we may induce that the fetishist fears that, should he let go of his object, he will lose his sexual agency and become a woman" (1991, 78–81). The penis, then, like the fetish in general and, indeed, like the fetish it literally becomes in the photographs of Mapplethorpe (and, as we see in the next chapter, in hard-core pornography), serves to protect against the fear of being a woman. But Davis also elides part of this argument. While her argument that not showing the erection displaces this function onto the metonymic fantasy and the action ideal of the entire body is perceptive, it diverts all attention away from the flaccid penis, which we do see. I would argue that the large penis itself partially fulfills this function; the specularity surrounding it *is* part of the metonymic fantasy. The erection that is never seen is displaced not only onto other sites of the body but also onto the sight of the unerect penis.

Kent, Moore, Gaines, and Davis all point to the importance of considering the work of male homosexual artists in relation to various spectator groups including heterosexual women. My analysis in Chapter 6 of certain structures in the films of Almodóvar and Fassbinder is relevant here. Some of the more provocative and unconventional sexual representations of the male body in cinema can be found in the work of such gay male directors. It would be a serious mistake, however, to presume that it is only relevant to study these films in relation to gay male spectators. In addition to the potential for contributing to homophobia, especially on the part of the heterosexual male spectator, such a stance marginalizes the issue of the sexual representation of the male body, which is exactly what patriarchy has always done, marking it only for homosexuals. On the contrary, I would suggest that we are all indebted to such work, which in many cases yields representational practices enabling all to understand better and see clear alternatives to dominant modes. Clearly the comparisons between male and female looking and desiring in Almodóvar's and Fassbinder's films show how male homosexual desire may function via a diegetic circuit that appears to be heterosexual female. Just as clearly, it would be a grave mistake to dismiss those films as a mere male or gay "appropriation" of female desire. As Fassbinder's and Almodóvar's careers make clear, these two filmmakers have nothing to hide. They have both openly acknowledged their homosexuality and have explored their sexuality in their films. Whatever else is the case, they do not use women to mask their desire. In fact, such an accusation would make more sense (though I think it would still be overly limiting and unproductive) aimed at heterosexual filmmakers and unacknowledged homosexual filmmakers working within the dominant style. Indeed, the analysis of cinematic penis-size jokes in Chapter 6, structured around beautiful women looking at or joking about men's genitals points to unconscious appropriation of the looking and joking woman by male writers and directors, who use the heterosexual veneer to safeguard their preoccupations from any possible homosexual implications.

By daring to break the conventional representations of the male body and the female gaze at it, such filmmakers as Fassbinder and Almodóvar place all spectators in the position of confronting and responding to significant alternatives to the norm. Chris Straayer (1986) has analyzed how lesbian spectators can read heterosexual films in pleasure-producing ways, even when the content of the scenes is overtly heterosexual. The scenes I have analyzed by Almodóvar and Fassbinder put into play structures that are likely to pull different spectators to them, but in entirely different ways. We should not place these readings within a hierarchy by simply establishing a correct one against which the others are willed "misreadings" or readings "against the grain." A heterosexual male spectator, for example, who reads the opening sequence in *What Have I Done to Deserve This?* as a way of perceiving the male body as an object of female desire is not misreading a scene that, some could argue, has nothing to do with female desire and everything to do with a gay male appropriation of such desire. Instead, the scene affords the heterosexual male spectator an opportunity to perceive the male body in a new way and one that may make him feel uncomfortable, since his gaze at the objectified body is routed through the desiring gaze of a woman. Some students have responded that way when I have shown the film in class. Other heterosexual males may find the reversal appealing, rather than disturbing. Some heterosexual female spectators respond, as Sarah Kent does to Mapplethorpe's photographs, by enjoying the opportunity to perceive the eroticized male body pleasurably, while others respond by feeling that the scene has nothing to do with their desire.

As I mentioned in Chapter 1, gay male spectators may read the scene as an in-joke between a gay male director and his target audience. This latter reading, however, should not imply that the scene, and others like it, speak only to gay males and that the issues raised are therefore applicable only to those spectators. Such thinking, in fact, enables patriarchal ideology to marginalize any work on the male body. The effectiveness of that marginalization is nothing short of scandalous, since all segments of the population have a stake in understanding and questioning the sexual representation of the male body. Even some issues in lesbian sexuality, ranging from clothing to the body (e.g., the "butch" image), are linked to male images. Although our culture tells heterosexual women that the male body is of limited importance in relationship to other male attributes (see the discussion of *Cyrano de Bergerac* in Chapter 1) and instills homophobic fear in heterosexual men, members of both groups stand to gain much by questioning and analyzing these assumptions. Interestingly, several of the women quoted in "Bringing Up Dick and Jane" remark that, were it not for *Dick Talk*, they would never have had the opportunity to discuss these issues with other women. In this context, the very existence of *Dick Talk* makes it an important and courageous tape.

THE "GIFT" AND THE "KEEPSAKE"

● ● ● ● ● ●

IN THE REALM OF THE SENSES: CASTRATION FANTASIES

In *Dick Talk* the women pass around hard-core pornographic magazines, discussing the way sex is represented in them and in hard-core films
and concluding that these are male forms and fantasies that have little or
nothing to do with women. While many women have dismissed these representations, the issue is of interest because hard-core pornography and its
related mainstream versions, such as *Playgirl,* are the only places within
contemporary Western arts and media where the male genitals are centrally
and explicitly sexually represented. Instead of covering up, or metaphorically displacing elsewhere onto the body, or talking incessantly about what
cannot be shown, hard-core dwells on the taboo image of the penis. It is important to explore hard-core's representational practices to understand how
the penis is represented on the rare occasions when the spotlight is directed
on it; if there are cultural reasons that the penis remain covered or only
glimpsed in special circumstances, we may expect to find a variety of rep-

resentational strategies that guarantee that awe and mystique surround the organ even when it is unveiled.

As I noted in Chapter 1, Scott McDonald has suggested that part of the heterosexual male viewer's pleasure of hard-core films comes from the unique opportunity to look at the penis, particularly erections and ejaculations, since these are things he cannot see elsewhere (1983). Stephen Prince has argued that the extent to which the male body and the male genitals are objectified in pornography simply invalidates Laura Mulvey's claim that the male spectator cannot bear to look at the objectified male body (1988). Prince's statistical data showing that male and female patterns of nudity are approximately equal in the hard-core feature will not surprise anyone familiar with the genre. Clearly, Mulvey's formulations are inadequate to understanding many features of hard-core pornography, but Prince bypasses all the critical ideological issues of representation, leaving the naive impression that hard-core treats male and female bodies equally because they share the spotlight for the same amount of time. I argue, on the contrary, that the statistical analysis of such imagery tells us nothing about how the male body functions regarding issues of equality in pornography. If the concept of the phallus structures the representation of the penis (and I think it does), its overwhelming presence may work to displace the usual inequality that results from dwelling more on the female than the male to another textual level. Equal time for men and women in pornography does not mean equal representational strategies.

Prince, equally naive in his assumptions about the representation of the female body, demonstrates that in the majority of porn scenes, women's bodies are not fetishized through the use of costume and paraphernalia. While this may be true (some of Prince's claims are valuable as they show that many commentators on pornography are content to make gross and unsupported generalizations), it falsely implies that women's bodies are not overwhelmingly fetishized in pornography. The porn star system clearly dictates that women cast in pornographic films be chosen in accordance with cultural norms of beauty (age, figure type, facial features, etc.), which are themselves part of a fetishistic regime. Furthermore, costumes are not needed to fragment and overemphasize parts of a woman's body. Posturing, lighting, camera positioning, and other representational devices can bring attention to the buttocks just as much as a flimsy pair of panties. Similarly, close-ups of women's faces, for many male spectators, may be among the most highly erotic moments in such films. What women say, the way they talk, and the sounds they make can be fetishized for male pleasure in a manner that has little to do with female subjectivity. Thus, whether women talk or how much they talk tells us little of significance about female subjectivity in pornography.

In her brilliant book *Hard-Core*, Linda Williams argues that many feminist assumptions about pornography must be reevaluated (1989). She finds some of the central elements of certain hard-core films unique in the way that, for example, they do not sadistically punish women for being sexual or the manner in which they posit female sexual desire and fulfillment as a legitimate need that males have to acknowledge. In her survey of recent pornography made by women for women and the couples market, Williams raises a number of questions that are pertinent to both the women's photographs of men discussed in the preceding chapter and to possible alternatives to dominant hard-core representations such as *In the Realm of the Senses* analyzed in this one:

> If a heterosexual woman's desire is for a man, and if the man's sexual difference resides primarily in the penis, then how shall we represent woman's pleasure in pornography? Can it be represented as anything but envy or submission to a penis that symbolizes phallic power and potency? Is it possible to represent the penis so that it is not also the phallus, that is, so that the penis is not asserted as the standard and measure of all desire? (1989, 247)

Williams points out that hiding the penis, as in soft-core pornography, is no solution because it merely shifts phallic dominance to other textual levels. As I noted in Chapter 1, ignoring the penis only intensifies the problem; this is just as true for critical practice as it is for artistic practice.

Nagisa Oshima's *In the Realm of the Senses* (1976) is a particularly useful film for analyzing the sexual representation of the male body in this context because it not only foregrounds the male body but also significantly departs from three separate traditions of representing it: the seventeenth- to nineteenth-century Japanese erotic woodblock, the late 1960s to mid-1970s Western hard-core pornographic film, and the dominant narrative film. *In the Realm of the Senses* noticeably displaces the usual pornographic emphasis on male sexuality and the powerful phallus, but replaces it with a contradictory structure. While this qualifies any simple reading of the film as a radical critique of patriarchy, it should not obscure the film's political significance for a reassessment of alternative ways of representing the male body.

In the Realm of the Senses tells the story of a sexual obsession between

Kichi, the married owner of a geisha house, and Sada, a woman who has come to work there. Their sexual encounters begin at the house, but they soon leave for the privacy of an inn, where they do virtually nothing but pursue their sexual desires. The specter of death hovers over their lovemaking as Sada first threatens to cut off Kichi's penis if he makes love again with his wife; then, repeatedly, after he initially requests it, she places her hands around his throat and nearly strangles him. Finally, she does strangle him and castrates his corpse. The period during which the action takes place is curiously ambiguous throughout most of the film. Noël Burch claims that "most of it could be set any time between 1900 and 1940" (1979, 343). To the Western viewer, the film simply appears to be set in traditional, rather than modern, Japan except in two instances in which Oshima clearly marks the time as the militaristic 1930s.

Narrative cinema in Japan and the United States (and indeed elsewhere) conventionally avoids showing the nude male. In the few exceptions, the nude male is usually involved in action (e.g., running or wrestling) or the view of his genitals is obstructed through the careful placement of objects in the composition. In order to take narrative cinema's powerfully ideal male body seriously, we must not see its literal truth. In both *The Terminator* (1984) and *The Terminator 2* (1991), for example, Arnold Schwarzenegger plays a cyborg of superhuman strength and appears fully nude in early scenes that establish an awe for Schwarzenegger's powerful, muscular body, which is clearly shown in long shot only from behind; frontal views are mid-shots from the waist up with one exception in the first film that includes a dimly lit, heavily shadowed long shot, somewhat like that noted in *The Deer Hunter*.

A glance at the surface structure of *In the Realm of the Senses* reveals strong similarities with hard-core pornography, and Oshima has acknowledged watching and being interested in the genre at the time he made the film (Lehman 1980). *In the Realm of the Senses* takes place almost exclusively indoors, as if the external world and its realities were of no consequence. Sex, which begins almost immediately and never stops, appears to be the sole focus of the film's interest. There is no character development to speak of, none of the motivation so carefully developed in the classical cinema to explain the characters' actions. Why, for example, does Kichi suddenly leave his wife to devote himself to seeking nothing but sexual gratification with Sada? What happened in his past to make him the kind of man who would pursue such a maniacally intense sexual relationship? One might as well ask similar questions of the telephone repairman or the pizza-delivery boy in a hard-core porn film. Nevertheless, Oshima marks Sada in a manner that accounts for her excessive sexuality. When Kichi remarks, "You're ready all the time," she responds, "But I'm not sick. I was worried so I went to see the doctor. He said that I was only hypersensitive." Finally, once Kichi and Sada are together, they do virtually nothing other than have sex, leading to a pattern of repetition and variation reminiscent of the hard-core porn film. The spectator awaits the inevitable "getting down to business" that comprises almost every scene typical of the genre.

Male sexuality lies at the center of the porn genre. Everything turns on affirming and satisfying male desires, and the hard-core scene typically ends immediately after the visual proof that this has occurred. Women's pleasure becomes merely a sign of their dependence on the phallus. The shots of women's faces as they receive pleasure affirm the sexuality of the men who give it to them. Women's pleasure thus becomes fetishized, not valued. Women frequently express their desire to have the man ejaculate on them so that the woman's pleasure apparently coincides exactly with the man's. For example, in *Charmed and Dangerous* (1987), a woman tells the man she is having sex with, "I want you to come all over me—my face, my lips, my tits, my pussy." Similarly, during the third sequence in the compilation film *A Taste of the Best* (1988), in the midst of intercourse the woman says, "I want you to pull out and bring it right here [indicates her breasts]. I want to jerk you off and watch you just come all over my tits. When you come all over me, I'm gonna lick your come of my tits like that. Huh? Yeah? You want to pull it out and give it to me? I want to see that cock shoot all over my nipples." In both films, each scene ends with the man ejaculating on the woman. Sometimes the structure is intensified, as when two women are involved. In *Torrid House* (1988), for example, the first scene climaxes (as usual, in both senses of the word) as one woman looks on, expressing her excitement and satisfaction as the man ejaculates on the other woman's buttocks and affirming the visible moment of the male's pleasure as her own pleasure, even though he is not even touching her! Similarly, in *Outrageous Foreplay* (1987) two women articulate their desire to see the male ejaculate and, watching him do so, the fulfillment it gives them. This common structure is an extreme instance of the way in which hard-core not only tells men that they are needed to make women feel good, but even goes so far as to tell them that male pleasure is so fully the standard of female desire that women want only to see his fulfillment.

The common occurrence of a lesbian scene in heterosexual pornographic films can best be understood in this context: The scenes fetishize at least two women's bodies for male spectator pleasure; sometimes (though as Prince reminds us, not nearly so often as is commonly thought) the women use a dildo, which is a reminder of and substitute for the absent penis. More important, these scenes are frequently presented as preludes to "the real thing," as in *Behind the Green Door* (1972), or as brief asides in predominantly heterosexual films, as in *The Wild Brat* (1988). In the first, Marilyn Chambers, after being abducted and forced onto a stage of a private club for a sexual performance, has "lesbian" sex, then a man dramatically enters and takes over. In *The Wild Brat*, a woman begins to make love to a man who falls asleep, and she then becomes involved in a lesbian scene. This scene is clearly marked as a replacement or substitute for the heterosexual scene and functions so that men can look on with pleasure as the women make love. The men who watch are diegetic equivalents of the male spectators of the film, and this doubling emphasizes the way in which "lesbianism" in hard-core is a spectacle for male heterosexual desire.

The soundtrack also contributes to this centering of male sexuality. As women desire the visibility of male ejaculation, they frequently express their desire for large penises—a statement of their dependence on the phallus for their pleasure—and they are frequently heard moaning with pleasure. These moans are the sound equivalent of the visual structures fetishizing the looks of pleasure on their faces, and both sight and sound affirm the phallus as the sole source of that pleasure. Sometimes the dialogue makes these connections explicit, as, for example, in *Toys 4 Us* (1987) in a scene where we see a woman and hear her say, "Wouldn't I love that big cock right between my tits [groans]. Oh, that cock looks good [groans]. It's turning me on." We then see her reach down and run her hands over a centerfold picture of a huge penis. She then masturbates with a dildo. Finally, a man appears, and she has sex with him. The progression of this scene is a remarkable condensation and summary of how these features of hard-core all combine to emphasize the centrality of the large penis–phallus and male sexuality.

I have used "penis" and "phallus" interchangeably here because hard-core pornography constantly attempts to link the penis to the phallus, a visual version of what Jane Gallop calls the pleonasm of the phallic penis (1982). The hard-core porn film depends on well-endowed male stars; this reliance is so pervasive that Linda Williams remarks on an exception in *Insatiable* (1980): "The delivery boy, for example, has no special desirability; even his penis is of ordinary length, a feature that is itself extraordinary in the genre" (1989, 175). I would qualify this observation for two reasons. First, the boy is presented as a totally comic figure. He is so flustered and comically incompetent that he does little more than look stupidly enthralled as Marilyn Chambers performs fellatio. He remains totally passive throughout the sequence, which ends after the oral sex; he never attempts to satisfy her, nor does she ever appear to get aroused during the encounter. Second, this comically unattractive character is named Goldberg, and his characterization is stereotypically anti-Semitic; he even fears retribution from his father for this dalliance. Thus the apparent exception proves the rule about penis size, since the "ordinary" man is comically portrayed as a sexually incompetent Jew. Something similar occurs in *Mary! Mary!* (1977); we see a man with a small, ordinary penis, and one of the two women who have sex with him mentions his size. He appears in only one scene, and is presented as comically inept because he is gay. These departures from the usual emphasis on large penises in porn films are simply the other side of the coin; they link smaller penises to Jews and gays and to comic ineptness. What would be truly extraordinary would be to characterize either of those men as sexually desirable and competent.

As I previously observed, penises in pornographic films are frequently shown erect or partially erect. In none of the heterosexual sequences of *Doubletake* (1988), for example, do we see the man's penis when he is taking off his clothes because the moment is either elided or because of the camera position or because the position of the woman blocks the view. If a man is shown unerect when he undresses, rather than dwell on this, the films usually show the woman arousing him immediately. This structure may even contrast the briefly seen flaccid penis with the significantly larger erect penis, which then occupies the remaining time of the scene. The genre cannot tolerate a small, unerect penis because the sight of the organ must convey the symbolic weight of the phallus. Again, the exceptions prove the rule. John C. Holmes (a.k.a. Johnny Wadd) who is notoriously large, even by porn standards, is frequently shown unerect because his flaccid penis is larger than many erect penises. This is true in his appearance in the final scene of *Insatiable* (1980). After Marilyn Chambers has had sex with a number of men, the attention shifts to a man who slowly appears out of the darkness as the framing and lighting emphasize what Williams characterizes as a "long and lanky penis" (1990, 179). We are obviously meant to be in awe of this penis even when it is flaccid. It is no coincidence that Holmes appears as the last man in the narrative, which is structured around the woman's insatiable desire of the title; if any man can satisfy her, the assumption is, he is the one.

In addition to being a defining feature of pornographic iconography, large penises figure in the narrative structure of porn films such as *Insatiable* in a manner that further highlights their significance. In *Deep Throat* (1972), for example, the central female character requires a man with an unusually large penis to satisfy her, since her clitoris is located deep within her throat. She meets such a man at the end of the film. In *The Resurrection of Eve* (1973), at the end of the film Marilyn Chambers leaves her husband for a larger, more virile black man. It is thus not just the organ that the women in porn films need for their fulfillment but its symbolic dimension. The symbolic dimension involves a complex association of strength, power, and size. The always-big penis is a requirement of a genre which represents the penis as the phallus.

Despite its surface similarity to the hard-core pornography film, Oshima's *In the Realm of the Senses* marks a profound departure from the genre in its representation of male sexuality and the male body. It does not, however, simply avoid or bypass phallic sexuality. In terms of casting and construction of both the visual image and the soundtrack, the film nearly always avoids the male-centered structures of the hard-core film. During most of the sex scenes, the erect penis is deemphasized. In fact, *In the Realm of the Senses* contains none of the hard-core porn genre's standard close-ups of the penis thrusting in and out of the vagina; what in industry terminology, Williams notes, is called the "meat shot" (1989). It does contain a number of shots of Kichi's unerect penis. There is no anxiety evident in any of these scenes, no attempt to make the penis "impressive." Oshima did not cast the part with the usual hard-core emphasis on an actor with a large penis nor does he show Kichi partially aroused. In one shot (19), Kichi is seen lying still on his back, his unerect penis visible in the lower foreground of the frame. In a variation of that shot, we see him lying in a reverse position with his head in the foreground (20). We never hear Sada or any other women articulate their need for or awe of big penises.

In one scene Oshima emphasizes a different view of the penis than that commonly found in hard-core. We see several close-ups of the unerect penis of an old man who is first taunted in the street by women and a child after the child exposes him and who then tries to have sex with one of the women but, due to impotence, fails. In addition to being "impressive," penises in

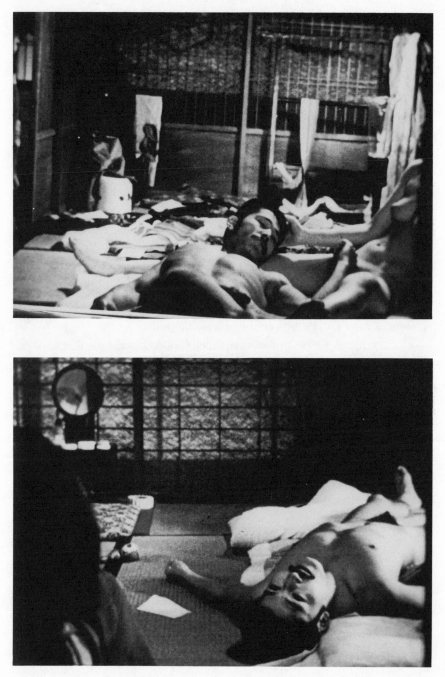

19

20

hard-core are always erect or become so in moments (this is even true of the gay man in *Mary! Mary!*). The close-up of the old man's flaccid penis after the woman has tried to arouse him is far removed from the spectacle of the phallicly powerful penis that dominates hard-core.

The film also lacks shots of the man ejaculating on the face or body of the woman, what Williams notes the pornographic industry terms the "money shot" (1989). After the first time Sada fellates Kichi, we see semen coming out of the corner of her mouth, and although the image may authenticate that actual sex rather than simulated sex has taken place (a crucial distinction in hard-core), it does not function to specularize male ejaculation. Although the most notorious instance of this sort of specularization occurs in an extended, close-up, slow-motion sequence in *Behind the Green Door* (1972), nearly all the sex scenes involving males in hard-core end with the man visibly ejaculating on the woman's face or body. I have checked this generalization over a large number of films, and this one is sound. In many films there are no exceptions (e.g., *Doubletake* [1988], *The Good, the Bad, and the Horny* [1985], *A Taste of the Best* [1988]), and in others, there may be the exception that proves the rule. A film may, for example, end with a brief scene that implies, like the conventional fade-out, that the sex continues after what we see ends (e.g., *Behind the Green Door*). Or in another variation, a comic moment may end the scene or the film. *Bringing Up Brat* (1987), for example, ends when, after a typically structured sex scene, the man falls into a swimming pool just as he is about to climax.

I have seen no hard-core features from this time period that do not prominently feature both the meat shot and the money shot. Prince's convincing data overturn many such generalizations but do not address either of these shots, which Williams has shown lie at the center of the iconography of the hard-core feature and reveal its phallocentric nature. Their absence, therefore, is symptomatic of the profound ways in which *In the Realm of the Senses* differs from the standard Western hard-core feature.

In the Realm of the Senses sounds different as well as looks different from the hard-core feature. We do not hear the usual moaning and groaning of women in ecstasy. Indeed, many of the moans in hard-core porn films are obviously dubbed in, a practice that intensifies them by exaggerating their frequency and loudness. Often when the sex scenes begin, the soundtrack shifts noticeably from the live or "realistically" dubbed sound of conversation and sounds present in the setting to a poorly synchronized mix of background music and moaning, and the sound editing further structures these moans to build with the visuals in a pattern geared to male sexual climax. The jarring quality of the sound shift is yet another difference between hard-core porn and the classical cinema. As with several visual structures (e.g., the actors looking directly into the camera and addressing the spectator), pornography sometimes abandons the invisible style of classical realism to intensify eroticism, the erotic payoff overriding the usual need to maintain believability. In contrast to the typical pornographic film, Sada's moans sound like an expression of her satisfaction, since they are not part of an orchestrated sound mix aimed at building the male spectator's pleasure. Instead, they come from within the diegesis as signs of the pleasure she is experiencing.

Because the narrative of *In the Realm of the Senses* explicitly raises the question of female sexual pleasure, the film replaces the usual pornographic visual emphasis on the impressive penis with a temporal structure that emphasizes the frequency and duration of Sada's desires. These concerns emerge repeatedly in the film's repetitive narrative structure and in Sada's words. Much of the sexual activity that we see in the film is represented as being done for Sada's pleasure. At several points, she talks of the pleasure she gets from Kichi's penis, though that talk is never couched in the characteristic tone or terminology of the porn film. This may relate to Audie Bock's claim that *In the Realm of the Senses* has "dialogue that appeals strongly to women" (1978, 337). The way in which the narrative is structured around Sada's pleasure has both similarities and differences with Western hard-core of the period. Williams has shown that women's pleasure emerged as a problem that had to be acknowledged and addressed by male filmmakers and their male audiences in hardcore during the 1970s, but I would argue that the solutions to the problem are formed within the overwhelmingly male-dominated structures. Hard-core pornography does have an emphasis, for example, on how long erections last, but it serves merely to prolong the visual spectacle and confer remarkable phallic power on the men. Oshima does not simply avoid the usual pornographic emphasis on the visual spectacle of male sexuality; he abandons it for a temporal dimension that speaks to a female desire about which pornography cares nothing.

As the film progresses, Kichi invites Sada to castrate and kill him if it will make her happy. Later, he tells her that he has heard that being slowly strangled increases sexual pleasure; she begins a series of such strangulations, but they are for her pleasure, not his, as an exchange between them makes clear. "Do you really want me to?" Sada asks. "No. But if it pleases you, yes," Kichi responds. Sada moans with pleasure during the ensuing act. "My body is yours. Do as you like," Kichi tells Sada after he has earlier stopped her when his pain was too great. "At least you should be happy," he adds. "Even if I kill you?" she responds. "Then I'm going to kill you. I'm going to kill you. It's extraordinary . . . it's marvelous. I'm going to kill you . . . I'm killing you." As soon as they have finished, Kichi asks, "Was it good?" His final strangulation takes place not because he wants to experience an intense orgasm as he dies but because she wants to kill him just as earlier she wanted to feel him in her as she slowly strangled him.

Sada's desire, however, centers almost exclusively on Kichi's penis. She can never get enough of it, even talking about it as if it were a being separate from Kichi. In the end that logic is carried to its extreme when, after strangling him to death, she cuts off his penis and testicles. In the final voice-over narration, we are told that she wandered around Tokyo for four days with her lover's genitals and that "when arrested Sada was resplendent with happiness." As I have summarized it thus far, *In the Realm of the Senses* decenters the usual phallic male sexuality that dominates the conventional pornographic film. The male in action and representation is not a powerful, impressive machine of phallic sexuality but an appealing body that is literally offered up to the woman for her pleasure.

The acting as well as the casting in *In the Realm of the Senses* differs from the usual porn film in which one constantly feels that one is watching performers, not characters. Although Williams has shown that there is a thematic structuring process at work, hard-core's flimsy narrative pretexts for sex combined with the lack of traditional character development foregrounds sex as performance for the pleasure of the spectating audience. The spectator watches Jamie Gillis, for example, rather than any fictionalized character Gillis might be playing in that particular film. This structure encourages an awe of the sexual performance of the male actor: how long he can last, and how hard and aggressively he can thrust. This has nothing to do with genuine concern for the woman's pleasure but is another sign of the man's power. In *In the Realm of the Senses*, however, we feel that we are watching the characters Kichi and Sada. Neither Kichi's sexual activities nor his body are primarily presented to impress us. Although Oshima does not present characters fully in the psychological realist tradition of the classical cinema, neither does he present sexual athletes who perform for us in the porn tradition. Instead, he presents actors who create characters that give each other pleasure in a way that takes precedence over the spectator's voyeuristic pleasure.

Stephen Heath has perceptively pointed out that much of *In the Realm of the Senses* is structured around female looks (1977). We constantly see women looking at sexual activity, and on several occasions what we then see is relayed through their gazes. Near the beginning of the film, two women watch through a cracked door as Kichi and his wife make love. The first time Sada and Kichi make love at an inn, a woman similarly watches through a cracked door. When Kichi and Sada make love outside in a courtyard, a woman scrubbing the floor watches them. Later, a serving woman watches in their room as they have sex, and on another occasion, a woman plays a musical instrument while watching them. Sada then watches while Kichi has sex with the musician. These scenes, of course, reverse the usual pattern of the view of the woman's body relayed through the desiring or controlling look of the man. Unlike Heath, however, I do not think that the structure of those looks creates a serious disruption of the conventional structures of vision, looking, and identification in the classical cinema. It seems to me to foreground the role of women's desire and pleasure in the film, and it helps to break the usual pornographic pretext of using that pleasure simply to affirm male sexuality. The women in this film look and act.

Many of Oshima's images of women watching the sexual act recall the seventeenth- to nineteenth-century Japanese erotic woodblock prints. The influence of these prints on the film has been either underestimated or misunderstood. Noël Burch observes, "The on-screen diegesis consists almost solely of the lover's sex-play. . . . The image is strongly connotative of the late nineteenth-century prints in the ukiyo-e tradition" (1979, 343). Burch's reference is so general that it does not help us understand specifically how Oshima uses the erotic woodblock tradition. Maureen Turim notes that

> the ukiyo-e, the Japanese woodblock, developed a significant genre based on the representation of sexual intercourse. Genitals not only were shown in these prints, they were exaggerated in size so as to dominate the composition, twisting the surrounding space into a surface designed to glorify their acrobatic feats of penetration. (1987, 36)

When the penis is shown in these prints, it is exaggerated in size as in Kunisada's *Koi no Yatso Fugi*, circa 1830–40 (21). *The Phallic Contest*, an anonymous nineteenth-century copy of a twelfth- or thirteenth-century original, shows two men with enormously large erections, one of which is being measured for length. The erection is represented as approximately as large as the man's head and torso. Some woodblock prints combine both the structure of looking and the exaggerated penis. *Frustration* by Utamaro (22), circa

21

22

23

1805, derives its title from the fact that it shows a man with a very large erection preparing to enter a young man from behind. He indicates puzzlement as to how something so large can penetrate an opening so small. In Kunimaro's *Ikuyo no Yumekoi no Tsurezuse* (23), in a virtually identical structure, someone (it could be a man or a woman) looks directly at the centered spectacle.

Turim concludes: "We can see in Oshima's mise-en-scène and his use of close-ups on genitals a filmic practice somewhat equivalent to the turned and exaggerated perspective on sexual anatomy in ukiyo-e" (1987, 37). Turim overlooks an important visual structure of the woodblock prints, namely that onlookers, frequently women, watch the central sexual activity (22 and 23).

Oshima seems to me to depart markedly from the woodblock tradition of representing the male body with, as in Western hard-core pornography, exaggeratedly large penises. The woodblocks, as Turim observes, feature views that emphasize the visibility of the penis as it penetrates the woman (21), but this is precisely the view that Oshima denies us. Penetration shots are entirely lacking in *In the Realm of the Senses*. Indeed, through most of the sexual scenes not only is the penis not emphasized but we do not even see it. Nor, contrary to Turim's claim, does the film stress close-ups of genitals. Ironically, her argument about exaggerated size, emphasis on penetration, and genital close-ups would much more accurately describe the contemporary Western hard-core pornographic film. The prints, like those porn films, represent an extremely phallic male sexuality, and the look of the woman in the prints poses no threat. She does not appear as someone who will enter the action and assert her desire; rather, she affirms the centrality of the phallic spectacle she watches. Thus Oshima uses the visual structure of the prints to create a different sexual ideology from that they possess themselves. He denies the exaggerated phallic spectacle of the male body and, in the character of Sada, changes the position of the woman who looks; she changes from one who admires, but does not threaten the sexual events, to one who threatens by acting on her desires.

Oshima himself finds historical significance in the fact that the film is based on an actual incident that occurred in 1936 (Polan 1985, 111). In one memorable shot, the absent historical context erupts as Kichi passes columns of marching troops. To die for his country is a man's proper patriarchal position; to die for a woman's pleasure threatens that patriarchy. There is, of course, another historical context: Japan in 1976. Oshima's turning back to the Japan of the 1930s must be understood within the postwar Japanese context. Western influence helped create a climate of shifting roles for women. At the time, Oshima hosted a very popular Japanese television program for women in which he gave advice on family problems. He has acknowledged that listening to contemporary women articulate their frustrations and problems prompted him to make *In the Realm of the Senses* (Bock 1987, 330).

While Oshima's account of why he made the film might be true, it does not go far enough. Oshima has remarked that Sada's castration of Kichi fulfills a fantasy of Japanese men that a woman could be so intense about them that she would act as Sada does (Lehman 1980, 58). His conception may at first seem to be the opposite of the common Western male response of horror at the sight of the woman cutting off the penis. And to offer it as an image of desire is far removed from the Western male dread of castration, where the image of the woman with a knife conjures up visions of the "castrating bitch."

Oshima's comment presents castration as a male desire. Although Sada castrates Kichi apparently to fulfill her desires, her desires are doubly in the service of men. Kichi first makes the offer to her that she may strangle him; Sada is, in some sense, following not only Kichi's suggestion but also giving expression to Oshima's desires when she acts. This castration fantasy wherein Oshima refers to the penis as a "keepsake" may not be as uniquely Japanese as he presumes (Lehman 1980, 58). In 1973, Robert Mel-

24

ville described Fuseli's 1785 wash drawing *My Lady Betty* (24), which shows a woman holding a severed, erect penis, in similar ways:

> The male sexual parts in the girl's hand have not been conventionalized into a symbolic device. They are drawn naturalistically; they look as alive and fresh as if they were still between a man's legs, and they undoubtedly symbolize her role as receiver (the penis is still in erection), but they are not bloodstained, and there is nothing in the treatment to suggest that someone has been castrated. Nor is there anything in the atmosphere of the drawing to suggest that the girl is a harpy or a succubus. She delights in intercourse; it is the genitals in good working order that matter to her, not the man's identity, and Fuseli has depicted her as a day-dreaming voluptuary. What she holds is not a sinister trophy but a symbol of sexual pleasure. If, as I think, Fuseli was in love with the act of love, *he has bestowed on this girl his own sexuality*. In view of the nature of the gift, I wish that Fuseli could have given it *greater visual impact. It could have been larger, a bit out of scale*. (1973, 269; emphasis added)

Melville unwittingly betrays himself in this reading of the drawing by expressing the desire that the penis be larger than it is, a desire that points to the need for the symbolic to reinstate itself over the literal. Although Melville recognizes the male structure that wants the woman to have this "gift" of the man's sexuality, he uncritically aligns himself with the pornographic concept of visual impact I have analyzed. Melville's nervousness is not unfounded. Betty holds a very ordinary-looking erect penis. In fact, her hand provides a scale that shows that were she to wrap her fingers around it, it would disappear from sight—the ultimate dread horror against which hardcore pornography (and much "serious" art that represents the penis) protects itself well.

But if Melville sounds contradictory in his praise and regret at how Fuseli has represented the penis, Oshima also has his moment of contradiction. In one scene in *In the Realm of the Senses*, Oshima breaks with his pattern of avoiding representing the penis as an impressive spectacle. It is, no doubt, not coincidental that this occurs during the graphic castration. In a long shot, we see Kichi's body after Sada has strangled him. His unerect penis is clearly visible (25). We then see a close-up of Sada as her knife actually cuts through the penis followed by a close-up of the severed penis (26), which bears little resemblance to the one we have just seen in the long shot; it is large and straight, almost as if erect.

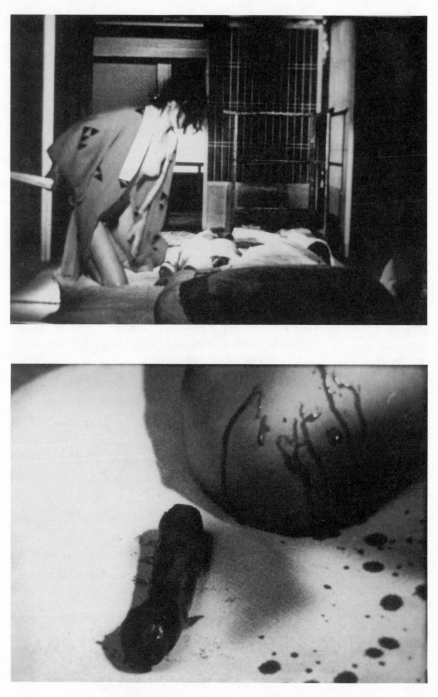

25

26

Is this a simple continuity error? Moments of intense contradiction in cinema are sometimes accompanied by continuity errors, as if the film acknowledges the gap between what it wants to show and what it should show. Representation is troubled for a brief moment. As we saw in the analysis of *Scarlet Street* in Chapter 5, such moments may have profound consequences for a study of gender ideology. The hurried action wherein Chris inexplicably knocks out Johnny asks us to accept this narrative development without careful scrutiny. Everything about the castration scene in *In the Realm of the Senses* similarly asks us not to scrutinize it too carefully. Most important, of course, is the tradition to which I referred in Chapter 1, wherein we are critically inclined microscopically to investigate every possible structure of fetishism of women's bodies (from details of figure type to hairstyle) and fashions (from lingerie to high-heeled shoes), but have no tradition for talking about the representation of the penis. Indeed, many commentators who really want to refer to the penis use the word "phallus," and they do so out of decorum rather than as a result of any significant terminological confusion between the organ and the psychoanalytic symbolic concept. We are even likely to respond to the consideration of how Oshima has represented the penis in the castration scene in *In the Realm of the Senses* by thinking, "That's something one doesn't talk about." No doubt Oshima would agree. To notice such a detail as a mismatch in the appearance of the penis in the scene might appear morbidly inappropriate. Yet it is precisely here that the ideological tension of the film cannot adequately mask itself. The scene is rich in the same sorts of gender implications I have suggested for the analogous scene in *Scarlet Street*. Oshima visually grants what Melville verbally wishes for in the Fuseli drawing. The gift is impressive. Kichi has died so that Sada may possess his penis. Oshima, perhaps unconsciously, grants the moment an element of centered visual spectacle unlike any he gave Kichi in life. But the penis is larger not just in terms of scale. In order to grant the keepsake the status he wants it to have, Oshima has to violate what we have seen throughout the film, including only moments before.

We could imagine an alternative thematic reading of the scene. Perhaps Oshima is suggesting that Sada has confused the literal and the symbolic, the penis and the phallus. After cutting it off, she thinks she possesses what she needs to gratify her desire and thus she is in ecstasy when caught by the police. Such a reading would shift the confusion from Oshima to Sada and grant the filmmaker remarkable control of and insight into the representation of the male body. But there is no indication in the film that we are seeing

Sada's point of view of the severed penis. There are no formal markers that the scene is a fantasy or distortion of any kind, such as there are in two other fantasy scenes in the film. Suddenly to read the castration scene as representing Sada's confusion is to miss Oshima's confusion.

Nor can we simply dismiss the scene as owing to medical confusion or sexual mythology. The erection a man gets on being hanged (and with which our culture is fascinated both pornographically and otherwise) comes from the shock to the nervous system when the neck is broken. Slow, near-strangulation is another matter, since it creates no such shock. The scenes where we see Sada almost strangling Kichi before releasing him make no sense if read as physiological explanations of giving him an exceptionally hard erection, though of course they make a great deal of sense psychologically. According to recent news reports, however, such cultural confusion does exist. Many cases of what had been thought of as teenage suicides are in actuality those of boys who have accidentally killed themselves while trying to experience intense sexual pleasure by almost strangling themselves to death by hanging. Some of the press accounts even attribute part of the misunderstanding to such films as *In the Realm of the Senses*.

A close examination of this scene shows that Oshima was not prey to any such myths, since the long shot of Kichi's body shows his penis limp. If Oshima wanted to suggest that Sada's strangulation gave Kichi the erection, he would have shown the erect penis prior to her cutting it off. And there is no cultural myth I know of that tells us that if a dead man's penis is cut off, it will become larger or erect. Either Oshima consciously chose to grant the penis a privileged visual emphasis, or he did not notice the representation of the penis. The distinction is not important for my purposes because such a neglect of detail would be consistent with my argument about sexual ideology. Such a seemingly insignificant detail is precisely where we should expect to find ideology speaking forcefully.

Even in the visual register, then, *In the Realm of the Senses* has this profoundly contradictory moment. It is as if the traditional Japanese and contemporary American visual spectacle associated with the penis, so carefully avoided by Oshima, returns with a vengeance at a critical moment of sexual tension. At one level, Melville's "gift" and Oshima's "keepsake" sound oddly similar, and ultimately *In the Realm of the Senses* remains caught in a contradictory critique of the phallus. Could a man's desire that a woman would want his penis as a keepsake lie entirely outside a phallocentric order?

In the Realm of the Senses raises broader issues about the relationship between East and West regarding the sexual representation of the male body. In his influential study *The History of Sexuality*, Michel Foucault has characterized two different historical conceptions of sexuality (1978). In the "*ars erotica*" tradition (which includes China, Japan, and India), the "truth" of sexuality comes from the practicing and experiencing of its pleasures. The secret of the art of this pleasure is the province of a master, who imparts it to a disciple. Contemporary Western civilization is the only one to practice "*scientia sexualis*," wherein the truth of sex is linked to knowledge and power. This tradition gives rise to the confession as opposed to the art of initiation. The modern sexology discussed in Chapter 7 is a medical discourse within this power–knowledge quest for the "truth" of sexuality. Foucault's argument is compelling and has been applied with great insight and skill by Williams in her analysis of hard-core. The danger in these kinds of classifications is that we will see only the differences and distinctions and overlook the commonalities. I am struck by the fact that most of the *ars erotica* cultures place an extraordinary emphasis on penis size, in a manner that is strikingly similar to that found within our *scientia sexualis*. I am not suggesting that big penises mean the same thing within both traditions, but that they are equally important. The woodblocks analyzed earlier are evidence of this in Japan, and next I turn briefly to an example from India and one from China.

The *Kama Sutra* of Vatsayana originally appeared in ancient India, and since Sir Richard Burton and F. F. Arbuthnot first published it privately in English translation in 1883, it has circulated widely in the West. Significantly, the section on sexual union begins with a discussion of the importance of size. Men are divided into categories of hare, bull, and horse, depending on the size of their penis; women are divided into deer, mare, and elephant, depending on the depth of their vagina. These divisions allow for nine kinds of union, three of which are equal and six of which are unequal. In a version of the present-day Western idea of the "perfect fit," equal unions were the most desirable. If the man was bigger than the woman, the resultant forms of union were called "high union" with the woman most remote from his size being the "highest." If the woman was bigger than the man, however, the result was "low union" with the man most removed from her size referred to as the "lower union": "Amongst all these, equal unions are best, those of a comparative degree, the higher and the lower, are the worst, and the rest are middling, and with them the high are better than the low" (Vatsayana 1982, 94). Though penis size is important in this scheme, bigger is not simply better, as was true with the examples in the last chapter. In this scheme, a hare and a deer are not an inferior match to a horse and an elephant. Penis size is of no great significance in itself, but only in relation to vaginal depth.

No such ambiguity exists in Li Yu's seventeenth-century Chinese novel *The Carnal Prayer Mat*. It tells the story of Vesperus, a newly married young man who seeks the truth of sexuality within the *ars erotica* tradition of which Foucault speaks and who introduces his wife to sensual pleasures through illustrated books. Still not satisfied, he goes away in search of erotic fulfillment. The novel places an extraordinary emphasis on penis size, much of which contradicts the *Kama Sutra*'s notion of the perfect fit.

We are told that penises and vaginas differ in length and depth and that a long penis and shallow vagina may lead to pain rather than pleasure for the woman, whereas if the vagina is deep and the penis only a little short, the woman will receive no pleasure. The latter situation can be corrected by bolstering the hips with pillows, but nothing can change thickness: "These facts explain why a short penis can be treated but not a thin one; why it is better to be short and thick than long and thin; and why the adept, in restructuring Vesperus's penis, had tried to make it thicker but not longer" (Yu 1990, 152). Women in the novel, however, are always noticing, desiring, and responding to large penises. Despite the many adventures that make reference to size, there are no exceptions to this. How, then, does size become so central to the novel?

Vesperus relies on the Knave, a notoriously successful thief and seducer who becomes his companion and helps him in his sexual quests. As he prepares Vesperus for seducing two married women who lack sexual desire, Vesperus suggests that they may lack desire in part because their husbands' penises are so small, but the Knave assures him that they are not. Vesperus smugly states that his own endowment is more than adequate. When the Knave persuades Vesperus to show his penis, Vesperus interprets the Knave's stunned expression as awe and boasts that he is even more spectacular when erect. Finally, the Knave breaks out in laughter, saying that he has inspected a few thousand penises, that Vesperus's is the smallest, that the women's husbands are two to three times as big, and that Vesperus can never seduce other men's wives.

Devastated, Vesperus, comparing himself to others at every opportunity, concludes that he is smaller and loses his sexual desire. Like Clint in *The Nothing Man* and Chris in *Scarlet Street*, he particularly fears laughter: "At least he [the Knave] is a man! I felt like hiding my face in shame when he laughed at me, but think how I'd have felt if I'd been having sex with a woman" (Yu 1990, 106). As a result, Vesperus determines to give up sex altogether when he comes across a poster that declares:

> A true man from a distant land
> Has come to teach the bedroom art.
> He can take a puny groin
> And turn it into a mighty part. (p. 109)

Clearly, even within *ars erotica* and its concept of the perfect fit, all penises are not equal.

At this point, the *ars erotica* master with knowledge of the secret truth of sexual pleasure becomes a character in the novel and speaks on penis size. A not particularly small penis can be increased by a third with medicines, but a very small one requires an operation to insert part of a dog's penis into the man's. According to the master, after this operation the patient's penis will be several times bigger than before; but during intercourse, like the dog's, it will become several times bigger again. The surgery leads to Vesperus's success as a seducer and lover, and in conquest after conquest, women respond to the size of his penis.

Even though *The Carnal Prayer Mat* involves fantasy, humor, irony, and moralizing, the fact remains that it both gives evidence to the general cultural importance of penis size in the Chinese *ars erotica* tradition and that it does nothing to discredit it. The women in the novel, for example, all are preoccupied with size. Vesperus was able to please his inexperienced wife only because she had no standards of comparison; after he leaves, she reads his books and learns to be dissatisfied. After reading of long and thick penises, she remarks, "My husband's is less than two inches long and two fingers thick" (Yu 1990, 207). Although the outcome is disastrous, the moral suggests not that big penises are not superior but that the quest for more pleasure can ruin the pleasures we already have. In other words, had Vesperus stayed home with his wife, everyone would have been happy because he had "formed" her vagina to fit his small penis and she knew no better for lack of experience. Bigger is indeed better, but the moral issue is whether we should always want more and better or be content with our lot in life.

Yu's novel is of particular interest both for including as a character the master of the *ars erotica* tradition and because it gives remarkable evidence that, as in the contemporary West, penis size was important in that ancient tradition; big penises were assumed to be important for a knowledgeable woman's pleasure. As the Knave says, "While endowment and stamina like yours are all right for keeping your wife on the straight and narrow, they are not enough to sustain any wild ideas about debauching other men's wives and daughters" (Yu 1990, 101). Indeed, as in the West (and the writings of the Marquis de Sade), size is linked to other notions of virility, such as "stamina" (i.e., how long the man can last). Also as in the West, and in Sade's writings, actual measurements are given. The Japanese woodblock print *The Phallic Contest* shows the measuring process taking place, and Yu gives measurements not only for Vesperus but also for the husband of one of the women he wishes to seduce whose penis is described as "over eight inches long and too big to be grasped" (1990, 209). As with France in the eighteenth century, such figures would not have the precise implications they have in the modern world since the impact of the sexology movement, but they do evidence a concern with measurement and size. The comparison in the print *The Phallic Contest*, for example, is not with standard scientific data but with the other men being measured at the event. The winner is chosen based on such measurement. Measurement in the *ars erotica* tradition, and this is true of the *Kama Sutra* and, most of the time, *The Carnal Prayer Mat*, is usually given in terms of finger breadth and spread, rather than precise numerical gradations.

Finally, it is worth noting that modern sexology has at least once addressed the varying cultural and historical representations of the penis in terms of precise measurement. In R. L. Dickinson's landmark *Human Sex Anatomy* (see Chapter 7), a section of a chapter is devoted to "Dimensions in Art" (1949, 76–77). He carefully computes penis size in representations by analyzing the length of the penis in relation to other body parts, such as the thigh, forearm, or foot, and the thickness in relation to the wrist, ankle, calf, or upper forearm. In typical contemporary scientific fashion, Dickinson gives his sample size, then precise data on penis size. He measured representations precisely as his sexology colleagues measured living subjects!

Analyzing fifty-nine samples of Greek representations with erect penises, Dickinson concludes that in twenty-six the penis averages six inches (which he notes is the modern average), in fourteen of those the length was five and a quarter inches (our lower average), in twelve the length averaged seven inches, in seven they averaged eight and a half inches, in two four and one half inches and in two fourteen inches. He includes Japanese erotic woodblock prints by Moronobu, Harunobu, Utamaro, Kunisada, and Karuosai, which illustrated books intended for brides (of the kind Vesperus shows his bride in *The Carnal Prayer Mat*) and apart from a set of "gross extremes," he concludes, "We find in these woodcuts an average length of penis of eight-and-a-quarter inches (21 cm) the range being from seven to ten inches (17.5 to 25 cm) in sixteen samples" (Dickinson 1949, 77). The represented diameters are even comparatively larger than those found in sexological data. Dickinson concludes: "This is doubtless conventionalized humor-esque treatment since we cannot suppose Nippon to exceed Europe by more than double the diameter" (1949, 77).

I have found only one instance where small penises may have been valued over large ones: K. J. Dover has analyzed the representation of penises on Greek vases within the context of his study of homosexuality in ancient Greece. Dover asserts that "it would be surprising if the Greeks had no criteria for the aesthetic-judgment of male genitals, and the visual arts show us what these were" (1978, 125). Dover's assumption is sensible but still remarkable in art historical and critical discourses. To the best of my knowledge, Dover's mature and intelligent treatment of this topic in Greek art is virtually unique. Leo Steinberg's "The Sexuality of Christ in Renaissance Art and Modern Oblivion" makes an extraordinary contribution to our understanding of representations of Christ's genitals in depictions of him as a child and of his crucifixion and death. Although Steinberg's subject illustrates why the representation of the penis was of immense importance, he does not consider the specific issues of the aesthetics of genital representation and their relation to assumptions about sexuality of the type Dover investigates.

Dover finds that the penises of young males in the vase paintings are typically thin and short and cites literary evidence that a small penis was desired along with a good complexion, broad shoulders, and big buttocks. The scrotum in these pictures is of normal size. Yet, Dover notes: "One consideration (by no means cogent physiologically, but artistically interesting) is that the erect penis, as depicted in vase painting, is of normal size, and if it was exceptionally small when flaccid the extent of enlargement on erection is surprising" (1978, 126). In contrast to the desired youths depicted in this fashion, old men and satyrs were depicted as having exaggeratedly large and misshapen penises. Dover interprets the satyrs' penises as powerful weapons and observes that in many combat depictions the human participants' swords, spears, clubs, etc., are visually linked to the penis through their placement in the composition.

Dover concludes that the convention of depicting youthful penises as pointed and horizontal indicates the youths' potential as warriors: "That it should be small sharpened the contrast between the immature male and the adult male; a small penis (especially if the existence of the corona glandis is not betrayed by any undulation in the surface of the penis) is an index of modesty and subordination, an abjuration of sexual initiative or sexual rivalry" (1978, 134). This ideal youthful penis was used to depict men, heroes, and gods as part of a celebration of youthfulness.

In many fundamental ways, then, Greek representation conforms to the usual assumptions about penis size. Small penises were valued by older men within a power disequilibrium—the smallness indicated the youths' subordination and passivity and situated them in relation to women. Moreover, when erect, their penises were not small, and Dover observes that "the smaller the penis, the greater the drama when it becomes erect" (1978, 134). Powerful warriors, in contrast, were celebrated in conventional terms with large, phallic weaponry. In a context such as this, the ideal smallness of the youthful flaccid penis reinforces rather than challenges the size assumptions operative in the many images I have analyzed here.

Foucault is correct in arguing that there are different erotic traditions in ancient China, Japan, and India from those in the modern West, but the stubborn fact remains that, in regards to the penis, the traditions are remarkably similar. There are "nothing men" within both.

CONCLUSION

RUNNING SCARED

From Nagisa Oshima in the last chapter to Roy Orbison in this one. Their differences in culture, media, and artistic temperaments would seem to defy any connection. Oshima, a Japanese avant-garde filmmaker, pushes to extremes the conventions of various styles of filmmaking; his films are frequently obscure and inaccessible to large, general audiences. Roy Orbison was a U.S. musician known primarily for a string of rock 'n' roll Top-40 hits between 1960 and 1964. Top-40 radio was then and remains notorious for its programming inflexibility. Mass commercial appeal is essential. The work of both artists, however, centers on the issues of masculine sexuality and the male body that are central to this book. Orbison's music provides a vehicle for connecting the themes I have been exploring, and one of his biggest hits suggests a fitting title for this study.

The previous chapters analyzed a potentially bewildering variety of texts, but my intention has not been comprehensiveness or inclusiveness. To conclude with Orbison's music helps, I hope, to show the need to continue to cast the net wide in future research on the male body. It should also dispel the tendency to make overly general statements about the monolithic nature of the representation of the male body because pop music in the early 1960s, perhaps as much as any other area of popular culture, has been the object of undiscriminating, sweeping generalizations; for many years, 1960s pop music was seen as little more than the wasteland between the time when Elvis Presley entered the army and the Beatles arrived to save rock 'n' roll. Yet it is precisely during that time that Roy Orbison created a body of work virtually unmatched for its richness and uniqueness in the history of U.S. popular music: His work touches on many of the themes that run through this book, including the polarities of a phallic spectacle of masculine power and its vulnerable, sometimes comic antithesis. The fear and anxiety about the entire masculine project that underlie these polarities are extraordinarily evident and well developed in Orbison's work.

The three years preceding Roy Orbison's death on December 6, 1989, and the years since then have seen the proliferation of a number of popular and critical discourses about this most talented and unusual singer–songwriter. Some of these discourses inflect previous ones in new ways and others introduce entirely new elements into the mix. Two books on Orbison have already appeared (*Only the Lonely: Roy Orbison's Life and Legacy* by Alan Clayson and *Dark Star: The Tragic Life Story of Roy Orbison* by Ellis Amburn) and a third is being written by Orbison's widow Barbara; three movies have been titled after his songs, which are also used on their soundtracks (the 1990 made-for-TV movie *Blue Bayou*; the 1990 box-office smash *Pretty Woman*; and the 1991 film *Only the Lonely*); two films about Orbison are in various stages of pre-production (a documentary and a theatrical feature to be produced by Warner Bros. and Home Box Office); and an all-star concert tribute was held in Los Angeles in February 1990 and cablecast later that year on Showtime. I briefly survey these things because they are related to and intersect with another discourse I wish to add to the mix: a discourse on masculinity and the male body in Orbison's music, star persona, and performance style.

After all of Orbison's hits had been written and recorded, a series of events occurred and were constructed into a discourse of tragedy that dominated Orbison's life story in the media and among the general public. The 1966 death of his first wife, Claudette, in a motorcycle accident, which occurred as she rode by Orbison's side, and the death of two of his three children in a fire in 1968 that destroyed his Nashville home were the events on which this discourse was built, and his emergency triple bypass heart surgery in

1978 quickly became part of it. Articles on the singer at the time of his death showed how extreme his image came to be. *People* magazine ran a front cover headline "The Haunted Life of Rock Legend Roy Orbison," and the tabloid *The Star* declared his death the final tragedy of a tragic life.

Recent years have also seen Orbison emerge as perhaps the most admired musician's musician in the history of rock 'n' roll. Shortly before Elvis Presley's death, he called Orbison the greatest singer in the world. As with nearly all these discourses, this one is not entirely new, though it is unprecedented in scope. This homage probably can be dated from Bruce Springsteen's 1975 reference to Orbison in "Thunder Road" on the "Born to Run" album and certainly culminated with the much celebrated and highly publicized 1988 Cinemax special *Roy Orbison and Friends: A Black and White Night* in which Springsteen, Elvis Costello, Tom Waits, and numerous other stars played and sang back-up for Orbison. The February 24, 1990, tribute concert, however, may well have been the culmination of this phenomenon when Bonnie Raitt, Emmylou Harris, k. d. lang, NRBQ, Stray Cats, Levon Helm, the Talking Heads (minus David Byrne and redubbed the Shrunken Heads), Larry Gatlin, Dwight Yoakum, Ricky Skaggs, John Fogerty, Harry Dean Stanton, Gary Busey, Patrick Swayze, Booker T. Jones, and Was (Not Was), among others, all performed versions of Orbison's songs.

His becoming a member of the Traveling Wilburys, along with Bob Dylan, George Harrison, Tom Petty, and Jeff Lynne, was related to this aspect of Orbison's career, as was his 1986 recording of *The Class of 55* with Johnny Cash, Jerry Lee Lewis, and Carl Perkins. Most critics, as well as the public, were totally surprised by this outpouring of admiration for Orbison's music by fellow musicians because his work had been largely ignored and forgotten over the past twenty-five years, and Orbison had never been critically acclaimed in the way that a Bob Dylan or a George Harrison had been even during his four-year period of commercial success (1960 to 1964).

In addition to the musicians who performed and recorded with Orbison in his final years, many others—such as Bryan Ferry, David Bowie, and Neil Young—have acknowledged their respect for him. This leads me to another related discourse, which I term the discourse of hyperbole. Musicians speak about Orbison in the kind of excessive language usually reserved for fans talking about musicians. Bono, the lead singer for U2, remarked of Orbison, "He was at the time of his death the finest white pop singer on the planet" (Zimmerman 1968, 2D). Emmylou Harris, who had years earlier claimed that she never wanted to sell her house after Orbison had sung in it, called him "one of the greatest singers that ever lived" (Zimmerman 1968, 1D). When asked what it was like being the opening act for Orbison, Chris Isaak remarked, "It's like doing card tricks before the second coming" (Holden 1991). Emerging from the *Black and White Night* concert, Patrick Swayze said, "I saw God and the Boss [Bruce Springsteen] on the same night" ("The Boss Is Just One of the Guys . . . 1987, 45).

This last remark points to what we can call, in the loose sense of the word, a religious discourse around Orbison. When he died, Billy Joel said, "He had the voice of an angel" and rock critic Dave Marsh said of the *Mystery Girl* album, "Roy sings like a god across the whole record" (1989a, 1). In a related vein, Springsteen said he had the ability "to sound like he'd dropped in from another planet." Near the end of his life, Orbison himself contributed to this discourse by repeatedly telling interviewers that his writing and singing were a direct gift from God and that he could not personally take credit for his accomplishments; God spoke through him. He also remarked that he often felt he was not long for this world; he was merely passing through. Though he did not bother to say where he came from or where he was going, such talk certainly combined with Springsteen's "visitor from another planet" imagery and the religious imagery to give Orbison a quality of otherworldliness.

Although Orbison received little critical attention during his lifetime, Dave Marsh's writing was a notable exception. His 1987 article on Orbison's music, occasioned by the release of "In Dreams: The Greatest Hits," hailed Orbison as one of the greatest rock singers of all time, a sentiment Marsh repeated when Orbison died and he called him "more than just the owner of the greatest white pop voice in the past 30 years" (1989b, 28). Marsh's comments in many ways parallel those of the auteurist film critics. He claims that Orbison created a personal and interconnected world in his songs: "These songs define a world unto themselves more completely than any other body of work in pop music" (1987, 7). Indeed, in a gesture reminiscent of Robin Wood and Peter Wollen in their respective analyses of the films of Howard Hawks, Marsh argues that Orbison's songs can be divided into two categories, dream songs and songs of loneliness. And as with the Hawks comedies and action films, Marsh argues that a complex relationship exists between them; the unbearable pain and isolation expressed in the songs of loneliness require an outlet in the world of dreaming, but the combination is a dangerous one wherein the lonely dreamer risks losing all connection with the real world. The last time that Orbison performed in New York, the *New York Times* reviewer Peter Watrous contributed to such an auteurist account of Orbison's music by calling him "a genuine American eccentric" and by observing that "he has perfected an odd vision of popular music, one in which eccentricity and imagination beat back all the pressures toward conformity" (Watrous 1988, 48).

In relation to this auteurist discourse, we find a high-art, classical music discourse. The extent of this is clear in David Gates's *Newsweek* obituary: "Orbison . . . elevated a bastard form of regional music into something approaching art song" (1988, 73). On the occasion of making *A Black and White Night*, Jackson Browne called Orbison's music symphonic and when he died, Bob Dylan simply said, "Roy was an opera singer. He had the greatest voice." Tom Waits similarly remarked that the songs were like "arias" and that "he was a rockabilly Rigoletto, as important as Caruso in sunglasses and a leather jacket." Songwriter Will Jennings said, "The nearest thing to Roy— there's nothing like it in rock music—the nearest thing is Verdi and Puccini in grand opera." ("Tributes," *Rolling Stone* 1989, 32–33). Toward the end of his career Orbison agreed that there might be some validity to comparisons between himself and what he called "the guys who wrote the concertos."

Finally, in relation to this discourse of the classical musician whose music is artistic, complex, and timeless was the discourse of "The Voice," a term that became a common nickname for Orbison in the world of rock. The Voice, of course, was a reference to the unusual vocal range, power, and nuance of phrasing of Orbison's voice, but one music magazine went to a logical extreme by indicating that, in death, The Voice was all that was left, freed from the body. From this perspective, Orbison's voice always somehow overshadowed the body and was on a trajectory to being severed from the body and soaring away on its own. If his body, as we later see, seemed troubled, unattractive, sickly, and frail, The Voice seemed strong and vital beyond compare in the world of rock.

David Lynch's notorious use of "In Dreams" in *Blue Velvet* (1986) helped initiate a new discourse of sexuality and "darkness" about Roy Orbison's music. Just how new this discourse was can be seen in the way in which Orbison has spoken about it. At first Orbison denied Lynch permission to use "In Dreams" in *Blue Velvet*; as Orbison would affectionately recall several years later, Lynch was "a persistent young man," and he used it anyway. Orbison claimed that he could not understand how such a "pretty song" could be used in this way, though he then took a print of *Blue Velvet* on the road with him and, after repeated viewings, decided it was a brilliant film. Lynch even persisted in his desire to work with Orbison and agreed to do anything to get into a recording session with him for a new version of "In Dreams." Lynch not only became co-producer of the song with Orbison and T-Bone Burnette but also became his friend. Orbison credited Lynch with profoundly revitalizing concert performances of his old songs. Lynch was even present at the tribute concert and came out on stage with Barbara Orbison for the closing group rendition of "Only the Lonely."

Bruce Springsteen's 1987 speech inducting Orbison into the Rock 'n' Roll Hall of Fame brought further public attention to this dark, sexual aspect of Orbison's music. Springsteen remarked of his first concert memory of Orbison, "He came out in dark glasses, a dark suit, and he played some dark music," music Springsteen characterized as the "underside of pop romance," which he liked to listen to "alone and in the dark."

This bizarre side of Orbison's music that Lynch and Springsteen so perceptively grasped is, I argue, part of a pervasive challenge in Orbison's career to many of the norms of dominant early 1960s rock 'n' roll, especially those norms involving masculinity and the male body. Orbison wrote songs that (as Springsteen has also observed) totally departed from the standard verse, chorus, and bridge structure of pop music. They were also difficult, if not impossible, to dance to or to be covered by amateur groups, something that further differentiated them from pop hits of the time. And Orbison sang those songs in a three-octave voice that eerily defied sexual difference as it imperceptibly soared into some of the highest notes in the history of rock 'n' roll. His 1987 duet of "Crying" with k. d. lang chillingly blends the male and female voices so that the listener is not always sure who is singing. Due to lang's boyish appearance and the use of initials rather than a first name, their live performance of this song on Johnny Carson's show even misled some viewers into thinking lang was a male. In performance, Orbison stood motionless, singing song after song without so much as a word to the audience. During his string of hits between 1960 and 1964, Orbison did not hire a publicist and was virtually unrepresented in fan magazines. Even his most successful albums ("Greatest Hits, Vols. 1 and 2") did not include any photos of him. Thus he minimized the spectacle of his body in performance and hid it from public view in the publicity discourse that normally surrounds rock stars. It is important to note that the image of him in the ever-present dark glasses did not achieve any magnitude until after his string of hits. Rather than have an image of mystery or darkness about him, he originally had no image. An early 1960s article in *Life* magazine, which appeared at the height of his popularity, referred to him as "an anonymous celebrity."

But Orbison's body nevertheless became a troubled site of attention. Once again, Springsteen was particularly evocative when he observed that on first meeting Orbison, he felt that he could reach out and put his hand through Orbison's body. Notice how these discourses intertwine. The image of Springsteen passing his hand through Orbison's body is not unrelated to Orbison's reference to himself as someone merely passing through this world. The body was somehow insubstantial, not entirely of this world. At the Roy Orbison tribute concert, Bernie Taupin referred to Orbison as "frail," not an adjective commonly applied to rock stars.

John Belushi's late 1970s "Saturday Night Live" parody of Orbison, however, touched on what became by the 1980s the two most notable aspects of the singer's body: its immobility and the dark glasses. In the first part of the skit, Orbison's wife tries to get his attention by removing his glasses, only to find another pair beneath them. And another and another in an endless regression. The skit ends with a concert performance of "Oh, Pretty Woman." Rigid as a board, Belushi falls over while singing and playing guitar. He never misses a note as band members pick him up, and he finishes the song totally expressionless.

This exaggerated, though perceptive, version of Orbison's appearance is related to his denial of the traditional masculine position in rock 'n' roll. Most rock singers of the period, as typified by Elvis Presley, strutted around the stage, posturing in sexually aggressive and self-confident *macho* style. Something of this dichotomy can be seen in *Hail! Hail! Rock 'n' Roll* (1988), a documentary about Chuck Berry, by comparing Orbison's scenes with those of Jerry Lee Lewis, another early rocker whose performance style was actively sexual. Lewis, with trademark cigar and bourbon in hand, talks in predictably braggadocio fashion about how Chuck Berry won his respect in a fight the two had, but Orbison quietly talks about how Berry's music influenced him as a singer and songwriter. Orbison also contributed to this discourse late in his career by referring to the early 1960s as a time, for example, when men were not supposed to cry. Coming out of his recording session of "Crying" with k. d. lang, he joked that he tried to be macho, but failed. By 1988, this discourse also begins to emerge in the press, as in the earlier cited Watrous *New York Times* review: "Of all the rock-and-roll singers of his generation, Mr. Orbison is the least obsessed with masculinity; the music and his voice and words are unmenacing and complex" (1988, 48).

Orbison's music and performance style might be more accurately described as *most* obsessed with masculinity, though with questioning and departing from its dominant late 1950s and early 1960s manifestation. Watrous is also correct that Orbison's music lacks sexual menace but it is important to distinguish this from Pat Boone's style of blandly watering down rock's sexuality to make it clean and safely middle class. Similarly, Orbison's motionless performance style cannot be reduced to a mere elimination of the usual sexual antics. Orbison's performance, in fact, evokes a fearful paralysis that starkly contrasts with traditional masculine strutting and is thus closely linked to the songs he wrote. This is perhaps most explicit in "Leah," (Roy Orbison, 1962) a dream song wherein the dreamer, diving for pearls for his lost love, suddenly begins to drown: "But something's wrong, I cannot move around / My leg is caught, its pulling me down." The very titles of songs such as "Crying" (Roy Orbison and Joe Melson, 1962) and "Running Scared" (Roy Orbison and Joe Melson, 1961) emphasize the uncharacteristic way in which his music acknowledges male fear and intense emotion. In the latter song, the singer–narrator stands fearfully immobilized by the phallic spectacle of his rival for the girl: "Then all at once he was standing there / So sure of himself, his head in the air." Instead of acting to win the girl by fighting this threat (think of the male persona evoked in "My Boyfriend's Back"), the man passively watches the drama unfold ("You turned around and walked away with me"). "Oh, Pretty Woman" (Roy Orbison and Bill Dees, 1964) originally ended with the woman walking away from the singer–narrator. Orbison agreed to change it when his producer thought it too depressing, but even the happy boy-gets-girl ending reveals total male passivity: "But wait, what do I see / Is she walking back to me?"

Similarly, in "Crying," the mere touch of a former lover's hand starts the man uncontrollably crying. These outbursts of male emotion are not limited to the lyrics in Orbison's songs; they affect the structure of the songs and Orbison's singing style. "It's Over," (Roy Orbison and Bill Dees, 1964) for example, builds to two emotional crescendos in two and a half minutes, the second more excessive than the first. Perhaps the most extreme of all these outbursts occurs in "The Crowd," (Roy Orbison and Joe Melson, 1962) which is, not coincidentally, the most operatic of all Orbison's songs, since the oft-noted operatic qualities of his music are linked to the intense outpouring of male emotion. At a time when other rockers reveled in their active desire for and control of women, and kept other emotions in check, Orbison's music gave vent to feelings so intense that the end of a love affair sounded like the end of the world.

These aspects of male sexuality interact with the various other discourses surrounding Orbison, for if his music is unusual in that area, it is part of a much larger context wherein nearly everything about his music, star persona, and performance style defies generalizations about the rock music of his era. By not creating and circulating sexually desirable images of himself in fan magazines and on record albums, by minimizing the sexual display of his body in performance and hiding behind impenetrable dark glasses, by singing in an eerie high range, and most of all by explicitly writing songs about male anxiety and excessive emotion, Roy Orbison created a significant alternative to the sexual image of traditional male rock stars.

Nearly all of the discourses reveal a sense of difference about Orbison. What I have called the discourses of hyperbole and the musician's musician doubly reveal this. The need to speak about him in such excessive language stems from a sense of difference or uniqueness. "There will never be another singer like Roy Orbison," Bonnie Raitt said at the tribute concert. And David Hinkley wrote: "All singers have someone who sounds like them—except Orbison. No one sounds even a little like Roy Orbison" (1988, D20). But the range and spectrum of the speakers is equally revealing: How could any single musician be hailed by such a startlingly diverse group of other musicians? They range from traditional pop, country and blues, to nearly every form of rock 'n' roll including punk, new wave and new country, as well as current political folk music. Robert Hilburn commented on this aspect of Orbison's music in his *Los Angeles Times* review of the tribute concert, when he noted that "the fact that artists as varied as Emmylou Harris, John Hiatt, Booker T. Jones, Joe Ely, Cindy Bullens, Michael McDonald and members of the Talking Heads can find common ground in the music of a single writer also underscores the richness and range of Orbison's grand musical legacy" (1989, F7). Symptomatically, the few records of his that could be found in stores during the 1970s and for much of the 1980s were in the country and western section, rather than the rock section. He was inducted into the Country Music Hall of Fame long before he was inducted into the Rock 'n' Roll Hall of Fame. He has been called everything from a rockabilly to a blues singer.

Nearly everything about Orbison was different. His concerts during the 1980s, for example, were virtually the same songs performed in the same order with the same arrangements; no concession was made to the fact that these songs were twenty-five years old. He did not "update" them, nor did he present them as nostalgia, as is common among older rock singers. He performed them as classics that did not have to be updated because they were never dated to begin with. From this perspective, an Orbison concert was closer to a classical song recital, for example, than to opera. The music was everything; the stage show, nothing. Instead of surprises and changes, a nuanced appreciation of an established body of work was encouraged. The songs were interconnected through a complex sense of pacing, certain rockers supplying a necessary counterpoint to the ballads, and so on. The audience was as still and quiet as the performer. There is virtually nothing about Orbison's music, star persona, or career that was conventional, including his form of masculinity and sexuality. It is perhaps in part because of the latter that he is so deeply loved now by such artists as k. d. lang and David Lynch. The work of both of these artists challenges comfortable, traditional gender distinctions. Perhaps Orbison, more than anyone else, was surprised to end his career in such company, but it was fitting.

I have detailed elsewhere the complex function that David Lynch gives "In Dreams" in *Blue Velvet* (Lehman 1987). The song, used twice a few minutes apart, appears at a point where the distinction within the film between the dream world and the real world breaks down and at a point where perverse and ambiguous sexuality reigns. Such breakdowns between the dream world and the real world had been explicitly acknowledged in Orbison's music in such songs as "Heartache" (Roy Orbison and Bill Dees, 1968) (which he recorded twice for different labels, first for MGM in 1968 and then for Mercury in 1975), where a desiring, dreaming man cries out, "I reach out to touch you, but you're not there." On his final album, *Mystery Girl* (1989), the song "In the Real World" (Will Jennings and Richard Kerr, 1987) is a late-period reflection on "In Dreams." The perverse, sexual ambiguity, however, was something Orbison had not dealt with explicitly, though he also returned to this on the *Mystery Girl* album. In the title song, "She's a Mystery to Me" (David Evans and Paul Hewson, 1989), a woman with dark eyes leads a man into darkness where a night of ambiguously, intense, and perverse sex is only obliquely described by the provocative line, "Fallen angel cries / Then I just melt away." The song makes clear the implicit association in Orbison's music between the dark side and sexuality.

A streak of masochism runs throughout the dark sexuality of Orbison's songs. It surfaces explicitly in such songs as "Crawling Back" (Roy Orbison and Bill Dees, 1965), where the male persona simultaneously describes the awful, painful things his lover does to him and affirms that, no matter how many times she does them, he will always come crawling back. Many of the songs, however, wallow in the much more generalized pain of loss in a manner so extreme as to imply that their male persona revels in the pleasure of his loneliness and is, in part, responsible for it. Like the men described by Gaylyn Studlar in Josef von Sternberg's films, the male personae in Orbison's songs (which are through the connection with his voice, one man—Orbison himself) seem to prefer never getting the woman or, if they do, losing her. Again, "Careless Heart" (Roy Orbison, Diane Warren, and Albert Hammond, 1989), the last song on *Mystery Girl*, makes this very clear when the male persona, "Alone with my lonely heart," acknowledges that *he* let it all "slip away." At the time of his death, several critics used the cliché that when listening to Orbison's songs of loneliness and lost love, "it never felt so good to hurt so bad." This feeling is in fact borne out by the underlying masochism that emerges over and over by the image of the lonely dreamer in the dark whose pain, as expressed by Orbison's beautiful voice, can only be called exquisite.

But the Orbison persona, when not reveling in the pain of a lost or unrealized love, is sometimes the object of laughter. In "Pantomime" (Roy Orbison and Bill Dees, 1966), an overlooked masterpiece from Orbison's MGM period, he makes the connection explicitly, "I play the lonely joker / I laugh when things aren't funny." This motif can be traced as far back as "The Actress" (Roy Orbison and Joe Melson, 1962), where Orbison sings, "You keep me around, to be your faithful clown / Till someone you can love comes along." Significantly, both songs develop their scenarios of love around theatrical motifs. In the latter, the clown, with full awareness, masochistically pledges his willingness to play the fateful "masquerade" to its very end, when he will be "a fool on parade." As with so many of the motifs in Orbison's work, this one also finds its most explicit expression on the self-consciously late-period *Mystery Girl*. In "The Comedians" (Elvis Costello, 1989), the male persona takes a ride on a ferris wheel with his girl friend only to find himself the victim of a cruel practical joke when she arranges to have the ride stopped, leaving him "dangling" from the top to watch her laughingly walk away with another man. "It's always something cruel that laughter drowns," he laments in a line that applies to the clown–lonely joker image that takes its place alongside the scared man and the masochistic man to complete the three main facets of the male persona in Orbison's music. Fearful, hurt, and humiliated, the male persona in Orbison's work is a far cry from the cocky, self-confident *macho* image associated with so much rock 'n' roll, especially with Orbison's contemporaries.

In "Chicken Hearted" (Bill Justis, 1957), an odd little song that he recorded for Sun Records years before he became famous, Orbison sings of his desire to be a lover, but laments that he does not have any girls, and sings of his desire to be a hero, but laments that he does not have the nerve; he's "chicken hearted." In an unreleased version of the song, he even sings, "I'm scared of my own shadow." That song is the earliest intimation of what was to come—an unusually candid portrait of a man terrified by the conventional notions of masculinity and roles for men that lay at the heart of his culture. Nearly every significant aspect of Orbison's career circles around this problem, and nothing more so than his body and the strange inflections he would give it in various phases of his career. In the late 1980s, *Playboy* magazine did a short piece on a new cultural sensibility, which they dubbed an aesthetic of weirdness. Some of the people included are obvious choices, but alongside the obvious "weirdos" was a picture and mention of Roy Orbison. If Orbison was in any way a pioneer of a "weird" sensibility, it came from the way he enshrouded his frail body in blackness, wrapped his eyes behind ever-present dark glasses, and had the audacity to perform intensely emotional songs of male fear and pain, frequently employing a remarkable falsetto with feminine connotations, and performing as if he himself were paralyzed by the very emotions of which he sung. This was neither party music nor innocent teen music.

Orbison's songs reveal a polarity that underlies all the images I have examined in this book: In "Running Scared," the rival boy friend is described as a powerful spectacle of masculinity—"His head high in the air"; in "The Comedians," the male persona is left "dangling" high in the air, the object of female laughter. Not being able or not wanting to become the proper, powerful phallic male, the male protagonist fears becoming the vulnerable butt of the joke and the object of women's laughter and scorn. Recall the woman who laughs at Chris Cross in *Scarlet Street*, the laughs Clint Brown in *The Nothing Man* imagines others will direct as his body when they discover he does not have a penis, the laughs and contemptuous sneers of the women who tell penis-size jokes in so many recent films, and the laughs of the actual women in *Dick Talk*, who delight in recalling the inadequacies of their lesser-endowed lovers. At the opposite extreme, the shadows of the powerful, phallic male have fallen across the pages of the works analyzed in this book:

the muscular figure of Tarzan swinging through the jungles and making love to Jane, the powerful John T. Chance played by John Wayne in *Rio Bravo*, the muscled and well-endowed models of Mapplethorpe's photographs and the super-hero sex machines from hard-core pornography. Indeed, the polarized representation of men parallels that of women; representations of the mother/the whore and the phallic hero/the vulnerable, laughable failure are profoundly restrictive. At the simplest extremes, we are asked either to be in awe of the powerful spectacle of phallic male sexuality or to feel pity for, be ashamed of, or laugh at its vulnerable, failed opposite. In such a context, men as well as penises are either big or small, powerful or weak, impressive or pathetic.

The pervasive anxiety that underlies the entire spectrum of imaging the male body is, then, not surprising. Fear permeates the works analyzed in this book: The feral-child narratives either fear acknowledging the disturbing reality of male sexuality or simplistically affirm a ludicrously comfortable version of it; the Hawks films fear everything from aging to wounding that can weaken the male body; the war wounds analyzed in the works of Hemingway and Thompson reveal a fear of how the glorious activity of male combat can instantly create the opposite, emasculated men. The fear of not measuring up to a quantifiable notion of masculinity underlying these more symbolic areas achieves its literal equivalent in the anxiety about penis size, which is so pervasive in our culture. Within this fear-riddled masculinity, the real or imagined sound of laughter rings persistently.

Where there is such extensive fear of measuring up, there is an intense fear of those who are perceived to threaten this quantifiable notion of masculinity: women and homosexuals. *Rio Bravo* clearly focuses this issue. Feathers (Angie Dickinson), the "guilty" woman, threatens John T. Chance and the male group. When Chance's attempt to send her out of town fails, he orders her to conform to his notions of propriety. Indeed, much of the narrative of *Rio Lobo* is structured around the male group's attempts to leave the women behind; men are constantly dropping women off and telling them where to stay and wait. Their failure in this project is clear both when one of the women enters the jail in which the men have secluded themselves and when another appears at the shoot-out and kills the villian before the men can do so.

This fear of women surfaces in the dominating wife and treacherous mistress of *Scarlet Street*, the women in the Hawks films who will not leave when they are told to and will not stay where they are put, the sexually evaluating women who laugh at men with their penis-size jokes, or the avenging women who kill or even castrate men in the rape-revenge films.

The oft-noted pattern of male bonding in the Hawks films also points to the unacknowledged homophobia that lurks within and beneath sexual representations of the male body. At times, disturbing homosexual aspects of male sexuality are repressed, as in Truffaut's ommission of central aspects of Itard's diaries in *The Wild Child*. At other times, male obsessions with sexual aspects of the male body are masked by an apparent heterosexual context that drafts women into the service of male fantasy, as is the case with many of the penis-size jokes and rape-revenge films analyzed in Chapter 6. Indeed, as I suggested in my introduction, the near-total silence by heterosexual men on issues of the sexual representation of the male body is itself a symptom of homophobia; this subject, the silence seems to say, can be of interest only to gay men. But analysis of the wide variety of artistic, scientific, and medical discourses I have examined in this book belies such a notion.

Some works, such as Oshima's *In the Realm of the Senses* and many of Orbison's songs, supply challenging alternatives in their historical and cultural contexts. *In the Realm of the Senses* breaks with crucial assumptions about the phallic centrality of male sexuality in the widely differing cultural traditions of Japanese erotic woodblock prints and contemporary Western hard-core feature films; and Orbison's music breaks the self-confident *macho* masquerade that was such a central feature of late 1950s and early 1960s rock 'n' roll. Nevertheless, the work of both artists remains caught within phallocentric contradictions and limitations. Oshima, as I have indicated, paradoxically centers the penis in his attempt to overthrow the phallus; Orbison, in some of his songs as well as in aspects of his persona, affirms conventional ideas about women and male sexuality even as his best music cries out in anguish about the cost of such notions to heterosexual men.

If much of this book speaks about male concerns, I have also suggested that some of the same contradictions emerge from women's work. *Dick Talk* is riddled with phallocentric discourse about the importance and awesome spectacle of the highly active male body and the large penis. In contrast, the photographs and writing of Sarah Kent show a significant, if once again contradictory, effort to understand and break free of the bipolar sexual representation of the male body. The gentle male body she envisions neither tries to impress nor risks becoming the vulnerable object of humiliation. It is precisely such a notion of gentleness that is lacking in *Dick Talk* and that

Watrous invokes in his *New York Times* review of Orbison's concert when he notes the music is free of any sexual "menace."

Orbison's music, however, is not free of humiliation, and this points to the final common thread that runs through many sexual representations of the male body. In a cultural context that defines a normative masculinity and sexuality as powerfully phallic, the opposite pole of vulnerability and humiliation frequently becomes the goal of a masochistic yearning, as if many men want to be punished for the brutally powerful masculinity they attempt to embody, or want to abandon the attempt and flee from it entirely. Thus, in many of the images and situations I have analyzed, men willingly make themselves the butt of joking women and the object of brutal physical harm by revenging women. Even within the complex and profound work, *In the Realm of the Senses*, one can detect a masochistic male desire to abandon the usual male role (i.e., to die for one's country) in favor of offering oneself up entirely to a woman (i.e., to die for a woman's pleasure). Similarly, the male personae in Orbison's music seem thrilled at the moment when the woman decides her pleasure. That moment is entirely outside the man's active control—as when "Running Scared" builds in emotional torment as the singer waits to see whether the woman will turn to him or his rival, or when, in "Oh, Pretty Woman," he exclaims in near disbelief, "But wait! What I do I see / Is she walking back to me?" If she chooses the singer, her decision is in no way linked to anything he has done to ensure it; if she does not, he is left alone to revel in the pleasures of loneliness and unfulfilled dreams. In the late-period "Windsurfer" (Roy Orbison and Bill Dees, 1989) ("He said, 'Let's sail away together.' She told him, 'No, no, never, no.'"), he even kills himself over the pain of the loss. In neither scenario does he enact conventionally powerful masculine roles, preferring instead to be passively accepted or rejected.

The odd combination of Oshima and Orbison serves to highlight the need for artistic and critical work on both the literal and the symbolic dimensions of the sexual representation of the male body. Oshima's film is so explicit that it caused great controversy in the United States at the time of its release and could not be shown at all in Japan. Orbison's entire work lacks even one sexually explicit reference. Yet, as I have tried to demonstrate throughout these chapters, where the male body is involved, there is a constant tension and interplay between the literal and the symbolic. We must pay careful attention to both if we wish to understand and alter those representational practices.

I do not think that merely examining issues of masculine subjectivity and symbolic aspects of the body will suffice. If we want to understand and change the representations of the male body, we must create new images of the sexually explicit. So much of our response to the male body in films, for example, is contingent on retaining the mystique surrounding the penis, and that mystique is totally dependent on either keeping the penis covered up or carefully regulating its representation.

The significance of the interplay between the literal and the symbolic is clear if we consider the star system. It is no coincidence that when rare moments of frontal male nudity occur in the U.S. cinema, they involve actors like Richard Gere, rather than Clint Eastwood. Despite the fact that they represent different notions of the hero, conventional male hero figures like John Wayne and Clint Eastwood simply could not be shown naked. Anything we would see would cause the collapse of the powerfully phallic male sexuality their character's embody. In Richard Dyer's terms, discussed earlier, just as the penis is not a patch on the phallus, the sight of the penis would invest these star bodies with a literal quality incompatible with their symbolic characterizations. Within the European art cinema, for example, no such generic connotations accrue around the body of an actor like Gérard Depardieu, and for that reason no particular problem arises when he appears nude in such films as *1900* (1977) or when he walks around nude for extensive periods of time in *The Last Woman* (1976).

The situation becomes even more problematic if we compare stars like John Wayne and Clint Eastwood with the muscle-building stars of the 1980s, such as Arnold Schwarzenegger. In an analysis of *Pumping Iron* and *Pumping Iron II*, Christine Holmlund perceptively notes:

> This is why, unlike the emphasis on tits and ass in *Pumping Iron II*, the camera never focuses on the bulge in Arnold's or Lou's bikinis or pans their naked bodies in the shower: to look might reveal too much or too little, threatening the tenuous equation established between masculinity, muscularity, and men. (1990, 45)

Although I think Holmlund's notion that there may be "too much" is mistaken, since anything is always too little where the penis–phallus relationship is involved, she perceptively draws attention to the way in which an already tenuous relationship is even more tenuous where muscle builders are concerned. For this reason, I would suggest, there is a cultural tradition of gossip about the penises of muscle builders. In the December 1978 issue of *Play-*

girl, there is a nude photograph of Richard Dubois, Mr. America of 1954, in which his genitals are exposed; the caption states that Mae West remarked of the man, "Umm . . . all that meat and no potatoes" ("X-Rated Sneak Peaks" 1978, 81). By grotesquely intensifying the symbolic phallic aspects of the body, male body builders risk tearing the mask off the facade by threatening to make conscious the realization that no man, no matter what he has, can be that impressively masculine.

It is significant that in the last few years a number of female and male artists have dealt very explicitly with penis imagery. As in the photograph that appears on the jacket of this book, Robert Flynt frequently juxtaposes rigid medical, scientific, or artistic grids or images with fluid and graceful bodies, which eloquently defy those fixed ways of understanding and representing them. The bodies he represents fit neither the stereotype of the powerful, phallic spectacle nor its opposite in pitiable vulnerability or comic failure. His works show the importance of creating new images of the male body and male sexuality.

Melody Davis has done a series of nudes that simultaneously focus attention on the genitals and yet seem remarkably free from representing them within the polarity that usually governs such photographs. Like Sarah Kent, she does not show the head of her model so that identification and narrativization are likewise blocked. The body and the genitals are thus objectified, but not in a conventional, judgmental fashion. Unlike Kent, she neither naturalizes her nudes by placing them in nature nor links them to the high-art tradition of such works as Michelangelo's *David*. The pictures thus fully and frankly acknowledge the photographer's erotic interest in the subject. None of the body poses involve traditional male postures; indeed, one of them shows the hips positioned in a manner with feminine connotations, not one that evokes traditional negative judgments but one that suggests that the conventional distinction between male and female nudes is overly dichotomized and rigidified. The penis is shown flaccid, semi-erect, and erect; in all states, it seems an object of contemplation, fascination, and beauty— nothing to be ashamed of or proud of, but something to be acknowledged by both men and women, heterosexual and homosexual (27). As with Flynt's photographs, one need only compare these to Mapplethorpe's to recognize her accomplishment. Davis has simultaneously produced a related series of photographs of construction sites that employs the same palladium–platinum printing technique that formally links them to the male nudes (28). Although not about the male body at all, these photographs show the need to pursue

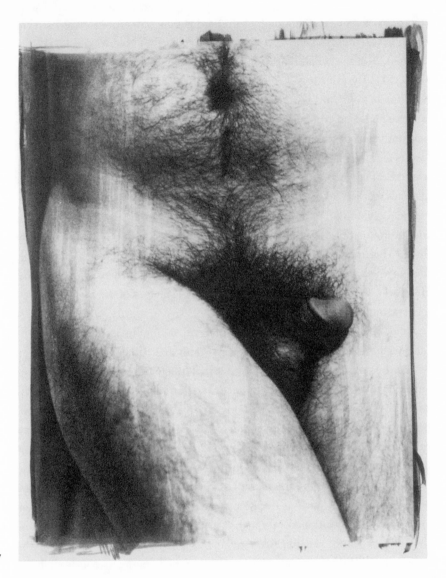

27

both literal and symbolic sexual representations of the male body if we are to understand them. She says: "In the second body of work, I have focused upon construction sites which I view as psychological spaces. . . . Given that gender is a space of construction and deconstruction—both ruinous and mysteriously grand, I feel that this body of work is of kindred spirit with the male nudes" (Davis 1991).

Dick (1991), an independent film by Jo Mennell, similarly extends the work of the anonymous producers of *Dick Talk*, analyzed in Chapter 8. In

approximately fifteen minutes, the film presents what it claims is a thousand Polaroid close-ups of male genitals and a commentary of one hundred women talking about such things as what they call penises, what they thought the first time they saw one, how they can tell by looking at a man what his penis will be like, and what they think about penis size. Visually the film is extraordinary in the range of represented penises. Within less than a minute of watching the film, the spectator becomes aware of how extremely limited and regulated all our representations of the penis are, whether they be in art, photography, cinema, or medicine. In terms of size and shape, these penises do not come close to conforming to any cultural notion of what a penis looks like; instead, they present a stunning variety that undermines the very notion of any such conformity. If one compares them with the images in modern sex education textbooks discussed in Chapter 7, one quickly realizes that the texts purportedly varied images are in fact bizarrely limited, being much more like each other than they are like the actual variety Mennell shows. As such, Mennell's work relates to Justine Hill's medical photographs in *Plain and Fancy Penises* discussed in Chapter 7. In direct opposition to much of *Dick Talk*, the women heard on the soundtrack in *Dick* speak in many voices. In the section on size, for example, we hear women who prefer small penises, women who believe there is no significant difference in the size, and women who prefer large penises. No narrator or moderator pursues her agenda, and there is no attempt to generalize along such lines as "women do not really care about size." Some care and some do not; some like big ones and some like small ones. As such, the soundtrack also helps participate in a discourse that destroys traditionally established and highly limited ways of talking about penises.

As well as paying careful attention to such alternative and frequently experimental work, future work on the sexual representation of the male body must also take into account the work of feature filmmakers who give prominent and frequently unusual treatment to it in their films. Although in this book I have not concerned myself with auteur issues, authorship studies on such directors as Paul Schrader, Paul Verhoeven, and Peter Greenaway are important areas of exploration. My analysis of *American Gigolo* in Chapter 1 points to a problem in Schrader's work that is central to such later films as *Mishima* (1985) and *Comfort of Strangers* (1991). The former film deals with a man who becomes totally preoccupied with his body, while the latter contains an extended scene in which a nude man walks around the room while a woman remains in bed and covered. Although lacking in frontal nudity, the scene bears comparison with a similar scene in *American Gigolo*. Furthermore, the film contains a remarkable scene in which the man and his girl friend are dining in a restaurant. Although he tells her that everyone is admiring her beauty, she tells him that, on the contrary, they are looking at him. The narrative centers on another man's obsession with photographing the central male character's body, and even the casting of the young couple emphasizes the physical beauty of the young man over that of the woman.

Similarly, the scene from *Robocop* that I analyze in Chapter 6 points to many similar scenes in Verhoeven's work, including his early European work and later Hollywood films. In *Spetters* (1980), we see frontal male nudity in a scene where two young men measure their penises to see who has the bigger one; in a scene in *Turkish Delight* (1974), a young man comes out of the bathroom and masquerades for a woman waiting for him in bed by parading around with a bra and "falsies" and his penis invisibly tucked between his thighs; and in *The Fourth Man* (1979), a man has a graphic castration nightmare. The central preoccupation of such futuristic films as *Robocop* and *Total Recall* (1990) turn on the spectacle of the male body as a powerful cyborg in the former and as a powerfully muscled weightlifter (Arnold Schwarzenegger) in the latter. In *Basic Instinct* (1992), we see a shot of the body of the first murder victim with his genitals clearly centered. Indeed, the preoccupation with the male body in Verhoeven's work is remarkably consistent, although his Dutch European Art films and his Hollywood blockbusters appear quite disparate.

Peter Greenaway's films (not discussed here) also feature a pronounced emphasis on frontal male nudity. The lover in *The Cook, the Thief, the Wife, and Her Lover* walks around nude for extended periods of time, and several men are shown nude in *Drowning by Numbers* (1987). *Prospero's Books* (1991) probably features more extensive male nudity than any other feature narrative film. Indeed, Greenaway's preoccupation with the male body and the penis surfaces in the dialogue of *Drowning by Numbers* several times. In one scene, a man sleeps naked on a bed; a woman asks the man's wife if it is true that all fat men have small penises. Just as she speaks the line, the overweight husband repositions his body in such a manner as to emphasize his penis. The moment is one of the very few in cinema where dialogue about a small penis actually accompanies the visual representation of it. A young boy in the film is preoccupied with circumcision. At one point he talks to his father about the representation of penises in an art book, and Greenaway cuts to the paintings being discussed. Later, the boy attempts to circumsize himself.

The scene in *Turkish Delight* where the man masquerades with his genitals tucked between his thighs points to another important direction for future research that departs from authorial perspectives. A similar image occurs in *Silence of the Lambs* (1991) when "Buffalo Bill," a deranged killer, parades around in makeup, earrings, and a woman's robe and with his genitals tucked between his thighs. In *Kinky Business 2* (1989), a hard-core pornographic film, a highly unusual scene within the genre occurs when a woman, dissatisfied with a potential lover who has fallen asleep, puts makeup on his face and then tucks his genitals between his thighs, an act that is shown in close-up. She then gets a long mirror, which she holds up to the side of the bed; when she awakens the man, he sees his image in the mirror and has a momentary panic about losing his penis. The appearance of this exact image within the European Art Cinema, Hollywood, and hard-core pornography suggests that it holds a particular fascination for men, a fascination that equates the invisible penis with a more generalized marking of the rest of the body as feminine (e.g., the bra and "falsies," the makeup, and the transvestism). All three films were directed by men, and all offer different narrative contexts that seemingly explain and justify what we are seeing: The man in *Turkish Delight* acts playfully for a woman; the man in *Silence of the Lambs* masquerades for himself in a manner that relates his sexual confusion to his criminal behavior; and the woman in *Kinky Business 2* acts out of revenge toward the man who does not satisfy her. The very diversity of these contexts suggests that they function in part as smokescreens that enable the representation of the male body with the genitals momentarily invisible.

What accounts for this persistent desire to show men without the most culturally sanctioned sign of their maleness visible? Does it represent a desire for men to be rid of the penis–phallus or a fear of such an occurrence? The answer, I believe, is both. To understand such multiple conflicting desires and fears fully, we need not only to be open to various psychoanalytic models but to clinical experience as well. Analysts report that it is not uncommon for adolescent boys to pose themselves in front of mirrors so that they may see what their own bodies look like without the genitals being visible. In some ways this act resembles Freud's analysis of the fort/da game because, like the infant, the young man pleasurably controls and perhaps feels a sense of mastery over the disappearance and reappearance of the object. The desire to view his body transformed into that of a woman's may have multiple levels of meaning for the young man, including castration anxiety, womb envy, and the fantasy that women may satisfy their sexual desires whenever they wish. Thus, while he must live in near-constant sexual frustration, he imagines that as a woman he would not. We should also wonder whether such images may hold any fascination or meaning for women. A woman told me that the image fascinated her by revealing how vulnerable a dangling, flaccid penis seemed, since, unlike a retracted penis, it could totally disappear in an instant, not even leaving a trace. Not surprisingly, the same image appears in Annie Leibovitz's photograph of Mark Morris. Pursuing such images of male sexuality across the works of diverse artists working in various media should complement authorial investigations of such artists as Jim Thompson and Peter Greenaway.

I want to conclude with two opposing assessments of current discourses about the penis in our culture, which appeared within a year of each other in the *Village Voice*. In an article appropriately entitled "Big: That's How the Men and Women of the Hung Jury Like It," Ellen Rapp profiles an organization devoted to matching men with large penises (no man with less than an eight-inch erection may join) with women who prefer such men. She begins her article by quoting Jim Boyd, the founder of the group: "Penis size is the scariest and most taboo subject on the planet Earth. It's scarier than Satanism" (Rapp 1990, 41). Boyd makes his comment in reference to why NBC canceled a planned episode of "Geraldo" on which he was to discuss the topic. Yet Scott Poulson-Bryant begins his review of *Dick* by noting almost the opposite: "Dicks, metaphorically or literally, are 'in.' " (Poulson-Bryant 1991, 48). Paradoxically, both perspectives may be correct. There is no doubt that the sexual representation of the male body in general and the penis in particular remains a strong cultural taboo, especially in any context involving homosexuality or women looking, objectifying, assessing, talking, or desiring. It is no coincidence that many of the recent public controversies, such as that involving Mapplethorpe's work, about the alleged pornographic nature of some art has focused on explicit sexual imagery of men. At the same time, there has been an unprecedented amount of artistic and critical work on penises, "metaphorically or literally." Indeed, this development warranted a 1990 *New York Times* article entitled "Bodies Go Public: It's Men's Turn Now" in which male nudity and penises are discussed (Williams 1990, C1, C6). *Dick Talk*, *Dick*, and Melody Davis's photographs all show artists significantly exploring and demystifying what may be the last great sexual taboo in our culture. Although the events are not causally related, I do not think it is meaningless coincidence that, as I discussed in Chapter 1, Maxine Sheets-Johnstone contemporaneously has mounted a serious critique about the silence surrounding the size of the penis in human evolution, or that Justine Hill has produced a slide show aimed at addressing that aspect of the male body in liberating terms. Increasingly, art, science, and medicine provide strong evidence that we cannot maintain the silence surrounding this taboo subject. As I have shown, many women have greatly contributed to this important work, and in his ground-breaking article on the male body in the cinema, Steve Neale (1983) correctly noted that most of the previous work in that area had been done from a gay male perspective, which remains vital. The situation is now changing. It is increasingly clear that nearly everyone has a stake in this scholarly and creative investigation. In 1991, Barbara de Genevieve perceptively observed: "Phallic masculinity as a system of inflexible values created in a heterosexist and eurocentric tradition is now being undermined by a cacophony of three voices, gay men, straight men, and women" (1991, 4). It is my hope this book adds to the cacophony and contributes to breaking that silence.

In *Body Invaders: Panic Sex in America* (1987), Arthur and Marilouise Kroker describe what they term "panic penis":

No longer the old male cock as the privileged sign of patriarchal power and certainly not the semiotician's dream of the decentered penis which has vanished into the ideology of the phallus, but the *postmodern penis* which becomes an emblematic sign of sickness, disease, and waste. Penis burnout, then, for the end of the world. (1987, 95)

They go on to describe a modern world in which the penis is outdated anyway because sex no longer involves secretions but technological systems: "The penis, both as protuberance and ideology, is already a spent force, a residual afterimage, surplus to the requirements of a telematic society" (1987, 95). There is something dangerously attractive in this kind of postmodern, apocalyptic writing that thrives on outrageous overgeneralization. Computerized phone sex, video porn, and the other technologies the Krokers invoke hardly justify the sweeping conclusions they draw about the outmodedness of the penis. No doubt it is tempting during the AIDS era to believe that just when we have come to fear secretions in sex, such secretions are outdated. Indeed, one might think that in a book entitled *Running Scared*, the term "panic penis" would be welcome. I have, after all, just finished arguing that fear about many things underlies the representations of male sexuality I have analyzed. Would it not be tempting to add fear of AIDS and bodily secretions to that list and herald the end of the patriarchal penis–phallus? Quite the contrary, what I fear is that in the name of postmodernism, the Krokers have performed the oldest trick in the book: They have just concocted a new reason for not talking about the penis. Fortunately, many different artistic and scholarly voices that insistently break this silence will not be deterred. It is the scandal of patriarchy that for so long so many have believed that the sexual representation of the male body could only be of limited interest to a group patriarchy would attempt to marginalize. What we should be running scared and panicked about is not that the penis is outmoded in a postmodern world of technological sex but that, just as artists and scholars are beginning to pursue inquiries into this and other areas of sexuality, the political and cultural climate in the United States threatens to repress, censor, and disrupt that work.

BIBLIOGRAPHY

Barthes, Roland. 1974. *S/Z*. Trans. Richard Miller. New York: Hill and Wang.

Becker, Robert E. 1974. "Quiz: A Monthly Feature." *Medical Aspects of Human Sexuality*, June, 169–170.

Becklard, Eugene. [1859] 1974. *Know Thyself: The Physiologist; Or Sexual Physiology Revealed*. Trans. M. S. Wharton. New York: Arno.

Berger, John. 1973. *Ways of Seeing*. New York: Penguin.

Bingham, Dennis. 1990. "Men with No Names: Clint Eastwood's 'The Stranger' Persona, Identification, and the Impenetrable Gaze." *Journal of Film and Video* 42, no. 4 (Winter): 33–48.

Bock, Audie. 1987. *Japanese Film Directors*. New York: Kodansha International.

"The Boss Is Just One of the Guys as an All-Star Band Salutes Rock 'n' Roll Great Roy Orbison." 1987. *People*, October 19, 44–45.

"Bringing Up Dick and Jane." 1986. *SPOT: A Publication of the Houston Center for Photography*, Fall, 12–13.

Burch, Noël. 1979. *To the Distant Observer*. Berkeley: University of California Press.

Burroughs, Edgar Rice. [1912] 1983. *Tarzan of the Apes*. New York: Ballantine.

Cauthorn, Robert. 1989. Review of *Tango and Cash*. *Arizona Daily Star*, December 22, F14.

Chesler, Phyllis. 1978. *About Men*. New York: Simon & Schuster.

Christie, Agatha. [1926] 1954. *The Murder of Roger Ackroyd*. New York: Harper.

Cohan, Steven, and Ina Rae Hark. 1993. *Screening the Male*. New York: Routledge.

Comfort, Alex. 1972. *The Joy of Sex*. New York: Simon & Schuster.

Coward, Rosalind. 1985. *Female Desires: How They Are Sought, Bought, and Packaged*. New York: Grove Press.

Crooks, Robert, and Karla Baur. 1990. *Our Sexuality*. 4th ed. (1987, 3rd. ed.; 1983, 2nd ed.; 1980, 1st ed.). New York: Benjamin/Cummings.

Davis, Melody D. 1991a. *The Male Nude in Contemporary Photography*. Philadelphia: Temple University Press.

―――. 1991b. "Statement Regarding Recent Work." Ms.

Dickinson, R. L. 1949. *Human Sex Anatomy*. 2nd ed. Baltimore: Williams & Wilkins.

Doane, Mary Ann. 1987. *The Desire to Desire: The Woman's Film of the 1940s*. Bloomington: Indiana University Press.

Dover, K. J. 1978. *Greek Homosexuality*. Cambridge: Harvard University Press.

Dubois, Jean. [1839] 1974. *Marriage Physiologically Discussed*. Trans. William Greenfield. New York: Arno.

Dyer, Richard. 1982. "Don't Look Now: The Male Pin-Up." *Screen* 23, nos. 3–4: 61–73.

———. 1986. *Heavenly Bodies*. New York: St. Martin's Press.

———. 1990. *Now You See It: Studies on Lesbian and Gay Film*. New York: Routledge.

Feuerbach, Anselm von. [1833] 1942. *Caspar Hauser: An Account of an Individual Kept in a Dungeon, Separated from All Communication with the World, from Early Childhood to about the Age of Seventeen*. Trans. Henning Gottfried Linberg. In *Wolf-Children and Feral Man*, ed. J.A.L. Singh and Robert M. Zingg. New York: Harper & Brothers.

Flitterman, Sandy. "Thighs and Whiskers: The Fascination of *Magnum, P.I.*" *Screen* 26, no. 2 (March/April 1985): 42–58.

Foucault, Michel. 1978. *The History of Sexuality*, Vol. 1, *An Introduction*. Trans. Robert Hurley. New York: Pantheon.

———. 1980. *Herculine Barbin*. Trans. Richard McDougall. New York: Pantheon.

Freud, Sigmund. [1905] 1960. *Jokes and Their Relation to the Unconscious*. Trans. James Strachey. New York: Norton.

———. [1909–1918] 1963. *Three Case Histories*. Ed. Philip Rieff. New York: Collier Books.

Gaines, Jane. 1990. "What Psychoanalysis Can't Tell Us about Fantasies of Race and Sex." Paper presented at the Society for Cinema Studies Conference, Washington, D.C., May.

Gallop, Jane. 1982. *The Daughter's Seduction*. Ithaca: Cornell University Press.

Gates, David. 1988. "The Voice That Sang in the Dark: Roy Orbison, Rock and Roll's Mr. Lonely: 1936–1988." *Newsweek*, December 19, 73.

Gebhard, Paul H., and Alan B. Johnson. 1979. *The Kinsey Data: Marginal Tabulations of the 1938–1963 Interviews Conducted by the Institute for Sex Research*. Philadelphia: Saunders.

Genevieve, Barbara de. 1991. "Masculinity and Its Discontents." *Camerawork* 18, nos. 3–4 (Summer/Fall): 3–5.

Gould, Stephen Jay. 1981. *The Mismeasure of Man*. New York: Norton.

Hansen, Miriam. 1986. "Pleasure, Ambivalence, Identification: Valentino and Female Spectatorship." *Cinema Journal* 25, nos. 4–6: 6–32.

Heath, Stephen. 1977. "The Question Oshima." *Wide Angle* 2, no. 1: 48–57.

———. 1978. "Difference." *Screen* 19, no. 3 (Autumn): 51–112.

Hemingway, Ernest. [1926] 1954. *The Sun Also Rises*. New York: Scribner's.

———. 1964. *A Moveable Feast*. New York: Bantam.

Hilburn, Robert. 1989. "The Big Surprise at Orbison Tribute." *Los Angeles Times*, February 26, F1, F7.

Hill, Justine. 1979. "Plain and Fancy Penises." San Francisco: Multi-Focus.

Hinckley, David. 1988. "Farewell to 'One of Those '50s Kids'." *New York Daily News*, December 9, D20.

Holden, Stephen. "The Pop Life." *New York Times*, April 17.

Hollick, Frederick. [18—] 1974. *The Marriage Guide: Or Natural History of Generation*. New York: Arno.

Holmlund, Christine Anne. 1989. "Visible Difference and Flex Appeal: The Body,

Sex, Sexuality, and Race in the *Pumping Iron* Films." *Cinema Journal* 28, no. 4 (Summer): 38–51.

———. 1990. "Masculinity as Masquerade: The 'Mature' Stallone and Stallone Clone." Paper presented at the Harvard Lesbian/Bi/Gay Conference on Pleasure and Politics, Boston.

Homer. 1963. *The Odyssey.* Trans. Robert Fitzgerald. New York: Doubleday Anchor.

Itard, Jean-Marc-Gaspard. [1801–1806] 1962. *The Wild Boy of Aveyron.* Trans. George and Muriel Humphrey. Englewood Cliffs, N.J.: Prentice Hall.

Kaplan, Ann E. 1980. "Patterns of Violence towards Women in Fritz Lang's *While the City Sleeps.*" *Wide Angle* 4, no. 2: 55–59.

———. 1983. "Ideology and Cinematic Practice in Lang's *Scarlet Street* and Renoir's *La Chienne.*" *Wide Angle* 5, no. 3: 32–43.

Kellogg, J. H. [1888] 1974. *Plain Facts for Old and Young: Embracing the Natural History and Hygiene of Organic Life.* New York: Arno.

Kent, Sarah. 1985. "The Erotic Male Nude." In *Women's Images of Men*, ed. Sarah Kent and Jacqueline Morreau. New York: Writers and Readers Publishing.

Kinder, Marsha. 1989. "Individual Responses." *Camera Obscura*, nos. 20–21: 199–204.

Kipling, Rudyard. [1894–1895] 1987. *The Jungle Books.* New York: Penguin.

Kroker, Arthur, and Marilouise Kroker. 1987. "Introduction: Panic Penis/Panic Ovaries." In *Body Invaders: Panic Sex in America*, ed. Arthur and Marilouise Kroker. New York: St. Martin's Press, 95–99.

Lane, Harlan. 1976. *The Wild Boy of Aveyron.* New York: Bantam.

Lauretis, Teresa de. 1984. *Alice Doesn't: Feminism, Semiotics, Cinema.* Bloomington: Indiana University Press.

Legman, G. 1968. *Rationale of the Dirty Joke: An Analysis of Sexual Humor.* New York: Grove Press.

Lehman, Peter. 1980. "The Act of Making Films: An Interview with Oshima Nagisa." *Wide Angle* 4, no. 2: 56–61.

———. 1986. "Talk Show." *SPOT: A Publication of the Houston Center for Photography* 4, no. 4: 10–12.

———. 1987. " 'You're Just Like Me': Reading *Blue Velvet.*" *SPOT: A Publication of the Houston Center for Photography* 4, no. 4 (Winter): 4–5.

———. 1990. "Texas 1868/America 1956: *The Searchers.*" In *Close Viewings: An Anthology of New Film Criticism*, ed. Peter Lehman. Tallahassee: Florida State University Press.

———. 1991. "Penis-size Jokes and Their Relation to Hollywood's Unconscious." In *Comedy/Cinema/Theory*, ed. Andrew Horton. Berkeley: University of California Press.

———. 1992. " 'Don't Blame This on a Girl': Female Rape-Revenge Films." In *Screening the Male*, ed. Steven Cohan and Ina Rae Hark. New York: Routledge.

Lehman, Peter, and William Luhr. 1981. *Blake Edwards.* Athens: Ohio University Press.

Lor. 1988. Review of *Thinkin' Big. Variety*, April 27, 24.

Luhr William, and Peter Lehman. 1989. *Returning to the Scene: Blake Edwards.* Vol. 2. Athens: Ohio University Press.

MacDonald, Scott. 1983. "Confessions of a Feminist Porn Watcher." *Film Quarterly* 36, no. 2 (Spring): 10–17.

Marsh, Dave. 1987. "All That You Dream." *Rock & Roll Confidential* 49 (August): 7–8.

———. 1989a. "Crying." *Rock & Roll Confidential* 69 (January): 1–2.

———. 1989b. "Music." *Playboy*, April, 28.

Mast, Gerald. 1982. *Howard Hawks: Storyteller.* New York: Oxford University Press.

Masters, William H., and Virginia E. Johnson. 1966. *Human Sexual Response.* Boston: Little, Brown.

Masters, William H., Virginia E. Johnson, and Robert C. Kolodny. 1988. *Human Sexuality.* 3rd ed. Glenview: Scott, Foresman.

Mellencamp, Patricia. 1986. "Situation Comedy, Feminism, and Freud." In *Studies in Entertainment: Critical Approaches to Mass Culture*, ed. Tania Modleski. Bloomington: Indiana University Press.

Melville, Robert. 1973. *Erotic Art of the West.* New York: Putnam.

Mercer, Kobena. 1986. "Imaging the Black Man's Sex." In *Photography/Politics: Two*, ed. Patricia Holland, Jo Spence, and Simon Watney. London: Comedia Publishing Group.

Metcalf, Andy, and Martin Humphries. 1985. *The Sexuality Of Men.* London: Pluto Press.

Modleski, Tania. 1984. "Time and Desire in the Woman's Film." *Cinema Journal* 23, no. 3 (Spring): 19–30.

Moore, Suzanne. 1989. "Here's Looking at You, Kid!" In *The Female Gaze: Women as Viewers of Popular Culture*, ed. Lorraine Gamman and Margaret Marshment. Seattle: Real Comet Press.

Mulvey, Laura. 1975. "Visual Pleasure and Narrative Cinema." *Screen* 16, no. 3 (Autumn): 6–18.

Neale, Steve. 1983. "Masculinity as Spectacle." *Screen* 24, no. 6 (November–December): 2–16.

Nin, Anaïs. 1986. *Henry and June.* New York: Harcourt Brace Jovanovich.

Parker, Rozsika. 1985. "Images of Men." In *Women's Images of Men*, ed. Sarah Kent and Jacqueline Morreau. New York: Writers and Readers Publishing.

Penley, Constance, and Sharon Willis. "Male Trouble." Special Issue of *Camera Obscura* 17 (1988).

People. "The Haunted Life of Rock Legend Roy Orbison, 1936–1988." 1988. December 19, cover.

Polan, Dana. 1985. *The Political Language of Film and the Avant-Garde.* Ann Arbor: UMI Research Press.

Poulson-Bryant, Scott. 1991. "Tool for Thought." *Village Voice*, August 20, 48–49.

Prince, Stephen. 1988. "The Pornographic Image and the Practice of Film Theory." *Cinema Journal* 27, no. 2 (Winter): 27–39.

Rapp, Ellen. 1990. "Big: That's How the Men and Women of the Hung Jury Like It." *Village Voice*, October 20, 41–42.

Reinisch, June M., and Ruth Beasley. 1991. *The Kinsey Institute New Report on Sex: What You Must Know to be Sexually Literate*. New York: St. Martin's Press.

Reuben, David R. 1969. *Everything You Always Wanted to Know about Sex—But Were Afraid to Ask*. New York: McKay.

Robinson, Paul. 1989. *The Modernization of Sex: Havelock Ellis, Alfred Kinsey, William Masters, and Virginia Johnson*. Ithaca: Cornell University Press.

Rodowick, D. N. 1991. *The Difficulty of Difference: Psychoanalysis, Sexual Difference, and Film Theory*. New York: Routledge.

Ryan, Tom. 1985. "Roots of Masculinity." In *The Sexuality of Men*, ed. Andy Metcalf and Martin Humphries. London: Pluto Press.

Sacks, Oliver. 1988. "The Revolution of the Deaf." *New York Review of Books*, June 2, 23–28.

Sade, Marquis de. [1785] 1966. *The 120 Days of Sodom and Other Writings*. Ed. and trans. Austryn Wainhouse and Richard Seaver. New York: Grove Weidenfeld.

Scheuer, Steven H. 1983. *Movies on TV, 1984–1985*. New York: Bantam.

Shattuck, Roger. 1980. *The Forbidden Experiment: The Story of the Wild Boy of Aveyron*. New York: Farrar, Straus and Giroux.

Sheets-Johnstone, Maxine. 1990. *The Roots of Thinking*. Philadelphia: Temple University Press.

Smith, Paul. 1989. "Action Movie Hysteria, or Eastwood Bound." *Differences* 1, no. 3: 88–107.

Steinberg, Leo. 1983. "The Sexuality of Christ in Renaissance Art and in Modern Oblivion." *October* 25 (Summer): 1–222.

Straayer, Chris. 1986. "The Hypothetical Lesbian Heroine in Feature Narrative Film." Paper presented at the Florida State University Literature and Film Conference, Tallahassee, January.

Studlar, Gay Lynn. 1988. *In the Realm of Pleasure: Von Sternberg, Dietrich, and the Masochistic Aesthetic*. Urbana: University of Illinois Press.

Thompson, Jim. [1954] 1988. *The Nothing Man*. New York: Mysterious Press.
———. [1953] 1991. *Savage Night*. New York: Vintage.

Thompson, Kristin. 1988. *Breaking the Glass Armor: Neoformalist Film Analysis*. Princeton: Princeton University Press.

Trall, R. T. [1881] 1974. *Sexual Physiology: A Scientific and Popular Exposition of the Fundamental Problems in Sociology*. New York: Arno.

"Tributes." 1989. *Rolling Stone*, January, 32–33.

Truffaut, François. 1973. "How I Made *The Wild Child*." Trans. Linda Lewin and Christine Lemery. In *The Wild Child: A Screenplay*. New York: Washington Square Press.

Turim, Maureen. 1987. "Signs of Sexuality in Oshima's Tales of Passion." *Wide Angle* 9, no. 2: 32–46.

Vatsayana. [1883] 1982. *Kama Sutra*. Trans. Sir Richard Burton and F. F. Arbuthnot. Ed. by Mulk Raj Anand and Lance Dane. Atlantic Highlands, N.J.: Humanities Press.

Verinis, J. S. and S. Roll. 1970. "Primary and Secondary Male Characteristics: The Hairiness and Large Penis Stereotypes." *Psychological Reports* 26: 123–126.

"Voice of an Angel: Rock 'n' Rollers Recall Roy Orbison." 1988. *Tucson Citizen*, December 8, 1C.

Walling, William H. [1904] 1974. *Sexology*. New York: Arno.

Walters, Margaret. 1978. *The Nude Male*. New York: Penguin.

Watrous, Peter. 1988. "Roy Orbison Mines Some Old Gold." *New York Times*, July 30, 48.

Waugh, Tom. 1987. "Gay Erotic Cinema in the Postwar Era." *CineAction* 10 (October): 65–72.

Westheimer, Ruth. 1990a. "Ask Dr. Ruth." *Arizona Daily Star*, June 25, B5.

———. 1990b. "Ask Dr. Ruth." *Arizona Daily Star*, July 25, B4.

Willemen, Paul. 1980. "Letter to John." *Screen* 21, no. 2: 53–66.

———. 1981. "Anthony Mann: Looking at the Male." *Framework*, nos. 15–17 (Summer): 16.

Williams, Lena. 1990. "Bodies Go Public: It's Men's Turn Now." *New York Times*, October 31, C1, C6.

Williams, Linda. 1984. "When the Woman Looks." In *Re-vision*, ed. Mary Ann Doane, Patricia Mellencamp, and Linda Williams. Los Angeles: American Film Institute.

———. 1989. *Hard-Core: Power, Pleasure, and the "Frenzy of the Visible."* Berkeley: University of California Press.

Wollen, Peter. 1972. *Signs and Meaning in the Cinema*. Bloomington: Indiana University Press.

Wood, Robin. 1981. *Howard Hawks*. London: British Film Institute.

———. 1986. *Hollywood from Vietnam to Reagan*. New York: Columbia University Press.

x. 1987. "Letters." *SPOT: A Publication of the Houston Center for Photography* 5, no. 1: 22.

"X-Rated Sneak Peaks." 1978. *Playgirl*, December, 77–83.

Yu, Li. [1657] 1990. *The Carnal Prayer Mat*. Trans. Patrick Hanan. New York: Ballantine.

Zimmerman, David. 1988. "His Voice Haunted a Generation." *USA Today*, December 8, 1D–2D.

ILLUSTRATION CREDITS

Illustrations 14 and 15 on pages 139 and 143, from R. L. Dickinson's *Atlas of Human Sex Anatomy*, 1971, are used with the kind permission of Krieger Publishing Company, Malabar, Florida.

Illustration 16 on page 162 is reproduced with permission. It was published in Sarah Kent and Jacqueline Morreau, *Women's Images of Men* (London: Writer and Readers Publishing, 1985).

Illustration 17 on page 163, Sarah Kent's *Male Nude California* (1982), is reproduced with permission of the artist.

Illustration 18 on page 164 is Copyright © 1977 by the Estate of Robert Mapplethorpe and reproduced here by permission.

Illustrations 21 and 23 on pages 182 and 183 appear courtesy of the Kinsey Institute for Research in Sex, Gender and Reproduction, Indiana University, Bloomington.

Illustration 24 on page 185, Henry Fuseli's *My Lady Betty*, is used here by courtesy of Weidenfeld & Nicolson, London.

Illustrations 27 and 28 on pages 214 and 215, untitled 1990 photographs by Melody Davis, are used with the artist's permission.

INDEX

European Art Cinema, 36, 44–45, 49, 217

Everyman for Himself and God against All. See *Kaspar Hauser*

Everything You Always Wanted to Know about Sex—But Were Afraid to Ask, 30, 71–72, 131

evolution, role of penis in, 24–28

Fassbinder, Rainer Werner, 30, 126–128, 166–167

female sexual pleasure, in *In the Realm of the Senses*, 179–180

feminist theory, representation of male body and, 4, 7

feminization of male hero: in *American Gigolo*, 18–20; in *A Moveable Feast*, 83; in *Scarface*, 64–68; in *Scarlet Street*, 88–104

feral-child narratives, 209; gender issues in, 39; sexuality in, 29, 36–54

Ferrer, José, 11

Ferry, Bryan, 199

fetishism, penis size and, 161–168

Feuerbach, Anselm von, 46

film *noir*, 73, 86

film theory: heterosexual male theory, 22–23; male body in, 7–8

Finch, Mark, 163

Fischer, Lucy, 9

Fitzgerald, F. Scott, 35, 81–83

Flashdance, 108, 119, 122, 124

Flitterman, Sandy, 7

Flynt, Robert, 213–215

Forbidden Experiment, The, 39–46

Foucault, Michel, 133, 189–190

400 Blows, The, 42

Fourth Man, The, 216

Fox and His Friends, 127–128

fragmentation of women's bodies, patriarchal regulation of, 4–5

Frears, Stephen, 73

French New Wave cinema, 37

Freud, Sigmund: fetishism and, 165–166; film theory influenced by, 32–34; fort/da game, 218; misinterpretation of, in film theory, 7–8, 32–33; on Oedipal complex, 55; on paranoia and homosexuality, 22–23; on smut and dirty jokes, 111–113, 128–129; on visibility of penis, 109

Frustration, 181–182

Fuseli, Henry, 184–188

Gaines, Jane, 163–164, 165–166

Gallaudet College, 38

Gallop, Jane, 174

gangster films, male representation in, 101–102

Gardens of Stone, 115

Garner, James, 95

Gates, David, 201

gay male culture: artists and directors in, 166–168; film theory and, 147–148; male representation in, 7; response to *What Have I Done to Deserve This?*, 10

Genina, Augusto, 11

Gentlemen Prefer Blondes, 9

"Geraldo," 219

Gere, Richard, 14–20, 212

Getaway, The, 73

Godard, Jean-Luc, 9

Godfather, The, 109, 115

Good, the Bad, and the Horny, The, 178

Gordon, Michael, 11

Gotham, 112

Gould, Stephen Jay, 142–144

Grahame, Gloria, 61

Greek art, penis in, 193–195

Greenaway, Peter, 216–218

Greystoke: The Legend of Tarzan, Lord of the Apes, 29, 37, 48–54

Grifters, The, 73

Hail! Hail! Rock 'n' Roll, 203

"My Boyfriend's Back," 204
My Lady Betty, 184–186
Mystery Girl, 200, 206–208
Mystery of Kaspar Hauser, The. See
    Kaspar Hauser

Naked Vengeance, 126
narrative cinema, nude male in,
    172–173
Neale, Steve, 7, 32–33, 154, 219
New German Cinema, 37
New Kids on the Block, 118
New York Times, 219
Newsweek, 38
Nicholson, Jack, 7, 107–108
Nightmare on Elm Street, A, 108
Nin, Anaïs, 158
1900, 212
Niven, David, 109
Nothing Man, The, 29, 72–83, 85–86,
    103, 105, 191, 208
Nude Male, The, 111
nudity: vs. nakedness, 19; use of
    frontal, male, in film, 8–20

Odyssey, The, 69
Oedipal complex, film theory and,
    33–34
"Oh, Pretty Woman," 203–204, 211
O Lucky Man, 116
Once Bitten, 116, 118
120 Days of Sodom, The, 142
Only the Lonely (film), 198
"Only the Lonely" (song), 202
*Only the Lonely: Roy Orbison's Life and
    Legacy*, 198
Opposing Force, 116, 118
Orbison, Barbara, 198–199, 202
Orbison, Roy, 31; changing percep-
    tions of, 210–211; dark qualities in
    work of, 198–199, 201–202, 204,
    206–207; innocent quality perceived
    in, 197–199; male representation in
    music of, 197–211; as musicians'
    musician, 199–201, 205; operatic

qualities in voice of, 201, 204–205;
    weirdness, Orbison associated with,
    208
orgasm, myths concering women's,
    26–27, 146
Oshima, Nagisa, 30–31, 171–173,
    176–189, 210–212
Our Sexuality, 141, 159
Outrageous Foreplay, 173

"panic penis," 219–220
"Pantomime," 207
Parker, Rozsika, 161
Paths of Glory, 73
patriarchal culture: concealment of
    penis in, 28; in gay male culture,
    166; representation of male body
    and, 5
Patrice, 161–165
Peckinpah, Sam, 73
penis: anthropological evolution
    of, 24–28; artists' imagery of,
    213–216; cultural taboos regarding,
    35–36, 219; discussed in *Dick Talk*,
    149–168; images of severed penises,
    184–189; injuries to, 72–83; and
    IQ measurement as related to penis
    measurement techniques, 142–144;
    jokes and brags about, 105–129;
    large, as feature of pornographic
    films, 174–178; as literal organ, 5;
    medical representation of, 131–146;
    size of, 10, 30, 81–83, 105–129,
    142–144, 174–178, 190–195, 218;
    visual and verbal representations of,
    29–30
"peniscope" cartoon, 109–110
Penley, Constance, 7
People magazine, 199
Perkins, Carl, 199
personal narratives, in *Dick Talk*,
    150–151
Petty, Tom, 199
Pfeiffer, Michelle, 107
Phallic Contest, The, 181, 193–195